The
Third
Culture Kid
Experience

The Third Culture Kid Experience

Growing Up among Worlds

David C. Pollock and
Ruth E. Van Reken

For information contact:
Intercultural Press, Inc.
PO Box 700
Yarmouth, Maine 04096 USA
207-846-5168

© 1999 by David C. Pollock and Ruth E. Van Reken

Design and production by Patty J. Topel

Printed in the United States of America

03   02   01   00   99   4   5   6   7   8

Library of Congress Cataloging-in-Publication Data

Pollock, David C.
   Third culture kids: growing up among worlds/David C. Pollock and Ruth E. Van Reken.
     p. cm.
   Includes bibliographical references
   ISBN 1-877864-72-2
   1. Social interaction in children—Foreign countries. 2. Social skills in children—Foreign countires. 3. Children—Travel—Foreign countries. 4. Children—Foreign countries—Attitudes. 5. Intercultural communication—Foreign countries. 6. Parents-Employment—Foreign countries. I. Van Reken, Ruth E., 1945–   II. Title.
HQ784.S56P65   1999
303.3'2—dc21   99–10851
                              CIP

For Betty Lou and David, our lifelong partners and unfailing supporters throughout our journeys. And to our children, who have taught us so much—TCKs "for true."

Table of Contents

Section Two—Maximizing the Benefits

Appendices

Foreword

It is an honor to have been asked to write the foreword to this perceptively written and valuable book in which Dave Pollock and Ruth Van Reken demonstrate their combined wisdom and their ongoing commitment to the TCK community. They do so with depth and sensitivity. Each has had a profound impact on my own personal and professional development and that of scores of others who live and work in the global corridor.

My association with Dave Pollock began at a SIETAR International conference (International Society for Intercultural Education, Training and Research) in 1984. At that time, Fanchon Silberstein and I gave the very first presentation on *global nomads*, a term I had coined as synonymous with *TCK*, and Dave was in the audience. Two years later he became a founding board member of Global Nomads International, serving as a source of insight and vision for that body. He is an esteemed colleague, mentor, and forever a friend. I am privileged to have worked with him and continue to enjoy the lively exchange of ideas and possibilities that have marked our collaboration over the years. Our interaction continues to inform my life and my work.

Dave Pollock works tirelessly on behalf of and with the TCK community. His presentations and consultations with TCKs and their families have literally changed lives. For this book he has distilled decades of direct experience with TCKs of all ages and numerous nationalities. The result is a highly distilled body of knowledge that is both anthropological and psychological in nature. Through this knowledge he gives voice to what so many of us have felt soul deep but often cannot articulate. As a result, the outcome of his work runs deeper than an "aha" experience. As lightening thrusts the power of electricity into the earth, so it is when this defining moment occurs in a group he is guiding—the impact of emotional grounding is palpable for those present. Clearly, for many who have grown up globally, having their past validated and placed in the clear context of a shared heritage brings with it a stunning sense of safe homecoming.

On a lighter side, watching spouses during Dave's presentations is a wonder in itself. They sit, wide-eyed and incredulous, listening intently as their beloved's peculiarities are described in detail by a total stranger. As Dave has said, this underlines the critical need for premarital counseling of TCKs and their intendeds. Indeed, too many assume that common nationality means shared culture; they thus unwittingly enter into what is, in actuality, an intercultural marriage.

My first memory of Ruth Van Reken reaches back to 1987 at the International Conference on Missionary Kids (ICMK) in Quito, Ecuador. It was at the Hotel Colon that I stayed up all night in an alcove off the lobby reading her first book, *Letters I Never Wrote* (now *Letters Never Sent*). I had sought refuge there so I could weep with abandon without waking my roommate of the moment. Suffice it to say, I, too, experienced the sense of catharsis commented on by those who have read her powerful personal story.

It was there, also, that Ruth displayed her remarkable ability to relate to others with great simplicity and authenticity. In one lengthy, private conversation during the conference, the two of us discussed being TCKs, the cultures of our respective sponsors—God and the corporation—and the stereotypes each expatriate subgroup smugly held of the other. We got quite the chuckle out of it, but we also decided that it was time to move beyond such judgments. The no-tion needed to be put forth that we were all grazing in the same pasture separated by—and seeing only—the fences marking boundaries dictated by our sponsorship. Now, as members of the global nomad/TCK community, it was time to look for the gate between our pastures, to understand the power of our shared heritage, and to draw on it for our benefit and for those who come after us. It was Ruth who articulated this vision to our action group the following day, in effect swinging that gate wide open and shepherding us through it.

Her actions there were testimony to her consistent willingness to risk emotionally. She is able to be with TCKs in a way that affirms their worth, draws them to awareness of common strengths as well as pain, and encourages their personal healing in the context of their own community. It is her gift to gently lead others beyond the superficial to the place of greatest vulnerability and growth, where one heart touches another. The Quito conference marked the beginning of what has been for me a valuable and enduring friendship.

What Ruth has done in crafting this book as a writer and a contributor, honing and refining it—yet staying intellectually fresh and emotionally present through its many iterations—demands our utmost respect. It is we readers who benefit most from her persistence and commitment.

Together these two extraordinary people have given us a well-organized, highly readable text that will prove to be a classic in the intercultural field.

For those of us who share the global nomad/TCK heritage, having this experience named, being able to say "I am a TCK," "I am a global nomad," is a powerful gift to our community. In the words of Nori Hsu in the *Global Nomad Quarterly*:

> Suddenly it came out, blurting like a geyser from the ground, I am a global nomad. Nothing has felt the same since. I now have a culture. After three decades of learning other peoples' cultures and still being an outsider, I look to the future.... The recognition has

been life-changing. For me, it is as if three quarters of
my life has emerged from shadow into full color.

The authors give us a deep understanding of the wide range of
hues in the palette of TCK experience. They enable us to add depth,
dimension, and definition to the personal portraits of our own lives
over time.

Most of us are, I believe, in a lifelong process of integrating our
globally nomadic upbringing into our present and our future. We
strive, to paraphrase Dr. Kathleen Finn Jordan, to make the pieces
of our complex puzzle fit. Just when we feel we have put the mobil-
ity/relationship piece securely in place, it is jostled by a pending
marriage, another move, a teenager's departure for college, or the
prospect of where in the world (literally) to retire. That same old
feeling wells up, only this time it's in a different context, buried in a
deeper place.

Whatever our life stage may be, then, this book resonates on
several levels. It affirms our experience and releases us from self-
imposed and external judgments about our TCK-based reactions and
behaviors. It offers the renewal born of insight and action. With con-
siderable care, Dave and Ruth have cleared the path, marked it, and
given us the tools for self-discovery. By the end of this book, T. S.
Eliot's words, elegantly expressed and certainly applicable to the
globally nomadic, could be our own:

We shall not cease from exploration.
And the end of all our exploring
Will be to arrive where we started
And to know the place for the first time.

Owing to the knowledge, skills, and global awareness born, as
Paul Seaman has said, of ordinary lives lived in extraordinary circumstances, we TCKs have great potential to effect change. We have
the capacity, as Margaret Pusch has said, to view the world whole.
So please—let the authors hear from you. Tell them what makes this
book work for you, what it sparks in you. Share it with your school,
university administrators, or coworkers. Use it as a reference for

writing an article for your alumni association. Encourage and support these institutions in acknowledging, valuing, and guiding the TCKs in their midst.

If you haven't already done so, consider the impact of the TCK/ global nomad experience on your life and how you can use it beneficially—within your family as well as locally and globally. After all, after awareness is raised about the characteristics and dynamics of being a TCK, then what? Not surprisingly, the authors take us to that next step—integration. The sections of the book that deal with exploring cycles of mobility, uncovering hidden losses and addressing them and reframing grief, for example, are brilliant. Enlightening suggestions are provided on how TCKs, family, friends, and counselors can engage in dialogue that clears emotional logjams and permits the lifestream to flow freely.

With this book, the authors add a new level of understanding, articulation, and visibility to an emerging interdisciplinary social science field—one with a focus on the children of the globally nomadic community. Undoubtedly it will prompt greater intellectual discourse and synergy.

With that in mind, I would add one cautionary note regarding the definition of *TCK*. The original intent of the term, used by Dr. Ruth Hill Useem in her research in the 1960s, referred to children whose parents' *work* took them abroad to live. The authors have included the children of what they term temporary refugees—those whose parents take them abroad to avoid civil strife, for example. They have also included those who have entered another culture (the Native American community) without leaving their country. In addition, Ruth Van Reken mentions that Dr. Useem herself now refers to TCKs simply as children who accompany their parents into another culture. These, then, broaden the definition of *TCK* to include the children of refugees, immigrants, and those whose experience is domestic, not global. As a result the term risks being diluted beyond use for both researchers and TCKs themselves. If researchers are to be able to exchange research data without contamination, they need clarity on who it is they have been researching. We can only assure this when we maintain the integrity and continuity of past terminology.

Further, in respecting original intent, we also securely establish the starting point for understanding the layering of other related experiences in a global nomad's life.

What are the implications, for example, for a family forced to flee its homeland—or risk death—only to find itself moving again as a result of a parent's career choice? The older children experience both the refugee layer of the journey—complete, perhaps, with all the trauma and violence often associated with such flight—and the TCK layer. Younger offspring, on the other hand, may directly experience only the TCK layer when a parent's job with the World Bank, for example, takes the family to several other elsewheres. These layers of family history, experienced both directly and indirectly, call different issues into play that influence the family dynamic. Clear terminology helps us to articulate the nuances.

As consultant Barbara Schaetti has commented, "We need to disentangle the layers so they can be more clearly understood, while at the same time *respecting their intersection within an integrated identity.*" From there we can explore how the dynamics of each affects the internationally mobile child and the adult she or he becomes.

Because each of us makes use of language in a different way, a healthy and vigorous debate on terminology, such as on the definitions of *TCK* and *global nomad*, has been going on for years—in groups, on listserves, in workshops, at conferences. This is as it should be. It is a dialogue and it, indeed, stimulates inquiry and encourages growth. We invite your participation in this ongoing discussion.

The authors have included two powerful pieces by Sophia Morton and Paul Seaman, both excellent writers. They are not to be missed. Those of you who are not TCKs, prepare to be moved by their stark honesty. Those of you who are TCKs will know well the place in the heart where they take you. Look for them in Appendix B.

Finally, in reflecting on this book, the *mola* as metaphor keeps pushing itself forward. Molas are embroidery pieces crafted in a style unique to the Kuna Indians of Panama. The symbolism inherent in their construction speaks to who I am as a global nomad. I offer it to you in closing.

Pieces of bright-colored fabric, as many as five to eight, are layered upon one another and attached temporarily at each corner. The seamstress cuts down to different layers, folds the edges under in the desired shape to reveal the color beneath, and stitches the folds in place. As she continues to cut, fold, and stitch, a multihued pattern slowly emerges, finally coming together in a richly vibrant image of a fish or a lobster, for instance. The end result is a piece that has a solid hue on one side and emerges brilliantly into full color on the other. Each has the stamp of the creator's individuality but is borne of a distinct cultural heritage.

So it is with our lives as global nomads, as TCKs. During childhood and beyond, all our experiences of mind, heart, body, and spirit—cultural, emotional, physical, geographical—all of the moves, the relationships, the places, the losses, the discoveries, the wonder of the world—are layered one upon another through time. Ultimately, to revel in the beauty of our personal mola-like tapestry means cutting, sometimes deeply, through these layers to reveal the richness and color beneath. This can be painful. It is the legacy of transition and change, and it is also the precursor to growth.

Sometimes the cut feels more like a tear, a violation committed with dull, badly nicked scissors. The stitches on ragged edges are crude. We feel powerless. Restitching takes longer and leaves deep scars on our souls.

Some of the transitions are surprisingly easy. The cut is cleaner. The stitches are neater. We heal faster and settle into the new layer of culture more comfortably. This is so for any number of reasons— good preparation, family interaction, and community support; better continuity (old friends in a new place); familiar routines in a new setting; or the stimulation of the new culture and country. Our mola takes on its own character, its own vibrancy and expression with each successive experience.

Some of us, upon returning home, turn our tapestry over, hide the brilliance of its colors and its uniqueness, deny our heritage or reveal it to few. Perhaps this is done to blend in and gain acceptance, perhaps to deny the impact of loss—what's past is past—perhaps because, frankly, it just seems easier. In that denial, we choose to present ourselves—to ourselves as well as others—as being of one hue.

Dave and Ruth encourage you in this book, as do I, to turn your "life mola" over, to reclaim and proclaim your TCK heritage fiercely. Your mola, unique and complex in its layering of events, emotions, and experiences, in what is folded back and what remains covered, in what is well stitched and what may need mending, is who you are. Hide it and you have little to show for a childhood like no other in its challenges and invaluable gifts. Display its richness, add to it, share it—and you may well change your life and your world, as have many TCKs before you.

—Norma M. McCaig
Founder, Global Nomads International
President, Global Nomad Resources

Acknowledgments

Without Lois Stück's original encouragement, transcriptions of seminar tapes, suggestions, and expert help throughout the initial creative process of this book, it would have remained only a dream. Without Professor Barbara Cambridge's guidance in the writing process or Professor Jon Eller's most helpful ideas about organization, the manuscript would never have gotten back to Lois or our publishers. Anthropologist Ken Barger; friends Lori Beuerman, Christine Dowdeswell, Janet Fischer, Stephanie Hock, Barb Knuckles, Ann Kroeker, Erica Lipasti, Paul Pedersen, Paul Seaman, Alan Shea, Francisco West, and Elisabeth Wood; wife Betty Lou Pollock; mother Betty Frame; and daughter Stephanie Van Reken Eriksen have all given most helpful suggestions while reading various drafts of the manuscript. Helen Fail's insights into international schooling have been invaluable. The list could go on and on.

Above all, without each TCK and ATCK who has shared his or her story with us through the years, without the honest dialogue we have witnessed among so many, there would have been no story to tell. In particular, we thank the Global Nomad chapter at Valparaiso University for the time they gave to engage in dialogue specifically designed to address issues we are raising in this book. And a huge thanks to "Erika" not only for letting us use her story, but also for helping in the early stages of writing it.

And many thanks to David Hoopes for having the vision that this is a topic whose time has come—to say nothing of his masterfully helping two people join their different thoughts and writing styles into one text. He did not have an easy job. Thanks also to Toby Frank for her further suggestions and Judy Carl-Hendrick for substantial help in the final editorial process. Without each of them this book couldn't have been written in the readable form we trust it now is. And thanks to Patty Topel for readying this manuscript for publication. We've decided it not only takes a village to raise a child but also to birth a book.

Last, but certainly not least, we thank God not only for life but for the richness of our lives. We have experienced much joy in our journeys as we have studied this topic and lived it as well.

Introduction

David C. Pollock

Third culture kids (TCKs) are not new, and they are not few. They have been a part of the earth's population from the earliest migrations. They are normal people with the usual struggles and pleasures of life. But because they have grown up with different experiences from those who have lived primarily in one culture, TCKs are sometimes seen as slightly strange by the people around them.

I have had the joy of working with TCKs since the mid-1970s. In 1986, when David Hoopes, editor-in-chief of Intercultural Press, first asked me to write about TCKs, I struggled with two concerns that still haunt me. First of all, there is much about the highly mobile, transcultural young person that we still don't know or that should be established through research. Second, since we are dealing with people, we are writing about process and progress, not a fixed entity. In the past two decades alone, dramatic changes related to the care of children and adults have occurred in the global nomad community, and undoubtedly new theories and practices will continue to evolve.

We must begin somewhere, however. After more than twenty years of virtually daily interaction with TCKs and their families, we have seen a set of patterns of behavior or reactions to life emerge that stem from the cross-cultural and high-mobility aspects of their upbringing. As I have shared these observations with TCKs, their parents, teachers, and caregivers throughout the world, I have observed a common type of response. Giggles start among the students in one corner of the room. In another, a parent pokes her child in the ribs. Teachers look at each other (and their students) with knowing glances. They all recognize the story. And as I've made this presentation to people in many different kinds of organizations and on every continent except Antarctica, a multitude of TCKs have validated that this is, indeed, their story.

Sometimes the third culture experience is unfairly blamed for problems it didn't generate. At other times it is viewed as a pathology for which therapy is needed and from which one must recover. It is my conviction that being a TCK is not a disease, something from which to recover. It is also not simply okay—it is more than okay. It is a life healthily enriched by this very TCK experience and blessed with significant opportunities for further enrichment.

Since the variety of experience is wide, let's acknowledge that breadth by recognizing that for some, growing up as a TCK has been very difficult, for others much easier. Someone whose experience has been close to ideal isn't in denial for seeing it as so. Someone whose experience has been difficult or painful isn't a wimp, a whiner, or a spoiled child for acknowledging it as such. And those who have known both are also within the normal range of human experience.

My appeal to you as the reader—whether a TCK of any age, a parent, a caregiver for TCKs, or an administrator of agencies with cross-cultural personnel—is that you read carefully and empathetically, act to make a positive difference in the lives of our TCK and adult TCK populations, and provide leadership and support to smooth the way and amplify the advantages for our future TCKs.

I hope the eyes of many will be opened by this book and that it will spark honest thought, sensitive discussion, and productive research into this topic. I pray too that the result will be positive action to help make the TCK experience a strong foundation on which TCKs can build a satisfying and productive adulthood.

A Beginning Word

Ruth E. Van Reken

Sometimes there is a specific moment in a specific day that creeps up so unannounced, it is hardly recognized for its significance, but ever afterward it marks the point when everything changed. Life is never quite the same again. I, and countless others who have grown up in countries and cultures outside that of our parents, have known such a moment. It is that first instant we learn we have a name—that we are third culture kids (TCKs) or adult third culture kids (ATCKs).

My moment came in 1984. It was a typically hot, muggy day in Monrovia, Liberia, where I lived with my husband, David, and our three daughters. I sat on the bed in David's study, sorting through the mail that had just arrived. Mail for me, as for anyone living overseas, was a precious commodity—one to be savored. It looked like a good day.

I organized the letters into piles according to the priority by which I would read them, including a letter from Mom. Ever since my years in boarding school, Mom hasn't missed a week of writing a letter to me when I'm away from her. Faithful as clockwork, never missing a beat. I should have known her letter would be here. It was Monday and the planes came from the States on Friday nights. Mom's letter went on the "slightly later" pile. If there were any earthshaking news, we would have gotten a radio message. Her letter could wait until I finished the rarer one from my school friend.

I read my friend's letter. Nice to get the news, to catch up on what's happening, but nothing particularly unusual. Now for Mom's letter.

"Open carefully, Ruth. Don't tear the stamps." The voice of my philatelist father echoed in my ear even six years after his death. Our mail had always come from so many different countries, each stamp had the potential to be a collector's treasure.

Along with Mom's letter came another two sheets of paper. I casually opened the extra papers to find a two-page article by David C. Pollock called "Ministering to the TCK (Third Culture Kid)." Presumably, Mom had sent it since we were working in what was then called a "Third World Country" and it must have something to do with that. While laying it aside, I wondered if she realized I worked with adults far more than with children. Still, it was nice she'd thought of me.

As I read Mom's letter, I almost forgot about the enclosure. After gathering the other letters and now empty envelopes, I stood up and the article fell to the floor. I bent over to retrieve it, thinking, I might as well read it now as later.

The article began, "He spent sixteen of his first eighteen years in a country where his parents were foreigners. He attended the community schools and spoke the language of the host country better than his parents.... When his parents traveled to the United States for furlough, they spoke of 'going home,' but when furlough was over and they returned to where they were foreigners, he went home."

I couldn't believe it. *This man is writing about me!*

As I continued to read, I was amazed at seeing expressed so many feelings I had experienced but never heard another person put into words. Somehow I had always thought to myself it was my fault for being so "out of it" when I returned to the States from Nigeria for eighth grade. Or when I felt so stupid for not knowing how to swim in high school. But here was someone actually naming some of these kinds of feelings—like always being a square peg in a round hole. Was I truly not the only one in the world to have gone through this? What *was* this third culture kid idea about anyway?

A crack had occurred in my armor that was to grow and later open the way to a whole new world. I didn't know it that day, but this was the moment my life took a new direction and changed forever.

Since then, I have talked to countless other adult TCKs and heard of the moment when they, too, first learned they had a name. That moment is a time to celebrate the many gifts of our backgrounds. It is also a time to begin to understand some of the particular challenges that a highly mobile international childhood can bring. Perhaps, above all else, we've found out we are "normal," whatever that means. Some of our experiences may have been different from those of others we know, but our humanity is the same.

Strangely enough, it took a little longer before I realized that my own father was also a TCK—an American born and raised in Iran. Then I realized I had aunts and uncles and cousins who were all TCKs and that my three daughters were TCKs—Americans reared for nine years in Liberia. Even my husband spent two of his preschool years in China. (And now my first two grandchildren are TCKs in Ghana.)

Since that time, I have discovered a world filled with TCKs from many backgrounds with whom I share a common bond. I hope each one who reads this will have as much joy in discovering his or her connection with this interesting world as I did.

Section One
The Third
Culture Kid
Experience

Part I
Understanding
the World of TCKs

1

Where Is Home? Erika's Story

As the Boeing 747 sped down the runway, Erika sat inside with seat belt secure, her chin propped against a clenched fist, staring out the window until the final sights of her beloved Singapore disappeared from view.

How can it hurt this much to leave a country that isn't even mine? Erika closed her eyes and settled back in the seat, too numb to cry the tears that begged to be shed. *Will I ever come back?*

For nearly half of her twenty-three years, she had thought of Singapore as home. Now she knew it wasn't—and America hadn't felt like home since she was eight years old.

Isn't there anywhere in the world I belong? she wondered.

Countless people of virtually every nationality and from a great variety of backgrounds identify with Erika's feeling of not belonging anywhere in the world. Like her, they may be Americans who grew up in Singapore. But they may also be Japanese children growing up in Australia, British kids raised in China, Turkish youth reared in Germany, African children living in Canada, or the child of a Norwegian father and a Thai mother growing up in Argentina. All of them have one thing in common: like Erika, they are spending, or have spent, at least part of their childhood in countries and cultures other than their own. They are third culture kids (TCKs) or, by now, adult TCKs (ATCKs).

Children are TCKs for many reasons. Some have parents with careers in international business, the diplomatic corps, the military, or religious missions. Others have parents who studied abroad. Still other families live for a period of time outside their home culture because of civil unrest and war.

TCKs are raised in a neither/nor world. It is neither fully the world of their parents' culture (or cultures) nor fully the world of the other culture (or cultures) in which they were raised. This neither/nor world is not merely an amalgamation of the various cultures they have known. For reasons we will explore, in the process of living first in one dominant culture and then moving to another one (and maybe even two or three more and often back and forth between them all), TCKs develop their own life patterns different from those who are basically born and bred in one place. Most TCKs learn to live comfortably in this world, whether they stop to define it or not.

TCKs are not a new phenomenon. They've been around since the beginning of time, but, until now, they have been largely invisible. This has been changing, however, for at least three reasons.

1. *Their number has increased.* In the last half of the twentieth century, the number of people involved in international careers of all types has grown dramatically. In her book *The Absentee American,* Carolyn D. Smith says,

   Since 1946, therefore, when it was unusual for Americans to live overseas unless they were missionaries or diplomats, it has become commonplace for American military and civilian employees and businesspeople to be stationed abroad, if only for a year. The 1990 Census counted 922,000 federal workers and their families living overseas, and the total number of

Americans living abroad either permanently or
temporarily is estimated at 3 million.[1]

That's a lot of people! But Smith is only talking about
Americans. Add to this the burgeoning number of citizens from
every other country working and living outside their home cultures and we can only imagine the total worldwide.

Not only do more people have international careers, but
now it's easier than ever before for these people to take their
children when they move to a new country. Traveling between
home and a host country rarely takes more than one day compared to the three weeks to three months it used to take on an
ocean liner. International schools exist everywhere; advanced
medical care is an airlift away (and soon may be even more
accessible via the Internet!). It is now normal for children to
accompany their parents overseas rather than to stay home.

2. *Their public voice has grown louder.* As these growing numbers of TCKs become adults, they are becoming more vocal.
   Through their alumni associations or organizations such as Global Nomads International,[2] they have formed visible, identifiable groups. Through writing or speaking out, their voices are
   beginning to be heard. As these TCKs and adult TCKs share
   their stories, they encourage others to do the same.

3. *Their significance has increased.* The TCK experience is a mi-
   crocosm of what is fast becoming normal throughout the world.
   Few communities anywhere will remain culturally homogeneous in this age of easy international travel and instant global
   communication. Growing up among cultural differences is already, or soon will be, the rule rather than the exception—even
   for those who never physically leave their home country. Soci-
   ologist Ted Ward claims that TCKs of the late twentieth century are "the prototype [citizens] of the twenty-first century."[3]
   Experts are trying to predict the outcome of this cultural jug-
   gling. Looking at the TCK world can help us prepare for the

long-term consequences of this new pattern of global cultural mixing.

The benefits of the TCK lifestyle are enormous. Many TCKs and ATCKs are maximizing the potential of these benefits in their lives. Unfortunately, others are not. For some the challenges of the TCK experience have been overwhelming, seemingly canceling out the many benefits—a sad waste for both the TCKs and the world around them. It is our hope that a better understanding of some of these benefits and challenges will help TCKs and ATCKs everywhere use the gifts of their heritage well. To this end, throughout this book we examine this paradoxical world of the TCK experience from a variety of perspectives.

We begin by returning to Erika for a better look at one young woman's true story. Only the names and places have been changed.

Erika didn't notice that the captain had turned off the "Fasten your seat belt" sign until a flight attendant interrupted her reverie.

"Would you like something to drink?" he asked.

How many Cokes and roasted peanuts have I eaten on airplanes? she wondered. Far too many to count. But today her grief outweighed any thought of food or drink. She shook her head, and the attendant moved on.

Erika closed her eyes again. Unbidden memories flashed through her mind. She remembered being eight years old, when her family still lived in upstate New York, Erika's birthplace. One day her father entered the playroom as she and her younger sister, Sally, performed a puppet show for their assembled audience of stuffed animals.

"Wanna watch, Dad?" Erika asked hopefully.

"In a few minutes, sweetie. First, I have something special to tell you."

Puppets forgotten, Sally and Erika ran to their dad, trying to guess what it could be. "Are we gonna have a new baby?" Sally began jumping up and down in excited anticipation.

"Did you buy me a new bike?" Erika inquired.

Erika's dad shook his head and sat in the nearby rocking chair, gathering one daughter on each knee. "How would you like to take a long airplane ride?" he asked.

"Wow!"

"Sure."

"I love airplanes."

"Where, Daddy?"

He explained that his company had asked him to move from the United States to Ecuador to start a new branch office. The family would be moving as soon as school ended that June.

A flurry of activity began—shopping, packing, and saying good-bye to relatives and friends. It all seemed so exciting until the day Erika asked, "Mom, how is Spotty going to get there?"

"Honey, it's not easy to take a dog. Grandma's going to take care of him 'til we get home again."

"Mom, we can't leave Spotty! He's part of our family!"

No amount of pleading worked. Spotty was sent to his new home, and finally, with a mixture of eagerness for the adventures ahead and sadness for the people and things they were leaving, Erika and her family flew off to their new world.

Wanting to stop this flood of memories, Erika opened her eyes, trying to focus on her fellow passengers. The diversion didn't work. As soon as she had adjusted her cramped legs and resettled in a more comfortable position, the flashbacks continued. It was almost as if every few seconds a button clicked inside her brain to advance her mental slide show. Pictures of Ecuador replaced those of New York. She had been so scared the first time her family flew into Quito. How would the airplane weave its way between the mountain ranges and find a flat place to land? Yet she remembered how, in time, those same Andes mountains gave her a deep sense of security each morning when she woke to see their towering peaks looming over the city, keeping watch as they had for centuries past.

But what did these memories matter now? She put on her headset, hoping that music would divert her thoughts. Unfortunately, the second channel she switched to carried the haunting music of the hollow-reed flute pipes that always evoked a twinge of melancholy whenever she heard it. The sound brought instant memories of going to fiestas with her Ecuadorian friends and dancing with them while the pipers played. Certainly, listening to this music wouldn't help her now. She took the earphones off, letting them dangle around her neck.

By now the images of the in-flight movie were on the screen in front of her, but Erika never saw them. Her own internal picture show continued with its competing images—the scene changing from towering mountains to the towering skyscrapers of Singapore. After two years in Ecuador, her father had been transferred once more, and for the thirteen years since then—including the four years she attended university in Wisconsin—Erika had considered Singapore her home. Now she knew Singapore would never truly be home. But the question continued to haunt her: where was home?

Still refusing to dwell on that topic, her mind searched for a new cassette of slides to look at. Pictures of countless scenes from other places she had visited with her family through the years appeared— the Kathmandu Valley in Nepal at the beginning of the rainy season, the monkey-cup plants in the Malaysian rain forest, the Karen tribal people in the hills of northern Thailand, winter on the South Island of New Zealand, the water-derrick wells of the Hortobagy in Hungary. One after another the frames appeared in her mind's eye. Even to herself, it seemed incredible how much she had done, seen, and experienced in her first twenty-three years of life. The richness and depth of the world she knew was beyond measure—but what good did that do her today?

Finally, the other pictures ended and Erika was left with the visions of life in Singapore that kept returning, insisting on a paramount spot in the show. Now instead of places, however, she saw people—her amazing collection of friends from the International School in Singapore: Ravi, Fatu, Sam, Kim Su, Trevor, Hilary, Mustapha, Dolores, Joe. One after another they came to her memory. How many races, nationalities, styles of dress, cultures, and religions did these friends represent? With diversity as their hallmark, who could say what was "normal"?

Erika never stopped to wonder that others might be surprised to know that the diversity among her friends reflected the norm rather than the exception of her life. Instead, she reminisced on how she had hated parting from them each summer, when her family returned to the States for vacation. (It was never America or the United States—simply "the States.") Somehow, she always felt much more like a fish out of water with her Stateside peers than she did in Singapore.

For the first time since the airplane had lifted off, a wry smile came to Erika's face. She remembered how strange she had felt the first time her American cousins had asked her to go "cruising." She presumed they meant some type of boat ride—like when she and her friends in Singapore rented a junk and sailed to a small island for a day of sunbathing, swimming, and picnicking. She was eager to go.

To her amazement, cruising for her cousins had nothing to do with boats and water. Instead, it meant endless driving about town with no apparent purpose. Eventually, they parked at a shopping mall and simply stood around. As far as Erika could see, it seemed their purpose was to block aisles rather than purchase any goods. What was the point?

For Erika "going home" meant something entirely different than it did for her parents. When her parents spoke of "going home," they meant returning to the States each summer. For her, "going home" meant returning to Singapore at the end of summer. But where was home now? The nagging question returned.

The temperature dropped inside the airplane as the short night descended. Erika stood up to grab a blanket and pillow from the overhead compartment, hoping for the comfort of sleep. But would sleep ever come on this journey? Not yet. Another set of pictures pushed their way into the muddle of her mind—now with scenes of the time she left Singapore to attend university in the States.

"Don't worry, darling. You'll be fine. I'm sure you'll get a wonderful roommate. You've always made friends so easily. I know you'll have no trouble at all," her parents had reassured her as she faced that transition.

But somehow it hadn't been that easy. Fellow students would ask, "Where are you from?" At first, Erika automatically answered, "Singapore." The universal reply was, "Really? You don't look like it," with the expectation of some explanation of how she was from Singapore.

Soon, Erika decided she would be from New York—where her grandparents lived. She hoped that would simplify these complicated introductions.

Eventually, as she adapted outwardly, picking up the current lingo and attire, others accepted her as one of them. By the end of her freshman year, however, she felt angry, confused, and depressed. How could anyone care so much about who won last week's football game and so little about the political unrest and violence in Bosnia or Rwanda? Didn't they know people actually died in wars? They couldn't understand her world; she couldn't understand theirs.

As time went on, Erika found a way to cope. Once she realized most of her peers simply couldn't relate to what her life had been, she no longer discussed it. Her relatives were happy to tell everyone she was "doing fine."

Just before graduating from university, however, she lost the last internal vestige of home. Her dad was transferred back to the States and her family settled in Dayton, Ohio. For school vacations, she no longer returned to Singapore. Erika closed that chapter of her life. The pain of longing for the past was just too much.

As she stared at the rhythmic, almost hypnotic, flashing red lights on the jet's wings, Erika continued her reflections. *That chapter on Singapore didn't stay closed for very long. When did I reopen it? Why did I reopen it?*

After graduation, she had decided to get a master's degree in history. Thinking about that now while flying somewhere over the Pacific Ocean, she wondered why she had chosen that particular field. *Was I subconsciously trying to escape to a world that paralleled my own—a world that was once exciting but is now gone forever?*

Who could know? All Erika knew was that her restlessness increased in graduate school, and she finally dropped out. At that point, Erika decided only a return to Singapore would stop this chronic unsettled-ness, this sense of always looking for something that might be just around the corner but never was. But also, she couldn't define what she wanted. Was it to belong somewhere? Anywhere?

Although her family no longer lived in Singapore, she still had many Singaporean friends who had often invited her to stay with them. Why not live her own life overseas? Surely it would be far better to live in a place where she belonged than to wander forever in this inner limbo.

Erika called a travel agent, who knew her well because of all her trips during university days, and booked a flight to Singapore. The next step was to call one of her former classmates still living in Singapore. "Dolores, I want to come home. Can you help me find a job? I'm coming as soon as I get my visa, and I'll need a way to support myself once I'm back."

"That's wonderful! I'm sure we can find some kind of job for you," came the reply. "You can stay with me until you get everything lined up." Erika was ecstatic! It felt so familiar, so normal to be planning a trip overseas again. She couldn't wait to return to the world in which she so obviously belonged.

When she arrived in Singapore, her dream seemed to have come true. What airport in the world could compare to the beauty of Changi? Graceful banners hung on the walls, welcoming weary travelers in their own languages. Brilliantly colored flowers cascaded down the sides of the built-in garden beds throughout the terminal. Trees grew beside waterfalls that tumbled over rocks to a pond below. The piped-in sounds of chirping birds completed her sense of entering a garden in paradise. How could anyone not love this place?

As she walked out of the terminal, she took a deep breath. How wonderfully familiar were the smells: tropical flowers and leaded petrol fumes—what a paradox! Living, life-giving plants, and dead, polluting fuel—intermingled. Was it possible her whole life was a paradox? A life full of rich experiences in totally diverse cultures and places, each experience filled with a special vibrancy that made her want to dance and celebrate the joy of life. And yet, a life in which she always felt a bit like an observer, playing the part for the current scene, but forever watching to see how she was doing.

Erika quickly brushed these thoughts aside. Those times of being an outsider were gone now because she knew where she belonged—in Singapore. How wonderful finally to be home!

As the days progressed, however, life seemed less familiar. She discovered that many things she had taken for granted as a child in the expatriate business community of Singapore were no longer hers to enjoy as a young, single, foreign woman living with a Singaporean family. No maid, no expensive restaurants, no car, fewer friends. Instead, she had to wash her clothes by hand, grab cheap rice dishes from street vendors, and get around the city by walking blocks in the hot sun to take a crowded bus.

While growing up, her family might not have been classified as wealthy, but there had always been enough money for them to be comfortable and not worry about paying the bills, taking little side trips or splurging on a particularly nice outfit. Now she had to consider seriously such mundane questions as how much lunch cost and how she could pay for her barest living expenses.

Finding a job was harder than she had guessed it would be. Jobs that paid enough for her to rent a reasonably modest apartment and buy food and clothes had to be contracted with international companies before entering the country. Now she realized that was what her father had done. To make matters worse, she learned that available jobs were next to impossible for a noncitizen to get. Because the government wanted to save jobs for Singaporeans, it rarely issued a work permit for local jobs to a foreigner. The jobs for local hires that she could find would not pay enough for her to live safely, let alone well. Because a young white woman was so visible in a cheap rent district with high crime rates, Erika feared she would present a far too easy target for someone bent on robbery or assault.

Here, in the world she had always thought of as home, Erika realized she was seen as a foreigner—an outsider. There was no such thing as an international passport.

The sad day came when she finally had to admit that she didn't fit in this country either. Sitting in her friend's tiny apartment in a world she had thought was home, despair swept over her. She was lost. The promises of big dreams seemed foolish and childish. She belonged nowhere. With a muffled sob she picked up the telephone and dialed her parents' number.

"Mom, I can't make it here, but I don't know what to do. I don't fit in Dayton, but I don't fit here either. Somehow I seem to have grown up between two totally different worlds, and now I've found out I don't belong to either one."

With infinite sorrow this time, she made one last airline reservation, and now she was here, forty thousand feet in the air, going—home?

Erika's story is only one of thousands we have heard from TCKs all over the world. The particulars of each tale are different, yet in a sense so many are the same. They are the stories of lives filled with rich diversity but mixed with an underlying question of where TCKs fit among all that diversity. What are some of the reasons for this common thread among TCKs? Who, indeed, are these TCKs and what are some of the benefits and challenges inherent in the experience they have had? These are the questions we will address in the chapters which follow.

Endnotes

[1] Carolyn D. Smith, *The Absentee American* (1991; reprint, Putnam Valley, NY: Aletheia Publications, 1994), 2.

[2] An organization formed by Norma McCaig in 1986 for TCKs of every background and nationality.

[3] Ted Ward, "The MKs' Advantage: Three Cultural Contexts," in *Understanding and Nurturing the Missionary Family,* edited by Pam Echerd and Alice Arathoon (Pasadena, CA: William Carey Library, 1989), 57.

2

Who Are "Third Culture Kids"?

Who or what exactly is a third culture kid? Here's the definition we like best:

> A Third Culture Kid (TCK) is a person who has spent a significant part of his or her developmental years outside the parents' culture. The TCK builds relationships to all of the cultures, while not having full ownership in any. Although elements from each culture are assimilated into the TCK's life experience, the sense of belonging is in relationship to others of similar background.[1]

Let's look at this definition in detail.

"A Third Culture Kid (TCK)..."

Some of the most vigorous discussions about TCKs start with a debate over the term itself. Over and over people ask, "How can you possibly say people with such incredibly diverse cultural backgrounds and experience can make up a 'culture,' when the word *culture*, by definition, means a group of people who have something in common?"

This is one of the strange paradoxes about TCKs. Looking at the differences among them—of race, nationality, sponsoring organizations, and places where they are growing (or have grown) up—you would think TCKs could have little in common. But if you attend a conference sponsored by Global Nomads International and watch the animated, nonstop conversation of the participants throughout the weekend, you will not question the powerful connection between them. What is this almost magical bond? Why have they been called third *culture* kids?

The Third Culture as Originally Defined

A common misconception about third culture kids is that they have been raised in what is often called the "Third World." While this might be true for some, the Third World has no specific relationship to the concept of the third culture. Two social scientists, Drs. John and Ruth Hill Useem, coined the term *third culture* in the 1950s, when they went to India for a year to study Americans who lived and worked there as foreign service officers, missionaries, technical aid workers, businessmen, educators, and media representatives.[2] While in India, the Useems also met expatriates from other countries and soon discovered that "each of these subcultures [communities of expatriates] generated by colonial administrators, missionaries, businessmen, and military personnel—had its own peculiarities, slightly different origins, distinctive styles and stratification systems, but all were closely interlocked."[3] They realized the expatriates had formed a lifestyle that was different from either their home or their host culture, but it was one they shared in that setting.

To best describe this expatriate world, the Useems defined the home culture from which the adults came as the first culture. They called the host culture where the family lived (in that case, India) the second culture. They then identified the shared lifestyle of the expatriate community as an *interstitial culture,* or "culture between cultures," and named it the third culture. The Useems called the children who had grown up in that interstitial culture *third culture kids.*

The Third Culture as Currently Defined

The Useems did their research when most Western expatriates lived in specific communal systems such as military bases, missionary compounds, and business enclaves. Identifying a visible, local expatriate community was relatively easy.

However, the world has changed since then. Today, many expatriates no longer live in defined communities. The Japanese families who live in Kokomo, Indiana, and work for Delco-Remy don't live in a Delco-Remy compound. Their children usually attend local schools instead of going off to boarding schools as TCKs often used to do. Because there are frequently no well-marked expatriate enclaves anymore, some argue that the terms *third culture* or *third culture kid* are now misnomers. How can there be a culture if people don't live together?

When we asked Dr. Useem what she thought about this, she said, "Because I am a sociologist/anthropologist I think no concept is ever locked up permanently…. Concepts change as we get to know more; other times concepts change because what happens in the world is changing."[4]

In her recent report on a survey of adult TCKs, Dr. Useem herself defined the third culture as a generic term to discuss the *lifestyle* "created, shared, and learned" by those who are from one culture and are in the process of relating to another one. In that same article, she defines TCKs simply as "children who accompany their parents into another society."[5]

These larger definitions are justifiable because if culture in its broadest sense is a way of life shared with others, there's no question that, in spite of their differences, TCKs of all stripes and persuasions in countless countries share remarkably important life experiences through the very process of living in and among different cultures—whether or not they grew up in a specific local expatriate community. Further, the kinds of experiences they share tend to affect the deeper rather than the more superficial parts of their personal or cultural being.

Like a double rainbow, two realities arch over the TCK experience that shape the formation of a TCK's life:

1. *Being raised in a genuinely cross-cultural world.* Instead of simply watching, studying, or analyzing other cultures, TCKs actually live in different cultural worlds as they travel back and forth between their home and host cultures. Some TCKs who have gone through multiple moves or whose parents are in an intercultural marriage have interacted closely with four or more cultures.

2. *Being raised in a highly mobile world.* Mobility is normal for the third culture experience. Either the TCKs themselves or those around them are constantly coming or going. The people in their lives are always changing, and the backdrop of physical surroundings may often fluctuate as well.

Members of this broad third culture community usually have other characteristics in common, including:

1. *Distinct differences.* Many TCKs are raised where being physically different from those around them is a major aspect of their identity. Even when external appearances are similar to either their host or home culture, TCKs often have a substantially different perspective on the world from their peers.

2. *Expected repatriation.* Unlike immigrants, third culture families usually expect at some point to return permanently to live in their home country.

3. *Privileged lifestyle.* Historically, employees of international businesses and members of missions, the military, and the diplomatic corps have been part of an elitist community—one with special privileges bestowed on its members by either the sponsoring organization or the host culture or both. Often, there are systems of logistical support or "perks": those in the military can use the commissary or PX; embassy or missionary compounds may employ home repair or domestic service person-

nel; diplomatic families may have chauffeurs to drive the children to school or around town. Even without the perks, there are entitlements such as worldwide travel to and from their post—all at the expense of the sponsoring agency.

4. *System identity.* Members of specific third culture communities may be more directly conscious than peers at home of representing something greater than themselves—be it their government, their company, or God. Jobs can hinge on how well the adults' behavior, or that of their children, positively reflects the values and standards of the sponsoring agency.

The first two characteristics of living in a cross-cultural and highly mobile world are true for virtually every third culture person. The degree to which TCKs may differ from their host culture, expect to repatriate, enjoy a privileged lifestyle, or identify with the organizational system varies a bit more depending on where and why their families are living outside the home culture.

A Sample Slice of the "Neither/Nor" Third Culture

ATCKs Rob and Heather are citizens of different countries who grew up on opposite sides of the globe. The only thing they share is the fact they were both raised outside their parents' home cultures. After hearing a lecture at a Global Nomads International conference about both the original and broader meaning of the term *third culture,* they talked together during a break.

> Rob spoke first. "I felt pretty skeptical before coming to this conference, but maybe there is something to this third culture bit. It never occurred to me that the military lifestyle I grew up in had a culture that was different from my home or host cultures. I just thought of myself as an American in Japan."
>
> "Why?" Heather asked.
>
> "I was nine when my family moved from Oregon to the 'American Bubble' in Japan—that's what everyone called our Army base. It seemed completely American.

Through the commissary or PX we could get Cheerios for breakfast, Nikes to run in, and even Pringles for snacks. The movies in our base theater were the same ones being shown in the States. Man, we even had tennis courts and a swimming pool just like I did at my YMCA in Portland!"

Heather looked at Rob with amazement. "I can't believe it!" she said. "I'm at least twenty years older than you, I've never been to Japan, my dad worked for the British government in Nigeria, but I can relate to what you're saying!"

"How come?" asked Rob.

"Well, I really don't know. I guess I never thought about it before. Maybe because we lived in a 'British Bubble'? We just didn't call it that. Although we didn't have a PX or commissary, we did have Kingsway stores in every major city. They imported all those wonderful British things like Marmite, Weetabix, and Jacob's Cream Crackers. We also had a swimming pool and tennis courts at the local British club. It all seemed very British and very normal."

Rob responded, "Yeah, well, I don't know about you, but for me, even with so many American trappings, life in Japan still wasn't like living in Portland. When I left the base and took the train to town, I suddenly felt isolated because I couldn't understand the people chattering around me or read most of the signs."

"I know what you mean," Heather responded. "With all our British stuff around, it still wasn't like living in England. I had a Nigerian nanny who taught me how to speak Hausa and how to *chiniki*, or bargain, for things as I grew up. I wouldn't have done that in England. But I probably got more into the local culture than you did, since we moved to Nigeria when I was two."

"Well, I got into the local culture too," Rob said, a bit defensively. "I mean, after a few months I found Japanese friends who taught me how to eat sushi, use chopsticks, bathe in an *ofuro*, and sleep on a futon. But my life wasn't like theirs any more than it was like life back in Portland. For one thing, I went to the local international school, where I studied in English instead of Japanese."

"I understand that, too!" Heather exclaimed. "My life wasn't the same as my Nigerian friends' lives either—even if I could speak their language. I had a driver who took me back and forth from school each day, while most of my friends had to walk long distances in the heat of the day to attend their schools."

"So did your life overseas seem strange?" Rob and Heather looked up in surprise to see that someone had joined them.

Both shook their heads at the same time in response to the stranger's question.

"Nope, not to me," said Rob.

"Me either," interjected Heather.

The newcomer persisted. "But how could you feel normal when you lived so differently from people in either your own countries or Japan or Nigeria? Seems to me that would make you feel somewhat odd."

Rob thought for a quick moment. "Well, I suppose it's because all the other American kids I knew were growing up in that same neither/nor world the speaker talked about today. All my Army and international friends had moved as often as I had. We were used to saying good-bye to old friends and hello to new ones. No big deal. That's life. Nothing unusual, since we were all doing it. I don't know—it just seemed like a normal way to live, didn't it, Heather?"

"Exactly. I lived the same way all my other British

and expatriate friends did. They had house help. So did
we. They flew from one continent to another regularly. So did I. When we went out to play, all of us
wore the same kind of pith helmets so we wouldn't
get sunstroke. To me, it's just how life was."

While both Rob and Heather happened to grow up in an easily identifiable expatriate community, third culture families who live in less
defined communities still find ways to keep some expression of their
home culture. In Indiana the Japanese community has organized
special swimming classes at the local YMCA for their TCKs because they want to maintain their traditionally more disciplined approach to training children. They also conduct Saturday classes, when
all academic subjects are taught in Japanese, so their TCKs maintain both written and verbal language skills.

But all this talk about the third culture should not distract us
from understanding the most crucial part of the TCK definition, the
fact that a TCK:

"...is a person..."

Why are these words critical to all further discussion on third culture kids? Because we must never forget that above all else, a TCK
is simply a person. Sometimes TCKs spend so much time feeling
different from people in the dominant culture around them that they
(or those who notice these differences) begin to feel TCKs are, in
fact, intrinsically different—some sort of special breed of being.
While their experiences may be different from other people's, TCKs
have the same need as non-TCKs for building relationships in which
they love and are loved, ones in which they know others and are
known by them. They need a sense of purpose and meaning in their
lives and have the same capacities to think, learn, create, and make
choices as others do. The characteristics, benefits, and challenges
that we describe later arise from the interactions of the various aspects of mobility and the cross-cultural nature of this upbringing,
not from some fundamental difference in them as persons.

"...who has spent a significant part..."

Time by itself doesn't determine how deep an impact the third culture experience has on the development of a particular child. Other variables such as the child's age, personality, and participation in the local culture have an important effect. For example, living overseas between the ages of one and four will affect a child differently than if that same experience occurs between the ages of eleven and fourteen.

While we can't say precisely how long a child must live outside the home culture to develop the classic TCK characteristics, we can say it is more than a two-week or even a two-month vacation to see the sights. Some people are identifiable TCKs or ATCKs after spending as little as one year outside their parents' culture. Of course, other factors such as the parents' attitudes and behavior or policies of the sponsoring agency add to how significant the period spent as a TCK is or was in shaping a child's life.

"...of his or her developmental years..."

Although the length of time needed for someone to become a true TCK can't be precisely defined, the time *when* it happens can. It must occur during the developmental years—from birth to eighteen years of age. We recognize that a cross-cultural experience affects adults as well as children. The difference for a TCK, however, is that this cross-cultural experience occurs during the years when that child's sense of identity, relationships with others, and view of the world are being formed in the most basic ways. While parents may change careers and become former international businesspeople, former missionaries, former military personnel, or former foreign service officers, no one is ever a former third culture kid. TCKs simply move on to being adult third culture kids because their lives grow out of the roots planted in and watered by the third culture experience.

"...outside the parents' culture."

The home culture is defined in terms of the parents' culture. Most often, TCKs grow up outside the parents' home country as well as culture, and the stories throughout our book predominantly feature this more typical TCK experience. It's important to recognize, however, that TCKs can be children who never leave their parents' country but are still raised in a different culture. Jennifer is one.

> Both of Jennifer's parents grew up in upper-middle-class suburbs of Toronto. When Jennifer was nine, they became teachers for five years on a First Nation (Native American) reservation near Vancouver. Jennifer went to school, played, ate, and visited with her First Nation playmates almost exclusively during those years—yet her lifestyle was not the same as theirs. For example, there were celebratory rituals in the First Nation culture that Jennifer's family never practiced. Her parents had rules for curfew and study hours that many friends didn't have, but Jennifer accepted these differences between her and her friends.
>
> When she was fourteen, Jennifer's parents returned to Toronto. They wanted her to have a more "normal" high school experience. Unfortunately, it wasn't as normal as they had hoped. For one thing, Jennifer's new classmates seemed to judge one another far more critically by what styles of clothes they did and didn't wear than she had ever experienced before. Far worse, however, it seemed to her that this emphasis on apparent trivia stemmed from a lack of concern for what she considered the *real* issues of life. When newspapers reported the ongoing conflict of land issues between the First Nation people and the Canadian government, she read the accounts with keen interest. She personally knew friends whose futures were directly affected by these political

decisions. But when she tried to discuss such things
with fellow classmates or their parents, the response
was almost dismissive. "I don't know what those
people are complaining about. Look at all we've
already done for them." The more she tried to explain
why this topic needed attention, the more they labeled
her as radical, and the more she labeled them as
uncaring. Jennifer sobbed herself to sleep many nights,
wishing for the comfortable familiarity of the world
and friends she'd known before.

Although she had never left Canada, Jennifer had become a TCK—
someone raised in that world between worlds—within her own country. Military children who have never moved outside their countries
may also share many TCK characteristics. The military subculture
(see Mary Edwards Wertsch, *Military Brats*) is quite different from
that of the civilian population around it. When military parents return to civilian life, their children often experience many of the same
feelings that internationally mobile TCKs describe when they return to their passport countries.

Raised on Navy bases in California and Washington,
DC, Bernadette was fourteen when her father retired
from the Navy and her family settled in the
midwestern town of Terre Haute, Indiana. Bernadette
later described the experience as one of total alienation from her peers, whose life experience was
completely foreign to her.

"...The TCK builds relationships
to all of the cultures, while not
having full ownership in any."

This brings us back to Erika.

As she flew back to the United States, Erika wondered
how it could be that life felt like such a rich dance in
and through so many cultures while at the same time

that same richness made it seem impossible to stop the dance. To land in Singapore would mean she could celebrate the hustle and bustle of that wonderful city she loved so much, but then she would miss the mountains of Ecuador and the joy of touching and seeing the beautiful weavings in the Otavolo Indian markets. To end the dance in Ecuador meant she would never again see the magnificent colors of fall in upstate New York or taste her grandmother's special Sunday pot roast. But to stop in New York or Dayton, where her parents now lived, meant she would miss not only Singapore and Ecuador but also all the other places she had been and seen. Erika wished for just one moment she could bring together the many worlds she had known and embrace them all at the same time, but she knew it could never happen.

This is at the heart of the issues of rootlessness and restlessness discussed later. This lack of full ownership is what gives that sense of belonging "everywhere and nowhere" at the same time.

"...Although elements from each culture are assimilated into the TCK's life experience,..."

Obviously, there are specific ways each home and host culture shape each TCK (Rob loves peanut butter and jelly, Heather prefers Marmite; Rob eats his Cheerios and speaks Japanese, while Heather eats Weetabix and speaks Hausa). But it's not only food and language that shape them. Cultural rules do as well.

- After living in London where his dad served as ambassador for six years, Musa had trouble with how people dealt with time when he returned to Guinea. Instead of relaxing as others from his home culture could when meetings did not begin and end as scheduled, he felt the same frustration many expatriates experienced. Musa had exchanged the more relational worldview of his home culture for a time-oriented worldview during his time abroad.

- At his summer job in Canada, Gordon's boss thought he was dishonest and lazy because Gordon never looked anyone in the eye. But where Gordon had grown up in Africa, children always kept their eyes to the ground when talking with adults.

Certainly cultural practices are incorporated from the unique aspects of both host and home cultures, but the third culture is more than the sum total of the parts of home and host culture. If it were only that, each TCK would remain alone in his or her experience.

"...the sense of belonging is in relationship to others of similar background."

Erika returned to Dayton, Ohio, after her long, final flight back from Singapore. She began teaching high school French and Spanish during the day; tutoring international businesspeople in English filled her evenings. Once more she tried to accept the reality that her past was gone. Life must go on, and she couldn't expect anyone else to understand her when she didn't understand herself.

Then a remarkable thing occurred. Erika met Judy.

One evening she went to see a play and got there a few minutes early. After settling in her seat, she opened her program to see what to expect.

Before she could finish scanning the first page, a middle-aged woman with curly, graying hair squeezed past her, sitting in the next seat.

Why couldn't she have a ticket for the row in front? That's wide open. Erika rolled her eyes to the ceiling. *All I wanted was a little space tonight.*

Then it got worse. This woman was one of those friendly types.

"Hi, there. I'm Judy. What's your name?"

Oh, brother, lady. I'm not into this kind of chitchat.

"I'm Erika. It's nice to meet you." *There, that's over with.* And she turned her eyes back to study the program again.

"Well, I'm glad to meet you too."

Why won't she let me alone?

The lady went on. "I come for the plays every month but I haven't seen you before. Are you new here? Where are you from?"

C'mon, lady. Erika was becoming more internally agitated by the moment. *This is the theater, not a witness stand. Besides, you don't really want to know anyway.* "I live here in Dayton," Erika replied, with cool politeness. *That ought to end it.*

But Judy continued. "Have you always lived here?"

Why does she care? Erika was definitely losing composure at this point. "No, I've only lived here for two years." *Now shut up, lady.*

"Oh, really? Where did you come from before that?"

With a sigh, Erika half turned to look at this pesky woman and said, "I've lived in lots of different places." *So there.*

"Hey, that's great. So have I! Where have you lived?"

For the first time, Erika looked Judy in the eye. She couldn't believe it. This lady genuinely wanted to know. Erika hesitated. "I lived in Ecuador and Singapore."

"How long?"

"Oh, about ten years between the two places, if you're talking about actually living and going to school there full-time."

"You're kidding! I grew up in Venezuela. I'd love to talk to you about it. It's not always easy to find someone here in Dayton who understands what it's like to grow up in another country."

Just then the curtain went up for the play, so they stopped talking. Afterward, they went for coffee and Erika found herself amazed. Here they were, two

women from two totally different backgrounds—
Judy's parents had been in the foreign service while
Erika's were in business; Judy had lived in Venezuela
and Erika had lived in Ecuador and Singapore. Judy was
forty-seven, married, the mother of four grown
children, while Erika was twenty-five, single, with no
children. Yet they were soon talking and laughing
together like long-lost friends.

"I remember when the CEO's wife first came to
our house for dinner," Erika said with a chuckle. "She
had just arrived in Singapore and kept talking about
how awful everything was. My sister and I made up all
sorts of stories about how big the roaches were and
how poisonous the spiders were just to scare her."

Judy laughed. "I know how you felt. I hated it when
new people arrived and complained about everything.
I always felt so protective for what seemed like my
personal Venezuela."

"Well, I guess it was kind of mean," Erika said, "but
we didn't like her barging into our world without
trying to understand the parts we loved so much. We
thought she was arrogant and narrow-minded and
didn't deserve to be there—and she probably thought
we were the same!"

They laughed together and continued talking for
three hours. Erika couldn't believe it. For the first time
in years she could speak the language of her soul
without needing a translator. A space inside that had
almost dried up suddenly began filling and then
overflowing with the joy of being understood in a way
that needed no explanation.

TCKs around the world instinctively feel this connection when they
meet each other. But why? How can someone from Australia who
grew up in Brazil understand that inner experience of someone from
Switzerland who grew up in Hong Kong?

A video of TCKs meeting at Cornell University clearly demonstrates this bond.[6] Among the TCK panelists are

- Kelvin—born in Hong Kong, raised in Nigeria and England;
- Marianne, a Danish citizen who grew up in the United States;
- Kamal, an Indian who lived in Japan as a child;
- a young Turkish man who spent his childhood in Germany, England, and the United States;
- one American who grew up in the Philippines; and
- another American reared in France.

Although each person in the video has differing points of identification with his or her host culture (e.g., the Turkish man feels he is extremely punctual as a result of living in Germany for many years), throughout the discussion it's obvious that their commonalities of feelings and experiences far outweigh their differences. It is equally obvious that they are delighted to finally find a forum where simply naming how they have felt in various circumstances brings instant understanding. No further explanation is needed to elicit a sympathetic laugh or tear from their peers.

But the question remains: what is it about growing up in multiple cultures and with high mobility that creates such instant recognition of each other's experiences and feelings?

Endnotes

[1] "The TCK Profile" seminar material, Interaction, Inc., 1989, 1.

[2] Ruth Hill Useem, "Third Culture Kids: Focus of Major Study," *Newslinks*, Newspaper of the International School Services 12, 3 (January 1993): 1.

[3] Ruth Hill Useem, "Third Cultural Factors in Educational Change," in *Cultural Challenges to Education: The Influence of Cultural Factors in School Learning,* edited by Cole S. Brembeck and Walker H. Hill (Lexington, MA: Lexington Books, 1973), 122.

[4] Personal letter to David C. Pollock, February 1994.

[5] Useem, "Third Culture Kids," 1.

[6] *Global Nomads: Cultural Bridges for the Future*, coproduced by Alice Wu and Lewis Clark in conjunction with Cornell University.

3

Why a Cross-Cultural Childhood Matters

I am
a confusion of cultures.
Uniquely me.
I think this is good
because I can
understand
the traveller, sojourner, foreigner,
the homesickness
that comes.
I think this is also bad
because I cannot
be understood
by the person who has sown and grown in one place.
They know not
the real meaning of homesickness
that hits me
now and then.
Sometimes I despair of
understanding them.
I am

an island
and
a United Nations.
Who can recognise either in me
but God?[1]

　　　　　　—"Uniquely Me" by Alex Graham James

Who Am I?

This poem by Alex, an Australian TCK who grew up in India, captures the paradoxical nature of the TCK experience—the sense of being profoundly connected yet simultaneously disconnected with people and places around the world. The question, however, is this: what makes Alex, like Erika and most TCKs, feel this way?

Before we can answer that question, we need to take a closer look at the world in which they grow up, a world filled with cross-cultural transitions and high mobility. These two related but distinct forces play a large role in shaping a TCK's life.

We recognize, of course, that TCKs aren't the only ones who experience cross-cultural differences or high mobility. In large metropolitan centers around the world, children may live their entire lives in one place with neighbors from a great variety of ethnic or racial backgrounds and become aware of cultural differences at an early age. Children may also experience high mobility within their own country for various reasons. Without doubt, these factors will shape a non-TCK's life as well. After Dave Pollock presented "The TCK Profile" in Washington, DC, one non-TCK said, "I'm an American who has never lived outside the States, but my dad climbed the corporate ladder while I grew up. We moved every two years or so, whenever he got his next promotion. I have all the challenges of the mobility issues without the benefits of the cross-cultural experience." We also realize that many adults experience both cross-cultural transitions and high mobility as they embark on international careers; their lives, too, are inevitably changed in the process.

So what makes the TCK experience different from that of these children or adults? Children who grow up amid people from many cultures in one locality usually learn to be comfortable with the diversity. It's a relatively stable diversity. The child isn't being chronically uprooted, and the unwritten rules for how the groups coexist and relate to one another are clearly defined and practiced. The difference for TCKs is that they not only deal with cultural differences in a particular location, but the entire cultural world they live in can change overnight with a single airplane ride. Relationships are subject to equally dramatic changes as they or others around them constantly come and go. When non-TCK children move within the same culture, they miss old friends and need to go through grief at losing familiar people and places, but they don't have to relearn basic cultural rules and practices when they unpack in the next city. The language remains the same, the currency still works, and they already know who the president is.

When people first go to another culture as adults, they experience culture shock and need a period of adjustment, but their value system, sense of identity, and the establishment of core relationships with family and friends have already developed in the home culture. They clearly see themselves as Americans, Australians, Kenyans, or Indonesians who happen to be living in another place or culture. Their basic sense of who they are and where they belong is intact. Unlike adults with similar experiences, however, for TCKs the moving back and forth from one culture to another happens before they have completed the critical developmental task of forming a sense of their own personal or cultural identity. A British child taking toddling steps on foreign soil or speaking his or her first words in Chinese with an amah (nanny) has no idea of what it means to be human yet, let alone "British." He or she simply responds to what is happening in the moment.

To have any meaningful discussion about TCKs, it is essential to remember that it is an *interplay* of these factors—living in both a culturally changing *and* highly mobile world during the *formative* years—rather than any single factor alone that leads to the evolution of both the benefits and challenges we describe as well as the personal characteristics. To better understand how the interplay of these factors works, we need to look at each one separately and in more depth to determine how a TCK's experience differs from that of the child who grows up among diverse cultures in one place or with high mobility alone. We will begin in this chapter by taking a look at the cross-cultural nature of the TCK's childhood. Then, in chapter 4, we will move on to high mobility.

The Significance of Culture

One of the major developmental tasks that help us form our sense of identity and belonging is to successfully learn the basic cultural rules of our society while we are children, to internalize those principles and practices as we move through adolescence, and then use them as the basis for how we live and act as adults. In order to look at this normal process and then why it is so significant for TCKs, we need to first answer these questions: What is culture? How do we learn it? Why is it important?

When we first think of the word *culture*, the obvious things such as how to dress and act like those around us come to mind. But learning culture is more than learning to conform to external patterns of behavior. Culture is also a system of shared assumptions, beliefs, and values.[2] It is the framework from which we interpret and make sense of life and the world around us. As cultural anthropologist Paul G. Hiebert emphasizes, culture is learned rather than instinctive behavior—something caught from, as well as taught by, the surrounding environment and passed on from one generation to the next.[3] Author and cross-cultural trainer and consultant L. Robert Kohls suggests we look at culture as a kind of iceberg, with one part clearly visible above the surface of the water and another, much larger part hidden below. The part above the water can be identified as the *surface culture* and includes behavior, words, customs, and traditions. Underneath the water where no one can see is the *deep culture,* and it consists of beliefs, values, assumptions, and thought processes. Here is a representation of Dr. Kohls' culture iceberg.

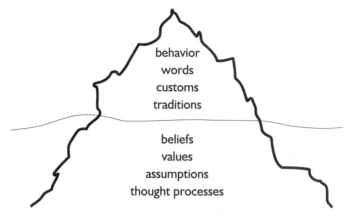

behavior
words
customs
traditions

beliefs
values
assumptions
thought processes

No group can be cohesive without its members sharing a basic consensus in the deeper dimensions of culture. Merely mimicking behavior—such as clothing styles or food preferences—will not hold a group together.[4]

Perhaps one of the best illustrations of the traditional role of culture is seen in *Fiddler on the Roof*, a musical about a farmer named Tevye and his Russian Jewish village of Anatevka. For years Tevye's culture has remained basically the same. Everyone knows where he or she fits in relationship to one another and to God. There have been no major outside influences. The way things have always been is the way things still are, with the milkman, matchmaker, farmer, and all others clearly aware of their assigned roles in the village. Roles assigned by whom? By *tradition*, which is another word for how cultural beliefs are worked out in practice. Tevye says,

> Because of our traditions, we've kept our balance for many, many years. Here in Anatevka we have traditions for everything—how to eat, how to sleep, how to wear clothes. For instance, we always keep our heads covered and always wear a little prayer shawl. This shows our constant devotion to God. You may ask, how did this tradition start? I'll tell you—I don't

> know! But it's a tradition. Because of our traditions,
> everyone knows who he is and what God expects him
> to do.... Without our traditions, our lives would be as
> shaky as—as a fiddler on the roof![5]

Tevye then laments that tradition is breaking down. During the story, as the old ways rapidly change, he loses his former sense of balance. His grip on life is slipping, his comfortable world shattered. Mentally and emotionally, Tevye can't keep up, and he begins to feel disoriented and alienated, even from his own children.

Why is *cultural balance*—that almost unconscious knowledge of how things are and work in a particular community— important? Because when we are in cultural balance, we are like a concert pianist who, after practicing for years to master the basics, now no longer thinks about how to find the right piano keys or when to pedal or how to do scales or trills. Those functions have become almost automatic responses to notations in the score of music, and this freedom allows the pianist to use these basic skills to create and express richer, fuller music.

Cultural balance gives us that same kind of freedom. Once we have stayed in a culture long enough to internalize its behaviors and the assumptions behind them, we have an almost intuitive sense of what is right, humorous, appropriate, or offensive in any particular situation. Instead of spending excessive time worrying if we are dressed appropriately for a business appointment, we can concentrate on coming up with a new business plan. Being "in the know" gives us a sense of stability, deep security, and belonging. Like Tevye, we may not understand *why* cultural rules work as they do, but we know *how* our culture works.

Conversely, when we are having to learn and relearn the basic rules by which the world around us is operating, our energies are spent in surviving rather than thriving. It's as if we are still figuring out the fingering for the scales on the piano while others around us are playing a Rachmaninoff concerto. Being out of cultural balance leaves us struggling to understand what is happening rather than fully participating in the event.

A World of Changing Cultures

Through the years, many TCKs have told us they wonder what is wrong with them, because they never seem to "get it." No matter what situation they are in, they often make what looks like a dumb remark or mistake. Others wonder at their apparent stupidity, while they are left with the shame that somehow they can never quite fit in socially as others do.

Perhaps ironically, the struggle many TCKs face in trying to find a sense of cultural balance and identity is not because they learn culture differently from the way others do. In fact, the real challenge comes *because* they learn culture as everyone does—by "catching it" from their environment rather than by reading a book or getting a master's degree in cultural anthropology. What TCKs and those who know them seem to forget is that their life experiences have been different from someone who grows up in a basically stable, traditional, monocultural community such as Tevye's. As TCKs move with their parents from place to place, the cultural values and practices of the communities they live in often change radically. What was acceptable behavior and thinking in one place is now seen as crude or ridiculous in the next. Which culture are they supposed to catch? Do they belong to all of them, none of them, or some of each of them? Where in the world (literally) do they fit?

Another factor for TCKs in finding cultural balance is that cultural norms are as unconsciously taught as they are caught. Parents, community, school, and peers are all part of the cultural teaching process, whether the members of those groups think about it or not. When everyone in a community such as Tevye's holds the same basic values and customs, each group unthinkingly reinforces the next group's instructions. For TCKs, however, not only do the overall cultural rules often change overnight, but equally often the individual members of these four basic groups in any given place may hold markedly different world- and lifeviews from one another. Let's take a look at how the normal process of learning cultural balance may be complicated by each of these groups in a TCK's life.

Parents

Parents communicate both the "above water" and "below water" cultural norms in various ways. They do it by example, dressing differently for a business meeting than for a tennis match, or speaking respectfully of others. They do it by correction: "Don't chew with your mouth open." "If you don't stop hitting your brother, you'll have to take a time-out." Or they do it by praise: "What a good boy you are to share your toys with your sister!"

Wherever TCKs are being raised, their families' cultural practices and values are usually rooted in the parents' home culture or cultures and may be markedly different from the practices of the surrounding culture. This includes something as simple as the style of clothing. Girls from the Middle East may continue wearing a head covering no matter which country they live in. Dutch children wear Western dress in the forests of Brazil. Of course, it's far more than that as well. Telling the truth at all costs may be a prime value at home, while shading the truth to avoid shaming another person is the paramount value in the host culture.

Increasing numbers of TCKs are also being born to parents who are in an intercultural marriage or relationship. In 1960 one-quarter of American children living overseas had parents from two cultures, according to Ruth Hill Useem.[6] In 1995 Helen Fail found that 42 percent of her ATCK survey respondents had grown up in bicultural families.[7] One young man, for example, was born in the Philippines to a German father married to a Cambodian mother, and they speak French as their common family language. That's a lot of cultures for a young child to learn, and it complicates this most elemental step of learning cultural rules and practices from parents.

Community

In a community like Tevye's, other adults reinforce what the parents teach at home because the rules are uniform. The same characteristics—such as honesty, hard work, and respect for adults—bring approval (or, in their absence, disapproval) from the community as well as from parents. No one stops to question by whose standards some cultural behaviors and customs are defined as proper and others as improper, but everyone knows what they are.

TCKs interface with different local communities, each having different cultural expectations, from the moment they begin their odyssey in the third culture experience. Unless they are isolated in a military, embassy, mission, or company compound and never go into the surrounding community, the host culture certainly affects them. They learn to drop in on friends without calling ahead. They call adults by their first names. When TCKs return to their home culture, they usually have to switch to a different set of cultural customs and practices. Now an unexpected visit becomes an intrusion. Addressing a playmate's mother or father by her or his first name is rude enough to be a punishable offense. Woe to the TCK who forgets where he or she is.

Besides the home and host cultures, in many situations TCKs are also conditioned by the overall expatriate community as well as the subcommunity—missionary, business, military, diplomatic corps—in which they grow up. Each of these groups also has its own subculture and clear expectations of behavior. In *Military Brats,* Mary Edwards Wertsch writes,

> Certainly by the time a military child is five years old, the values and rules of military life have been thoroughly internalized, the military identity forged, and the child has already assumed an active stage presence as an understudy of the Fortress theater company.[8]

Whatever the rules are in any TCK's given subculture—be they matters of correct dress, correct faith, or correct political views—TCKs know that to be an accepted member of that group, they must conform to those standards.

School

Although culture isn't taught from a book, no educational system develops in a cultural vacuum. A curriculum, along with how it is taught, is a direct reflection of the cultural values and beliefs of the society. Those who believe in the curriculum do so because they feel the values and practices it emphasizes are correct. As long as the community is in basic cultural agreement, the school will reinforce its views and practices because teachers and administrators (who also come from that community) will make choices for what is taught that are consistent with what parents and others in the community believe and teach.

For many TCKs, however, what and how things are taught at school may be vastly different as they shift from school to school while moving from one place to another. In addition, in an international community the individual teachers themselves often come from many different cultures. This can add significant confusion to the TCK's cultural development. Joe's story is an excellent example.

> My siblings and I found ourselves the only Americans in an Anglo-Argentine culture and we went to British schools. But the Argentines also thought their education was pretty good, so Peron mandated an Argentine curriculum for every private school and, with what time was left over, the school could do what it wanted. We went to school from 8:00 to 4:00 with four hours in Spanish in the morning and four hours of an English public school in the afternoon.
>
> Meanwhile, our parents fought desperately to keep some semblance of Americanism at home. They lost the battle of the "crossed 7s." They lost the spelling battle. Worse, when they were told that in a given year there would be a focus on North American history, geography, and literature, they discovered, to their dismay, North America meant Canada.[9]

It isn't only Americans going to British-oriented schools who struggle. Some of the most difficult situations are those of children who are from non-English-speaking countries who go to American-oriented schools. One Norwegian girl who attended such a school writes:

Norway became my well-kept secret. I was a fiercely patriotic little girl, and every May 17 I would insist on celebrating Norway's independence day. My American classmates had their Thanksgiving and Halloween parties. I was never invited, except for once, when I left the party in tears because I didn't understand the English in the video they were watching. Little did it help that we had a teacher from Texas who taught us U.S. history that year. When I put Florida on the wrong side of the map she scolded me for it. That memory is still very vivid in my mind. I was forced to hear about the wonders of America, and no one cared to hear about Norway. No one seemed to care that English wasn't my first language, and the school wouldn't give us time to learn Norwegian during school hours—we had to study Norwegian during our vacations. I used to think that was really unfair.[10]

If school is a place for learning the values as well as the behavior of culture, what happens when children attend a school with completely different customs, values, or religious orientation from that of their parents? This often occurs for globally nomadic families when the choices for schools that teach the academic curriculum of their home country may be limited to schools based on a belief system which does not match their own.

TCKs who go to boarding school experience another distinct subculture twenty-four hours a day rather than only during school. Without question, different rules are needed to organize scores of children in a dormitory environment rather than two or three in a home. Some TCKs talk of being raised by their peers more than by adults in such a setting. Some consider this the most positive thing about boarding school; others say it was the most difficult. Either way, it is a different experience from going to a day school and returning to parents each night.

Peers

When children play together, they instinctively parrot the cultural rules they have been taught: "You're cheating!" "Don't be a sissy!" As children grow, shaming one another this way enforces the norms of the community.

Most TCKs attend school and play with peers from many cultures—each culture valuing different things. Some friends practically live and die for soccer and cricket; others love American football and baseball. Some children are raised to believe that academic success is the highest priority; others value peer relationships over high grades. How does a child decide which is really most important?

While virtually all children learn culture from their parents, community, school, and peers, TCKs often have two additional sources of cultural input: caregivers and sponsoring agencies.

Caregivers

Some TCKs are left with a caregiver for perhaps as long as all day, five days a week, while both parents work. These caregivers are often members of the host culture and may speak only their national language. A German child being cared for by a Scottish nanny will likely hear no German during the time they spend together. Methods of child care in various cultures can be radically different. Instead of being pushed in a pram, Russian children raised in Niger will be carried on their African nanny's back until they can walk. Shaming may be the main method of training a child in the host culture rather than the positive reinforcement typical of the home culture.

Caregivers inevitably reflect their culture's attitude toward children and life. The story goes that when Pearl Buck was a child in China, someone asked how she compared her mother to her Chinese amah. It is said that Buck replied, "If I need to hear a story read, I go to my mother. If I fall down and need comforting, I go to my *amah*." One culture valued teaching and learning while the other placed a greater value on nurture, and as a child, Buck instinctively knew the difference.

Sponsoring Agencies

Many TCKs' parents belong to sponsoring agencies that have special behavioral or philosophical expectations of not only their employees but of the employees' families as well. This may result in situations that people in the home culture could never imagine. Two examples follow.

- A child's indiscretions (such as spraying graffiti on the wall of a public building) in a foreign service community might be written up and put in a parent's file, forever influencing future promotions, while that same behavior wouldn't cause a ripple in a parent's career if it happened in a suburban community in the home country.

- In the military, if a parent doesn't come in for a teacher-parent conference, the teacher can speak with the parent's officer-in-charge and the officer will require the parent to come in. If a military child does something as serious as getting drunk in school or setting off a firecracker, for example, he or she might be sent back to the home country, the parent won't be promoted that year, and the incident goes on the parent's permanent record.

In addition to such specific expectations for families in certain organizational subcultures, we have historically often neglected to look at how the root or home culture of the sponsoring agency itself may affect TCKs, particularly those who come from a different culture. The increasing internationalization of organizations throughout the world will soon force us to do so. When the policies and operational processes of an agency are rooted in a nationality or culture other than an employee's home culture, it means that without very careful planning, the decisions made by the executives of that organization which deeply affect the employee and his or her family may no longer coincide with the TCK's parental culture. Look at Ilpo's story to see what a major effect this one factor alone can have on a TCK's life. This relates to schooling options provided for him.

Ruth Van Reken met Ilpo, a Finnish TCK who had grown up in Taiwan, while he was finishing his medical residency program at the University of Chicago. He had completed all his post-secondary school education in the United States, including medical school. She asked why he had chosen to come to the United States rather than returning to school in Finland.

"Well, it sort of just happened," Ilpo replied. "My folks taught in a seminary in Taiwan, but the other missionaries were from America and Norway. Even though the curriculum for our little mission school was supposedly an international one, we had an American teacher, so all our classes were in English." Ilpo went on to explain how at age twelve he had gone to the American boarding school in Taichung and he lived in a small dorm run by the Finnish mission. Although he spoke Finnish in the dorm, his classes and interactions with fellow students took place in English. It was about this time that Ilpo faced his first cultural crisis. If he had been in Finland, after ninth grade he would have competed with all other Finnish students in a special test to decide who could continue their academic schooling and who would go to a trade or vocational school. When the time came for Ilpo to take that exam, he encountered a major problem. His education had been in English and the exam was in Finnish. Although he spoke Finnish fluently with his family, his written language skills in that language and his knowledge of the curriculum content from which the tests came were deficient. Ilpo knew he wanted to be a doctor, but if he went back and competed with students who had been studying in Finnish schools, the chances of his scoring high enough to attend university were slim. Ultimately, he felt his only option was to attend university in the States within the educational system he knew. But that also meant he had to stay in the United States for medical training because in Finland, medical training begins during university, not after it.

When Ruth asked Ilpo where he expected to live after his training, he said it would be very difficult to go back to Finland. Not only was its system different, but he didn't know medical vocabulary in Finnish. Even if he learned that, fellow physicians would look down on him because he had trained somewhere else. Ruth asked how he felt about that and Ilpo said, "That's what I'm coming to grips with now. I didn't realize before how nearly impossible it would be ever to return to Finland. It's a choice that slipped out of my hands. I feel like my world slipped away."

TCKs in Relationship to Surrounding Dominant Culture

There is another aspect of cross-cultural living that has a significant influence on a TCK's life—the changing nature of how he or she fundamentally relates to the surrounding dominant culture, be it the home or host culture. Sometimes people presume we only mean a TCK's relationship to the host culture when we talk of his or her relationship to the "dominant culture," but they forget that one of a TCK's most stressful times may be trying to sort out the relationship to the home culture itself. So let us be clear—the patterns of how a TCK relates to the surrounding culture that we are about to describe are possible in both host and/or home cultures.

We said earlier that no group can hold together for long if they share only the visible or surface parts of culture such as dress, language, behavior, and traditions. That is true. Traditionally, however, people have used their surface culture (e.g., tribal scarifications, heraldry, or the chador) to identify themselves as people who also share a common deep culture; in other words, they have similar beliefs, assumptions, and values. In some places, various tribes and nationalities may have coexisted side by side, but everyone readily knew by appearance who was and was not part of his or her group and, thus, who did or didn't share a common outlook in the deeper culture values as well.

Things are not so simple anymore. Across the world, external patterns of behavior are changing. TV, videos, and the Internet expose people all over the world to similar styles and fashions. Traditional garb is replaced by business suits (or blue jeans). Increased contact through trade, communication, and travel also causes the influences of music, food, and language to spread from one place to another with dizzying speed. We are careening toward the global village Marshall McLuhan and Bruce R. Powers predicted, where the campfire in the middle is a TV set telling us what we should all buy and how we should all look.[11]

But the deeper levels of culture that Kohls mentions are far slower to change than the surface ones. This creates a major problem. Why? As long as we look different from another person, or have some way to quickly and easily identify that we are different, we don't expect the other to behave or believe as we do. But when a person looks and acts much like us on the outside, we assume sameness on the inside and fully expect that other person to respond in a situation as we would. The truth is, the *appearance* that we are the same hides the fact that in those deeper places of culture—the ones from which we make our life decisions—we may be as different as ever. This actually increases cultural stress. We are far more offended if people who look like us don't behave as we assumed they would than if we never have any expectations of similarity in the first place.

How does this characteristic of cultural interaction affect the TCK experience? And how does that relate to our discussion of cultural differences?

Despite the fact that our world is becoming more of a global village, whatever country TCKs live or travel in, there is still a predominant national or local culture. The language and currency used for trade, the view of the elderly, whether tasks or relationships are most valued, and the racial or ethnic makeup of the majority of the population are examples of what might be part of the prevailing, overall cultural milieu. Wherever a TCK lives, he or she may or may not resemble the physical appearance of the majority of the members of that culture. In addition, the pervading cultural beliefs and assumptions may or may not be the same ones from which the TCK operates. In other words, wherever they live, at both the superficial and deeper levels of culture, TCKs either appear similar to and/or think like members of the surrounding dominant culture or they appear different and/or think differently from members of that culture. This means that there are four possible ways they relate to the surrounding culture, be it the home or host culture. For our purposes, we have called these relational patterns *foreigner, adopted, hidden immigrant*, and *mirror*.

Foreigner Look different Think different	**Hidden Immigrant** Look alike Think different
Adopted Look different Think alike	**Mirror** Look alike Think alike

1. *Foreigner—look different, think different.* This is the traditional model for TCKs in the host culture. They differ from those around them in both appearance and worldview. They know and others know they are foreigners. In a few cases (e.g., international adoption), this category may apply to TCKs in their official home culture as well.

2. *Adopted—look different, think alike.* Some TCKs appear physically different from members of the surrounding culture, but they have lived there so long and immersed themselves in the

culture so deeply that their behavior and worldview are the same as members of that culture. While TCKs may feel very comfortable relating to the surrounding culture, others may treat them as foreigners.

3. *Hidden immigrant—look alike, think different.* When TCKs return to their home culture, or when they grow up in countries where they physically resemble the majority of the citizens of that country, they appear like those around them, but internally these TCKs view life through a lens that is as different from the dominant culture as any obvious foreigner. People around them, however, presume they are the same as themselves inside, since they appear the same outside.

4. *Mirror—look alike, think alike.* Some TCKs not only physically resemble the members of their host culture, but they have lived there so long that they have adopted the deeper levels of that culture as well. No one would realize they aren't citizens unless they show their passports. TCKs who return to their home culture after spending only a year or two away or who were away only at a very young age may also fit in this category. Although they have lived abroad, their deeper levels of culture have remained rooted solidly in the home culture and they identify with it completely.

Of course, non-TCK children and adults may fall into one or another of these boxes at any given time, but the difference for TCKs is that throughout childhood they are constantly changing which box they're in depending on where they happen to be. They may be obvious foreigners one day and hidden immigrants the next. To complicate the matter further, many TCKs do not make a simple move from one culture to another but are in a repetitive cycle of traveling back and forth between at least home and host cultures throughout childhood. But why does that matter? Because as they move in and out of various cultures TCKs not only have to learn new cultural rules, but more fundamentally, they must understand who they *are* in relationship to the surrounding culture.

Defining this relationship is relatively simple when they are in the foreigner or mirror categories. In both cases, they are who they seem to be. Those in the foreigner box look around and realize that the people around them are different from themselves. People in the community look back at the TCKs and realize they are different as well. Neither TCK nor the member of that culture expects the other person to necessarily think or act like he or she does; they automatically know they are not the same—and they're not. Of course, TCKs in the mirror box look at the community and the community looks back and both expect the other to share similar fundamental principles for life as they do—and they are right again. In both the foreigner and mirror categories the expectations of who others are in the deeper levels as well as superficial levels of culture matches reality—for both TCKs and those in the community.

When TCKs are in the adopted or hidden immigrant categories, however, the expectations no longer hold true. What they and those around them presume is not what they get. Sometimes adopted TCKs feel frustrated when community members overexplain simple things they already know or speak to them slowly, presuming they can't understand the local language. Community members don't realize that in spite of physical differences these TCKs are remarkably like them inside. On the other hand, community members look at the hidden immigrant TCKs, presuming they can do every common task others around know how to do. A Cameroonian TCK who is raised in London and then returns to Cameroon at fourteen, however, probably has no idea how to husk a coconut just off the palm tree like other Cameroonian children can. Members of the community wonder how one of its own could be so ignorant. That same TCK may also be shocked, however, that friends at home don't yet know how to surf the Internet. Based on similar appearances, both TCKs and those in the community are expecting the others to be like themselves in every basic way. This time their expectations are wrong, but neither side forgives the other as they would a true immigrant or obvious foreigner for unexpected behavior or even ignorance. Relating as a hidden immigrant in any culture may be one of the greatest cultural challenges that many TCKs face.

It's not hard to see how growing up cross-culturally can affect a child's attempts to understand who he or she is in relation to the world around, but how does the highly mobile nature of a TCK's childhood also influence the very development of who they are? This will be the subject of chapter 4.

Endnotes

1 Alex Graham James, "Uniquely Me," in *Scamps, Scholars, and Saints*, edited by Jill Dyer and Roger Dyer (Kingswood, SA, Australia: MK Merimna, 1991), 234.

2 Paul G. Heibert, *Cultural Anthropology*, 2d ed. (Grand Rapids, MI: Baker Book House, 1983), 28–29.

3 Ibid., 25.

4 L. Robert Kohls (unpublished manuscript). Used by permission.

5 Book by Joseph Stein, music by Jerry Bock, lyrics by Sheldon Harnick, based on Sholom Aleichem's stories, *Fiddler on the Roof*, 4th Limelight Edition (New York: Crown Publishers, 1994), 2, 9.

6 Useem, "Third Cultural Factors," 126.

7 Helen Fail, "Some of the Outcomes of International Schooling" (master's thesis, Brookes University, Oxford, England, 1995), 76.

8 Mary Edwards Wertsch, *Military Brats* (1991; reprint, Putnam Valley, NY: Aletheia Publications, 1996), 6.

9 Joseph McDonald, MK e-mail communication, October 1995. Used by permission.

10 Personal correspondence from TCK to David C. Pollock, November 1995. Used by permission.

11 Marshall McLuhan and Bruce R. Powers, *The Global Village: Transformations in World Life and Media in the 21st Century* (New York: Oxford University Press, 1989).

4

Why High Mobility Matters

I had adored the nomadic life. I had loved gallivanting
from Japan to Taiwan to America to Holland and
onward. In many ways, I had adapted well. I had
learned to love new smells and vistas and the myster-
ies inherent to new cultures.... I had conquered the
language of internationalists, both the polite exchange
of conversation in formal settings and the easy intimacy
of globetrotters. I was used to country-hopping. To
move every couple of years was in my blood. In spite
of the fact that foreign service life is one long continuous meal of loss—loss of friends and beloved places—I
loved it. The warp of my life was the fact of moving
on.[1]

—Sara Mansfield Taber

We have looked at the cross-cultural nature of the TCK experience
in some detail. We also want to clarify how we define the term *high
mobility* and why it is the second major factor in the life of most
TCKs.

People often ask how we can say that high mobility is one of the
two nearly universal characteristics for TCKs when mobility patterns vary so widely among them. Some move to a different country
every two or three years with parents who are in the military or

diplomatic corps. It's obvious that their lives are highly mobile. Others stay in one country from birth to university, and mobility wouldn't appear to be an issue for them.

All TCKs, however, deal with mobility issues at one level or another. Children of parents in business like Erika or those with parents in the foreign service usually take home leave each summer. Missionaries' children may only go on furlough every four years, but they usually stay away from the host country for a longer period of time, sometimes up to a year. Each leave means good-bye to friends in the host country, hello to relatives and friends at home; then good-bye to those people a short time later, and hello again to the host country friends—if those friends are still there. TCKs who attend boarding school have other major patterns of mobility. Whether they go home once or twice a year or spend three months at school followed by one month at home, each coming and going involves more greetings and farewells—and more adjustments. Paul Seaman describes this pattern of mobility well.

> Like nomads we moved with the seasons. Four times a
> year we packed up and moved to, or back to, another
> temporary home. As with the seasons, each move
> offered something to look forward to while something
> had to be given up.... We learned early that "home"
> was an ambiguous concept, and, wherever we lived,
> some essential part of our lives was always someplace
> else. So we were always of two minds. We learned to
> be happy and sad at the same time. We learned to be
> independent and [accept] that things were out of our
> control.... We had the security and the consolation
> that whenever we left one place we were returning to
> another, already familiar one.[2]

Besides a TCK's personal mobility, every third culture community is filled with people who continually come and go. Short-term volunteers arrive to assist in a project for several weeks and then they are gone. A favorite teacher accepts another position a continent away. Best friends leave because their parents transfer to a new post.

Older siblings depart for boarding school or university at home. The totality of all these comings and goings—of others as well as the TCKs themselves—is what we mean when we use the term *high mobility* throughout this book, and any time there is mobility, everyone involved goes through some type of transition experience as well. To understand better why high mobility is the second major factor in a TCK's developmental process, we need to look at the normal process of transition.

The Transition Experience

In a certain sense, life for everyone, TCK or not, is a series of transitions—a "passage from one state, stage, subject, or place to another."[3] Each transition changes something in our lives. Some transitions are normal and progressive—we expect them, as in the transition from infancy to childhood or from middle age to old age. Sometimes these life transitions include physical moves from one place to another, such as when a young person goes off to university in another state. In most cases, we know these transitions are coming and have time to prepare for them.

Other transitions, however, are sudden and disruptive—such as the unexpected loss of a job, a serious injury, or the untimely death of a loved one. Life after these transitions is drastically different from what it was before. The abruptness of the change disorients us and we wonder, "What am I ever going to do?"

TCKs also experience expected and unexpected transitions. There are two important reasons, however, why this topic deserves special focus in a discussion on TCKs. First, because of the high mobility inherent in their lifestyle, TCKs go through major transitions far more frequently than those born and raised in one basic area. Psychologist Frances J. White says, "Because of the nature of their work, [third culture families] are particularly vulnerable to separations. They experience not only the...usual share of situational separations faced by the world at large but also a number of partings idiosyncratic to their profession."[4]

Second, TCKs not only go through the transition process more often than most people, but when it involves their personal movement from one location to another, TCKs usually change cultures as well as places. This increases the degree of impact from that experience as the issues related to what is commonly referred to as *culture shock* are piled on top of the normal stress of any transition.

Although there are many types of transitions, for our purposes we will concentrate on describing transition within the context of physical mobility. In any particular transition, of course, we may be a member in the sending or receiving community, but our discussion will primarily focus on how the process takes place from the perspective of the one who is leaving. Basically, each transition experience goes through these five predictable stages:

1. Involvement
2. Leaving
3. Transition
4. Entering
5. Reinvolvement

Involvement Stage

We barely recognize this first stage of transition because life seems too normal to be a "stage." We feel settled and comfortable, knowing where we belong and how we fit in. Under ideal circumstances, we recognize we are an *intimate* part of our community and are careful to follow its customs and abide by its traditions so that we can maintain our position as a valued member. We feel a responsibility to be involved in the issues that concern and interest our community, and we're focused on the present and our immediate relationships rather than thinking primarily about the past or worrying over the future.

Involvement is a comfortable stage for those around us as well. People hear our name and instantly picture our face and form. They know our reputation, history, talents, tastes, interests, and our place in the political and social network.

Leaving Stage

One day life begins to change. We learn we will be leaving, and deep inside we begin to prepare. At first we may not realize what's going on—especially if our departure date is more than six months away. With shorter warning, however, the mostly unconscious leaving process starts immediately. We begin loosening emotional ties, backing away from the relationships and responsibilities we have had. We call friends less frequently. We don't start new projects at work. During the last year before graduation from high school or university, this leaning away is called "senioritis."

While it may be normal—and perhaps necessary—to begin to detach at some level during this stage, it is often confusing as well to both our friends and ourselves. This detachment can produce anger and frustration in relationships that have been close or in the way we handle our job responsibilities.

> During one transition seminar, Dave Pollock talked about this loosening of ties as part of the leaving stage. Soon he noticed a general buzz in the room. One gentleman sat off to the side, blushing rather profusely as others began to laugh. When Dave stopped to ask what was happening, the blushing gentleman said, "Well, I guess I better confess. I'm the manager here, and just yesterday those working under me asked to meet with me. They complained about my recent job performance and told me I don't seem to care; I take far too much time off; I'm unavailable when they need me, and so on. As you've been talking, I just realized what's been happening. Last month, my CEO told me I would be transferred to a new assignment, so mentally I've already checked out."
>
> "That's pretty normal," Dave said rather sympathetically.

> "I know," he replied. "The only problem is I'm not
> due to leave for two more years. Maybe I'd better
> check back in again!"

We may not upset an entire office staff as this man did, but unless we consciously choose to maintain and enjoy relationships and roles as long as possible, at some point all of us will back away in one form or another. It's part of the state of denial that comes during the leaving stage as we unconsciously try to make the leaving as painless as we can. Other forms of self-protective denials surface as well.

Denial of feelings of sadness or grief. Instead of acknowledging sadness, we begin to think, "I don't really like these people very much anyway. Susie takes way too much of my time with all her problems. I'll be glad when I'm out of here and she can't call me every day." We can also deny our sadness at leaving by focusing only on what is anticipated. We talk about the wonderful things to do, eat, and see in the next location and seemingly make a mental leap over the process of getting there.

> One Canadian ATCK began to weep at this point in a
> transition seminar. Later he said, "Dave, I feel terrible.
> I grew up in a remote tribe in Papua New Guinea.
> When I left to return home for university, I could only
> think about how much I'd enjoy having Big Macs, TV,
> and electricity. I looked forward to new friends. When
> my PNG friends came to say good-bye, they started to
> cry, but I just walked away. Now all I can think about is
> them standing there as my little plane took off. They
> thought I didn't care. I want to go back and hug them
> one last time. What should I do?"

Of course, there was nothing wrong with this TCK developing a positive view of the coming move, but when he didn't acknowledge the losses involved in the leaving, he had no way to deal with them. Denying our feelings may get us through an otherwise painful moment, but the grief doesn't go away, and we simply hold on to it into the next stage of transition.

Denial of feelings of rejection. As friends plan for future events (e.g., next year's annual company picnic or the school play), we suddenly realize they are talking around us. No one asks what we would like to do or what we think about the plans. We have become invisible. Of course, we understand. Why should they include us? We'll be gone. In spite of what we know, however, we can still feel intense rejection and resentment. If we deny those feelings and push them aside as ridiculous and immature behavior (obviously we *shouldn't* feel like this), then that underlying sense of rejection and resentment easily produces a seething anger, which results in almost unbelievable conflicts—especially with those who have been close friends and colleagues. Failing to acknowledge that we are beginning to feel like outsiders (and that it hurts) only increases the chances that we will act inappropriately during this stage.

We may not consciously realize it, but as we're loosening our ties to the community, it's loosening its ties to us. Not only do people forget to ask our opinion about future events, they begin giving our jobs to others. They choose someone else for committees and announce the name of the teacher replacing us next year. The same types of denials we use are being used by them. Suddenly our flaws as friends or coworkers seem glaringly obvious, and they secretly wonder why they've maintained this relationship for so long in the first place.

Denial of "unfinished business." The closer we come to separation, the less likely we are to reconcile conflicts with others. We talk ourselves out of mending the relationship, unrealistically hoping that time and distance will heal it—or at least produce amnesia. Once more, the unfortunate reality is that we arrive at our next destination with this unfinished business clinging to us and influencing new relationships. Bitterness in one area of our lives almost always seeps out in another.

Denial of expectations. To prevent disappointment or fear, we may deny anything we secretly hope for. "It doesn't matter what kind of house I get; I can live anywhere." We deny we would like people to give us a nice farewell. We presume that if we have no expectations, we can't be disappointed. In reality, however, we all have expectations for every event in our lives. When they are too high, we're disappointed. When they're too low, we create fear, anxiety, or dread for ourselves.

One thing, however, helps save the day for everyone. This is the time when communities also give us special attention. There are ceremonies of recognition—a watch presented for years of faithful service or a plaque given to say thanks for being part of a team. Graduation ceremonies remind us this school will never be the same without our shining presence. This special attention and recognition help us forget for a moment that even though we are promising never to forget each other, already there is a distance developing between us and those we will soon leave behind.

Transition Stage

At the heart of the transition process is the transition stage itself. It begins the moment we leave one place and ends when we not only arrive at our destination but make the decision, consciously or unconsciously, to settle in and become part of it. It's a stage marked by one word—*chaos!* Schedules change, new people have new expectations, and living involves new responsibilities, but we haven't yet learned how everything is supposed to work. Norma M. McCaig, founder of Global Nomads, says the transition stage is a time when families moving overseas become at least temporarily dysfunctional. This dysfunctionality doesn't last (we hope), but it can be painfully discomfiting at the time.

First, we and all family members making the move with us lose our normal moorings and support systems at this point. Suddenly we aren't relinquishing roles and relationships—they're gone! We've lost the comfort they gave but haven't formed new ones yet. We're not sure where we fit in or what we're expected to do.

Second, this sense of chaos makes us more self-centered than normal. We worry about our health, finances, relationships, and personal safety to a far greater degree than usual. Problems that aren't generally a big deal are exaggerated. Headaches become brain tumors and sneezes become pneumonia. The loss of a favorite pen causes despair. We know we'll never find it again because the usual places we would look for it are gone.

Third, parents who are focusing on their own survival often forget to take time to read their children stories, stop to pick them up, or sit on the floor with them for a few minutes as they did in the past. Children wonder what's happening. The insecurity of each family member contributes to everyone's chaos. Family conflicts seem to occur for the smallest reason and over issues that never mattered before.

The enormous change between how the old and new communities take care of the everyday aspects of life—banking, buying food, cooking—can create intense stress. To make matters worse, we may be scolded for doing something in the new place that was routine in the old one.

> TCK Hanna grew up in an area of chronic drought.
> The local adage for flushing the toilet was "If it's
> brown, flush it down. If it's yellow, let it mellow."
> Breaking that rule meant serious censure from her
> parents or anyone else around.
>
> Unfortunately, Hanna's grandma in the States had
> never heard this wonderful rule. At age thirteen,
> Hanna visited her grandma. Imagine Hanna's chagrin
> and embarrassment when Grandma pulled her aside
> and scolded her for not flushing the toilet.

A severe loss of self-esteem sets in during this transition stage. Even if we physically look like adults, emotionally we feel like children again. Not only are we getting scolded for things about which we "should have known better," but, particularly in cross-cultural moves, it seems we have to learn life over practically from scratch. As teenagers and adults, probably nothing strikes at our sense of self-esteem with greater force than learning language and culture, for these are the tasks of children. Suddenly, no matter how many decibels we raise our voices, people don't understand what we're trying to say. We discover gestures we have used all our lives—like pointing someone out in a crowd using our index finger—have completely opposite meanings now (in some cultures, it's a curse). Our cultural and linguistic mistakes not only embarrass us but make us feel anxious and ashamed of being so stupid.

Initially, the community may welcome us warmly—even overwhelmingly. But in every culture the newcomer is still exactly that—and newcomers by definition don't yet fit in. Our basic position in the new community is one of *statuslessness*. We carry knowledge from past experiences—often including special knowledge of people, places, and processes—but none of that knowledge has use in this new place. No one knows about our history, abilities, talents, normal responses, accomplishments, or areas of expertise. Sometimes it seems they don't care. Soon we question whether our achievements in the previous setting were as significant as we thought.

People may now see us as boring or arrogant because we talk about things, places, and people they have never heard mentioned before. We feel the same way toward them because they talk about local people and events about which *we* know nothing.

Even with an initial warm welcome, we may discover it's not as easy as we thought it would be to make close friends. Circles of relationships among our new acquaintances are already well defined, and most people aren't looking to fill a vacant spot in such a circle. It's easy to become resentful and begin to withdraw. Fine, we say inside, if they don't need me, I don't need them.

Sadly, this type of withdrawal results in more feelings of isolation and alienation, for it continues to cut us off from any hope of making new friends. This increasing sense of loneliness can lead to more anger—which makes us want to withdraw even more.

The transition stage is a tough time because we often feel keenly disappointed. The difference between what we expected and what we're experiencing can trigger a sense of panic. All connection and continuity with the past seem gone, and the present isn't what we had hoped it would be. How can we relate the different parts of our lives into a cohesive whole? Is the orderliness of the past gone forever? We look longingly to the future—hoping that somehow, sometime, life will return to normal.

Entering Stage

> Standing on the edge of the Quad at Houghton College, TCK Ramona quietly said to no one in particular, "I think I'll go to my dorm and unpack my suitcase...and my mind."
>
> Ramona had graduated from an international school more than a year before. For fifteen months she'd been traveling and visiting relatives while working at short-term jobs. Without her own place to nest, Ramona could never finish the transition stage. Finally, with her arrival at school and the decision to settle in, she began the entering stage of the overall transition process.

During this stage life is no longer totally chaotic. We have made the decision that it is time to become part of this new community: we just have to figure out how to do it. Although we very much want to move toward people in this new place, however, we still feel rather vulnerable and a bit tentative. What if we make a serious social faux pas? Will others accept us? Will they take advantage of us? We often deal with these fears through an exaggeration of our normal personality traits as we begin to interact with others in our new location. People who are usually shy, introverted, or quiet may become more so. Normally gregarious or outgoing individuals may become loud, overbearing, and aggressive. Then, of course, we're mad at ourselves for acting so "stupid" and worry even more that people won't like us.

This stage is also when we feel a lot of ambivalence. We start to learn the new job, feel successful on a given day, and think, "I'm glad I'm here. This is going to be all right." Next day, someone asks us a question we can't answer, and we wish we were back where we knew most of the answers. Our emotions can fluctuate widely between the excitement of the new discoveries we're making and the homesickness that weighs us down. When we say *boot* and *bonnet* instead of *trunk* and *hood* (or vice versa), everyone laughs and tells us we're so funny. We laugh with them, but inside there is that feeling that nobody thought this was strange in our last place. There we were "normal," not different. On the other hand, tomorrow we catch ourselves just before we say the wrong word and use the local term instead. When it passes without a flicker from those around us (in spite of how strange it sounds to our ears!), we realize we are actually beginning to learn how life works here.

Entering is the stage, more than any other, where we need a good mentor. While we'll discuss that in detail later, suffice it to say that the day finally comes when we actually recognize someone from our new community in the grocery store and can call that person by name. We drive to the other side of town, down quiet, unmarked streets, without anyone telling us where to turn—and we find the house we are looking for! Someone calls with a procedural question at work and this time we *do* know the answer. Hope begins to grow that we will, in fact, one day have a sense of belonging to this community.

Of course, we must not forget that this entry stage is a bit uncomfortable for members of our new community as well, although they may have been eagerly anticipating our arrival. Before we came, everyone's roles were clear. Relationships—whether positive or negative—were established. Life functioned without explanation. We show up, and life changes for them too. Now *everything* seems to need an explanation. They also have to adjust their social order at least slightly to help us find our way in. In the end, however, people in the community begin to remember our names, include us in the events going on, realize we are here to stay rather than simply visiting, and start to make room for us in their world.

Reinvolvement Stage

And then the day finally comes. The light at the end of the proverbial tunnel is that in any transition, cross-cultural or not, a final, recognized stage of reinvolvement is possible. Although there have been moments of wondering if it will ever happen, given enough time and a genuine willingness to adapt, we will once again become part of the permanent community. We may not be native to that community, but we can ultimately belong.

We have learned the new ways and know our position in this community. Other members of the group see us as one of them, or at least they know where we fit in. We have a sense of intimacy, a feeling that our presence matters to this group. We feel secure. Time again feels present and permanent as we focus on the here and now rather than hoping for the future or constantly reminiscing about the past.

This is the normal process of transition. Knowing about the various stages doesn't keep them from happening, but it does help us to not be surprised by what happens at each stage, to recognize we are normal, and to be in a position to make the choices that allow us to gain from the new experiences we encounter while dealing productively with the inevitable losses of any transition experience.

****

Just as TCKs learn culture in the same ways others do, so they are quite as capable as anyone else of navigating their way through these stages of transition and being enriched by them. As with the cultural overlay, however, we need to be aware of some extra stresses TCKs may encounter during the transition process because of their particular lifestyle. Some globally nomadic families make international moves every two years or so, and their TCKs may chronically move from the leaving to entering to leaving stages without knowing the physical or emotional comfort and stability of involvement, let alone reinvolvement. When a tree is transplanted too often, its roots can never grow deep. So it is with these young people. Some TCKs refuse to get involved in a new place because they fear that liking this new place would mean betraying the friends and places they have known and loved before. Others don't settle in as a protection against being hurt again in a future move they know will inevitably come. If they refuse to make close friends, it won't matter when they have to say good-bye next time.

All of this raises the question, "How can any child survive so much cultural confusion and chronic change?" Perhaps one of the strangest things about TCKs is that for most of them this type of lifestyle itself becomes normal. Even the mobility becomes part of the routine. What Pico Iyer describes as the international culture[5] is, in fact, their world and, like Rob and Heather, our American and British ATCKs, they have found a comfortable place and sense of identity and security in it.

What we have also discovered, however, in doing seminars around the world is that because theirs is an intangible world, not tied to one visible place, most TCKs have lived their experience without the words to define it. Our presentations are often not so much about giving new information as much as they are about putting words to matters TCKs and their families already know without realizing they know it. They just never had words to describe their total life experiences before. With the hope that this book will do the same for many more, we proceed to look at the specific benefits and challenges as well as other characteristics we have observed through the years and call "The TCK Profile."

Endnotes

[1] Sara Mansfield Taber, *Of Many Lands: Journal of a Traveling Childhood* (Washington, DC: Foreign Service Youth Foundation, 1997), 1.

[2] Paul Seaman, *Paper Airplanes in the Himalayas: The Unfinished Path Home* (Notre Dame, IN: Cross Cultural Publications, 1997), 7–8.

[3] *Merriam-Webster's Collegiate Dictionary,* 10th ed., *s.v.* "transition."

[4] Frances J. White, "Some Reflections on the Separation Phenomenon Idiosyncratic to the Experience of Missionaries and Their Children," *Journal of Psychology and Theology* 11, no. 3 (Fall 1983): 181–88.

[5] Pico Iyer, "The Empire Writes Back," *Time,* 8 February 1992, 48.

Part II
The TCK Profile

5

Benefits and Challenges

Besides the drawbacks of family separation and the
very real adjustment on the permanent return to the
[home country], a child growing up abroad has great
advantages. He [or she] learns, through no conscious
act of learning, that thoughts can be transmitted in
many languages, that skin color is unimportant...that
certain things are sacred or taboo to some people
while to others they're meaningless, that the ordinary
word of one area is a swearword in another.

We have lived in Tulsa for five years...I am struck
again and again by the fact that so much of the sociol-
ogy, feeling for history, geography, questions [about]
others that our friends' children try to understand
through textbooks, my sisters and I acquired just by
living.[1]

—Rachel Miller Schaetti

Introduction: The TCK Profile

In Part I we focused primarily on defining third culture kids and
describing their world. Now we want to look in depth at the specific
benefits and challenges of this experience. Then we will examine

the character traits this lifestyle fosters along with how it affects interpersonal relationships and developmental patterns. Because this is a group profile, not every characteristic will fit every person. But the "Aha!" moment of recognition, which we have seen among countless TCKs and ATCKs, tells us these characteristics are valid as an overall representation of their world.

The often paradoxical benefits and challenges of this profile are sometimes described as being like opposite sides of the same coin, but in reality they are more like the contrasting colored strands of thread woven together into a tapestry. As each strand crosses with a contrasting or complementary color, a picture begins to emerge, but no strand alone tells the full story. For example, the high mobility of a TCK's life often results in special relationships with people throughout the world, but it also creates sadness at the chronic loss of these relationships. That very pain, however, provides opportunity to develop a greater empathy for others. A TCK's expansive worldview, which enriches history classes and gives perspective to the nightly news, also makes the horror of the slaughter of Hutus and Tutsis in refugee camps a painful reality. That same awareness can be what motivates a TCK's concern for solving those kinds of tragic problems. And so it goes.

Some of the characteristics as well as the benefits and challenges are primarily a result of the cross-cultural nature of the third culture experience. Others are more directly shaped by the high mobility of the lifestyle. Most of the profile, however, is this weaving together of these two dominant realities. We begin by discussing some of the most common general benefits and challenges we have seen among TCKs, but before we do, let us make clear that when we use the word *challenge*, we purposefully do not infer the word *liability*. A challenge is something people have the choice to face, deal with, and grow from. A liability can only be something which pulls someone down. Some may say we concentrate too much on the challenges, but if that criticism is valid, it is for a reason. We have seen the benefits of this experience enrich countless TCKs' lives, whether or not they stop to consciously define or use them. Many have also found unconscious ways to deal with the challenges and make them a productive aspect of their lives in one way or another. We have also seen, however, that for some TCKs (and those around them) the unrecognized challenges have caused years of frustration as they struggle to deal with matters that have no name, no definition. It is our hope that in not only naming these challenges but also offering suggestions on how to deal with them productively, many more TCKs will be able to maximize the great gifts that can come from their lives and not be trapped by the challenges. We begin.

Expanded Worldview versus Confused Loyalties

Benefit: Expanded Worldview

An obvious benefit of the TCK experience is that while growing up in a multiplicity of countries and cultures, TCKs not only observe firsthand the many geographical differences around the world but they also learn how people view life from different philosophical and political perspectives. Some people think of Saddam Hussein as a hero; others believe he's a villain. Western culture is time and task oriented; in Eastern cultures, interpersonal relationships are of greater importance. The TCK's awareness that there can be more than one way to look at the same thing starts early in life. Once we listened to some rather remarkable stories during a meeting in Malaysia with younger TCKs—ages five to twelve.

> "You know, last year we had to hide on the floor for four days because of typhoons."
>
> "We couldn't go out of our compound in Bangladesh for a week when everybody in town started fighting."
>
> "On our vacation last month we got to ride on the backs of elephants and go look for tigers."
>
> "Well, so did we!" countered another seven-year-old from across the room. "We saw six tigers. How many did you see?"

> And so it went.
>
> Eventually New Year's Day came up as part of a
> story. We asked what we thought was a simple
> question. "When is New Year's Day?" Instead of the
> simple "January 1" that we expected, many different
> dates were given—each young TCK trying to defend
> how and when it was celebrated in his or her host
> country. We knew that if we had asked most groups of
> five- to twelve-year-olds in the United States about
> New Year's Day, this discussion wouldn't be occurring.
> Most of them probably had no idea that "New Year's
> Day" could mean anything but January 1.

This may seem like a small detail, but already these children are
learning how big and interesting the world they live in is and how
much there will be to discover about it all through life.

Challenge: Confused Loyalties

Although their expanded worldview is a benefit, it can also leave
TCKs with a sense of confusion about such complex things as politics, patriotism, and values. Should they support the policies of their
home country when those policies are detrimental to their host country? Or should they support the host country, even if it means oppos-
ing policies of their own government?

Joe, the American TCK raised in Argentina and educated in a
British school, writes about divided loyalties:

> When I came to the U.S., there was the matter of
> pledging allegiance to the American flag. I had saluted
> the Union Jack, the Argentine flag, and now I was
> supposed to swear loyalty to a country which, in 1955,
> didn't even have decent pizza or coffee. Worse,
> Americans, many of them, were still McCarthyites at
> heart, and feared anything tainted with foreignisms.
>
> The unfortunate side effects of a multicultural
> upbringing are substantial, of course. Whose side are
> you on? I had a dickens of a time with my loyalties
> during the Islas Malvinas war (no, make that the

Falkland Islands war). After all, as an eleven-year-old I had sworn undying fealty to Juan Domingo Peron and his promise that he would free the Malvinas from British enslavement. After the army booted him out of Argentina, I figured I was off the hook. But could I really be sure? On the other hand, I whistled "Rule Britannia" at least three times a week and really felt proud to know that a massive British force was headed to the Falklands and that British sovereignty would be asserted, unequivocally. I was dismayed by the profound indifference to this war exhibited by Americans.[2]

Confused loyalties can make TCKs seem unpatriotic and arrogant to their fellow citizens. If Joe is a good American, how could he ever pledge allegiance to Argentina and Britain—or be angry with his own country for not getting involved in someone else's war? If British TCKs who grew up in India try to explain negative remnants of the colonial era to fellow classmates in England, they can seem like traitors.

In *Homesick: My Own Story*, Jean Fritz writes of her experiences as an American TCK in China during the 1920s. She attended a British school in China but defiantly refused to sing "God Save the King" because it wasn't *her* national anthem. She was an American, although she had never spent a day in the United States in her life. Throughout the growing turmoil that led to the revolution in 1927, Jean dreamed of her grandmother's farm and garden in Pennsylvania, fantasizing over and over about what it would be like to live and go to school in America. Finally, after an endless boat ride and many struggles, Jean arrived at that long-awaited first day in an American school. Here's what happened.

"The class will come to order," she [Miss Crofts, the teacher] said. "I will call the roll." When she came to my name, Miss Crofts looked up from her book. "Jean Guttery is new to our school," she said. "She has come all the way from China, where she lived beside the Yangs-Ta-Zee River. Isn't that right, Jean?"

"It's pronounced *Yang-see*," I corrected. "There are just two syllables."

Miss Crofts looked at me coldly. "In America," she said, "we say *Yangs-Ta-Zee*."

I was working myself up, madder by the minute, when I heard Andrew Carr, the boy behind me, shifting his feet on the floor. I guess he must have hunched across his desk, because all at once I heard him whisper over my shoulder:

"Chink, Chink, Chinaman
Sitting on a fence,
Trying to make a dollar
Out of fifteen cents."

I forgot all about where I was. I jumped to my feet, whirled around, and spoke out loud as if there were no Miss Crofts, as if I'd never been in a classroom before, as if I knew nothing about classroom behavior. "You don't call them Chinamen or Chinks," I cried. "You call them *Chinese*. Even in America you call them *Chinese*."

"Well, you don't need to get exercised, Jean," she [Miss Crofts] said. "We all know that you are American."

"But that's not the *point!*" Before I could explain that it was an insult to call Chinese people *Chinamen*, Miss Crofts had tapped her desk with a ruler.

"That will be enough," she said. "All eyes front."[3]

Which country had Jean's greatest loyalty and devotion—the United States or China? Did she know? All her life she had thought of herself as American—now here she was defending the Chinese. Certainly Miss Crofts and Jean's classmates couldn't understand why she would want to defend a people and a country halfway around the world from them—particularly at the expense of getting along with people from her own country.

More difficult than the questions of political or patriotic loyalties, however, are the value dissonances that occur in the cross-cultural experience. As we said earlier, TCKs often live among cultures with strongly conflicting value systems. One culture says female circumcision is wrong. Another one says female circumcision is the most significant moment in a girl's life; it is when she knows she has become an accepted member of her tribe. One culture says abortion is wrong. Another says it is all right for specific reasons up to certain points in the pregnancy. Still other cultures practice abortion based on the gender of the baby: males are wanted; females are not.

In each situation, which value is right? Which is wrong? Is there a right and wrong? If so, who or what defines them? Conflicting values cannot be operational at the same time, in the same place. How do TCKs decide from all they see around them what their own values will and won't be?

This expanded worldview and its resulting confusion of loyalties and values can be a problem for those who return to cultures that remain relatively homogeneous. In a study of Turkish TCKs, Steve Eisinger discovered that "the statistics regarding public opinion…indicate that this expanded worldview may not be necessarily viewed as a positive characteristic."[4] The new ideas that the TCKs bring back, and their refusal to follow unthinkingly the cultural patterns of preceding generations, can make them unwelcome citizens in their own countries.

Three-Dimensional View of the World versus Painful View of Reality

Benefit: Three-Dimensional View of the World

As TCKs live in various cultures, they not only learn about cultural differences but they also experience the world in a tangible way that is impossible to do through reading books, seeing movies, or watching nightly newscasts alone. Because they have lived in so many places, smelled so many smells, heard so many strange sounds, and been in so many strange situations, throughout their lives when they read a story in the newspaper or watch it on the TV screen, the flat, odorless images there transform into an internal 3-D panoramic picture show. It's almost as if they were there in person, smelling the smells, tasting the tastes, perspiring with the heat. They may not be present at the event, but they have a clear awareness of what is going on and what it is like for those who are there.

> Each summer Dave Pollock leads transition seminars for TCKs. During one of these, he asked the attendees, "What comes to your mind if I say the word *riot*?" The answers came back, "Paris," "Korea," "Iran," "Ecuador."
>
> Next question. "Any details?"
>
> More answers: "Broken windows," "Water cannons," "Burned buses," "Tear gas, mobs," "Burning tires."
>
> Burning tires. Who would think about burning tires except somebody who had smelled that stench?
>
> "Tacks."

Anyone might think of guns in a riot, but why tacks? Because this TCK had seen tacks spread on the streets of Ecuador to flatten tires, so people couldn't travel during a riot. Makes sense, but probably only someone who had seen it would name it.

Having a 3-D view of the world is a useful skill not only for reading stories but for writing them. For TCKs who like to write, their culturally rich and highly mobile childhoods give them a true breadth of hands-on experiences in many places to add life to their work. In a feature article for *Time* called "The Empire Writes Back," Pico Iyer gives an account of an entirely new genre of award-winning authors, all of whom have cross-cultural backgrounds.

> Authors from Britain's former colonies have begun to capture the very heart of English literature, transforming the canon with bright colors and strange cadences and foreign eyes. They are revolutionizing the language from within. Hot spices are entering English, and tropical birds...magical creations from the makers of a new World Fiction.[5]

Iyer goes on to describe the great diversity of each writer's background and then states,

> But the new transcultural writers are something different. For one, they are the products not so much of colonial division as of the *international culture* that has grown up since the war, and they are addressing an audience as mixed up and eclectic and uprooted as themselves.[6]

Without ever using, or perhaps knowing, the term *third culture kids*, Iyer has conveyed vividly the richness of their experience.

Challenge: Painful View of Reality

With this three-dimensional view of the world, however, comes the painful reality that behind the stories in the news are real flesh-and-blood people—not merely flat faces on a TV screen. When an airplane crashes in India, TCKs find it appalling that U.S. newscasters only say how many Americans died—as if the other lives lost didn't matter. As they watch a Serbian woman weep for her child who has been killed in war, TCKs know her loss is as painful as their own would be if they were in that situation. Many of them know that when bombs drop on Iraq, people scream with fear and horror there just as they do when a bomb explodes in Oklahoma City. Many TCKs have seen war or faced the pain of evacuation and its disruption of their world, school, and friendships. Others have parents living and working in dangerous areas of the world, while they themselves are back in the home country.

> During the Gulf War, Courtney's American parents lived in Saudi Arabia, while she lived with relatives and attended secondary school in the States. Unfortunately, her parents' home in Saudi happened to be in a target area for SCUD missiles. Naturally, she felt anxiety and fear for her family. While other friends waited to hear the headlines on the evening news, Courtney checked the news throughout the school day so she could keep up with events in Saudi.

Although her worry for her folks was intense, one of the hardest things about the experience came when she realized that none of her American friends could relate to what she felt. To Courtney, the desert images on the television were home; to most of her friends, the war was far away and incomprehensible. She found herself resenting her classmates for their seeming lack of interest in not only her family, but all the Saudis, Iraqis, and Kuwaitis who were suffering as well.

Cross-Cultural Enrichment versus Ignorance of the Home Culture

Benefit: Cross-Cultural Enrichment

TCKs usually have a sense of ownership and interest in cultures other than just that of their passport country. During university they run to the radio whenever they hear their host country named. They have learned to enjoy many aspects of the host culture others might not appreciate so highly. While the smell of the Southeast Asian fruit, *durian*, would precipitate a gag reflex in most of us, TCKs who grew up in Malaysia inhale the scent with glee, for it is the smell of home. TCKs from India use chapatis (a flat bread) to pick up the hottest curry sauce. Still other TCKs sit cross-legged on the floor whenever they have a choice between that and a lounge chair. TCKs consider these aspects of their lifestyle part of the wealth of their heritage.

Perhaps more important than what they have learned to enjoy from the more surface layers of other cultures, however, is the fact that most TCKs have also gained valuable lessons from the deeper levels as well. They have lived in other places long enough to learn to appreciate the reasons and understanding behind some of the behavioral differences rather than simply being frustrated by them as visitors tend to be. For example, while a tourist might feel irritated that the stores close for two hours in the middle of the day just when he or she wants to go shopping, most TCKs can understand that this custom not only helps people survive better if the climate is extremely hot, but it's a time when families greet the children as they return from school and spend time together as a family. Many TCKs learn to value relationships above convenience as they live in such places, and it is a gift they carry with them wherever they may later go.

Challenge: Ignorance of the Home Culture

The irony of collecting cross-cultural practices and skills, however, is that TCKs may know all sorts of fascinating things about other countries but little about their own.

> Tamara attended school in England for the first time when she was ten. Until then she had attended a small American-oriented school in Africa. In early November, she asked her mother, "Mom, who is this Guy Fawkes everybody's talking about?"
>
> Tamara's mom, Elizabeth, a born and bred Englishwoman, tried to hide her shock at her daughter's ignorance. Tamara seemed so knowledgeable about countless global matters—how could she not know a simple fact about a major figure in British history? And particularly one whose wicked deed of trying to blow up the Parliament was decried each year as people throughout the country burned him in effigy? Elizabeth hadn't realized that while Tamara had seen the world, she had missed learning about this common tradition in her own country.

TCKs are often sadly ignorant of national, local, and even family history. How many rides to various relatives' homes are filled with parents coaching TCKs about who is related to whom? Many kids simply haven't been around the normal chatter that keeps family members connected.

Although this may be changing in the Internet age, TCKs have also often missed the rise to renown of the currently famous—movie stars, politicians, musicians, and other public figures. Household names in one country mean nothing in another.

> In 1958, TCK Jordan returned to the States at age thirteen and heard friends discussing Elvis. Imagine the look on their faces when he innocently asked, "Who's Elvis?"

When people switch cultures, humor is another unknown. Jokes are often based on a surprise, an indirect reference to something current, or a play on words with a double meaning specific to that culture or language. Few things make anyone, including TCKs, feel more left out than seeing everyone else laughing at something they can't understand as funny. Or conversely, they try to tell a joke that was hilarious in their boarding school, but none of their new friends laughs. Adelle writes,

> Early in my dating relationship with my [now] husband, something happened and he hummed the theme to the TV show, "The Twilight Zone." I guess I didn't react properly so he said, "You don't know what that is, do you?" I replied, "I know it's supposed to be funny, but I don't know why."[7]

Probably most TCKs have some story about getting caught in an embarrassing situation because they didn't know some everyday rule of their passport culture that is different in their host culture. One TCK couldn't pay her bill because she had forgotten to mentally add the tax to the amount listed on the menu. Another was shamed by his visiting relatives because he came into the room and sat down before making sure that all the oldest guests had found their places. Not knowing cultural rules can also be dangerous.

> In the village in Mali where Sophie had grown up, passing anyone—male or female—on the street and not saying hello created instant social disfavor. In New York the rules were different, as she learned in a police seminar on rape prevention during her first semester at university. "Never look a stranger in the eye," the

policeman said. "After attacking someone, a man often accuses the woman of having invited him with her look." And Sophie had been smiling at strange men all over the city!

All the above benefits and challenges are a mere beginning of the TCK Profile. We continue our discussion by looking at common personal strengths and struggles many TCKs seem to share.

Endnotes

1   Rachel Miller Schaetti, comments from a questionnaire for Jack O. Claypoole, George Williams College, 1957. Used by permission of the Schaetti family.

2   Joseph McDonald, e-mail message on MK Net, October 1995. Used with permission.

3   Jean Fritz, *Homesick: My Own Story* (Santa Barbara, CA: Cornerstone Books, 1987), 148–50.

4   Steve Eisinger, "The Validity of the 'Third Culture Kid' Definition for Returned Turkish Migrant Children" (report submitted upon the partial completion of research done in the country of Turkey, 31 August 1994), 16.

5   Pico Iyer, "The Empire Writes Back," *Time,* 8 February 1992.

6   Ibid., 48. Italics ours.

7   Adelle Horst Ward, personal e-mail to Ruth E. Van Reken, November 1995. Used by permission.

6

Personal Characteristics

The benefits of this upbringing need to be under-
scored: In an era when global vision is an imperative,
when skills in intercultural communication, linguistic
ability, mediation, diplomacy, and the management of
diversity are critical, global nomads are better
equipped in these areas by the age of eighteen than are
many adults.... These intercultural and linguistic skills
are the markings of the cultural chameleon—the
young participant-observer who takes note of verbal
and nonverbal cues and readjusts accordingly, taking
on enough of the coloration of the social surroundings
to gain acceptance while maintaining some vestige of
identity as a different animal, an "other."[1]

—Norma M. McCaig
Founder, Global Nomads International

Norma M. McCaig, one of the true pioneers in raising global awareness of the issues facing TCKs, is a business ATCK herself and now
works with international companies preparing employees and their
families for overseas assignments. In this chapter and the next we
will discuss many of the characteristics and skills (their benefits and
their corresponding challenges) of the TCK that she mentions, beginning with the cultural chameleon McCaig describes above.

Cultural Chameleon: Adaptability versus Lack of True Cultural Balance

Benefit: Adaptability

TCKs usually develop some degree of cultural adaptability as a primary tool for surviving the frequent change of cultures. Over and over TCKs use the term *chameleon* to describe how, after spending a little time observing what is going on, they can easily switch language, style of relating, appearance, and cultural practices to take on the characteristics needed to blend better into the current scene. Soon their behavior is almost indistinguishable from longtime members of this group and they feel protected from the scorn or rejection of others (and their own ensuing sense of shame) that often comes with being different from others.

Cultural adaptability may begin as a survival tool, but it also has immensely practical benefits. TCKs usually learn to adjust with relative calm to life where meetings may start the exact minute for which they have been scheduled or two hours later, depending on which country they're in. Partly because of the frequency with which they travel and move, TCKs learn to think on their feet and can often "roll with the punches," even in unusual circumstances.

> Nona and her ATCK friend, Joy, waited in vain for a bus to carry them from Arusha to Nairobi. They finally found a taxi driver who would take them to the Tanzanian/Kenyan border and promised to find them a ride the rest of the way. At the border, however, the driver disappeared. Night was approaching, when travel would no longer be safe.
>
> As Nona watched in amazement, Joy walked across the border to find another taxi. She soon came back to the Tanzanian side, got Nona and the bags, and returned to a waiting driver who took them to Nairobi. Later, Nona complimented Joy, "If it was me by myself, I'd still be sitting at the border, waiting for that first driver to come back."

Joy replied, "Well, there are times when all I can think is that this is going to make a great story in three months, but right now it's the pits. But I always know there's a way out if I can just think of all the options. I've been in these kinds of situations too many times to just wait."

Challenge: Lack of True Cultural Balance

Becoming a cultural chameleon, however, brings special challenges as well. For one thing, although in the short term the ability to "change colors" helps them fit in with their peers day-by-day, TCK chameleons may never develop true cultural balance anywhere. While appearing to be one of the crowd, inside they are still the cautious observer—always checking to see how they are doing. In addition, others may notice how the TCK's behavior changes in various circumstances and begin to wonder if they can trust anything the TCK does or says. It looks to them as if he or she has no real convictions about much of anything.

Some TCKs who flip-flop back and forth between various behavioral patterns have trouble figuring out their own value system from the multicultural mix they have been exposed to. It can be very difficult for them to decide if there are, after all, some absolutes in life they can hold on to and live by no matter which culture they are in. In the end, TCKs may adopt so many personas as cultural chameleons that they don't know who they really are.

Ginny returned to Minnesota for university after many years in New Zealand and Thailand. She looked with disdain on the majority of her fellow students, who seemed to be clones of one another, and decided she would be anything but like them. She struck up an acquaintance with another student, Jessica, who was a member of the prevailing counterculture. Whatever Jessica did, Ginny did. Both wore clothing that was outlandish enough to be an obvious statement that they weren't going to be swayed by any current fads.

Only years later did Ginny realize that she too had been a chameleon—copying Jessica—and had no idea of what she herself liked or wanted to be. She had rejected one group to prove she wasn't like them, but she had never considered the possibility that among their styles of dress or behavior there might be some attributes she did, in fact, like. Since she had totally aligned herself with Jessica, Ginny never stopped to think that some of Jessica's choices might not work for her. Was it all right for her to like jazz when Jessica didn't? What types of clothes did she, Ginny, really want to wear? It was some time before she was able to sort out and identify what her own gifts, talents, and preferences were in contrast to those she had borrowed from Jessica.

Hidden Immigrants: Blending In versus Defining the Differences

While virtually all TCKs make cultural adaptations to survive wherever they live, traditionally, most TCKs—such as the children of early colonialists—were physically distinct from members of the host culture and still easily recognizable as *foreigners* when living there. Even today, the child of the Norwegian ambassador in China would never be mistaken for a citizen of the host culture. As mentioned earlier, when TCKs are obvious foreigners, they are often excused—both by others and by themselves—if their behavior doesn't exactly match the local cultural norms or practices. No one expects them to be the same based on their appearance alone. Only when these TCKs, who are true foreigners in their host culture, re-enter their home culture do they face the prospect of being the hidden immigrants we described in chapter 3.

A frequently overlooked factor, however, is that in our increasingly internationalizing world, many TCKs are becoming hidden immigrants in the host culture as well. British children in Canada appear the same as most of their classmates; a Ugandan diplomat's child may look just like the African Americans in his classroom in Washington, DC. So, why is this an important issue? For one thing, being a hidden immigrant gives those TCKs who desire it the choice to not only be *cultural* chameleons, but *physical* chameleons as well. Often people around them have no idea they are actually foreigners, and the TCK may like this type of relative anonymity. A second reason for noticing this new development in the TCKs' world, however, is that those TCKs who prefer *not* to totally adapt to the surrounding scene have to find some way other than their skin color or facial features to proclaim they are different from others. This may explain what otherwise might seem like rather bizarre behavior. Take a look at three TCKs who were hidden immigrants in their host cultures.

Benefit: Blending In

The first is Paul, an international business TCK who was born in Alaska and then lived in California and Illinois until he was nine. At that time his family moved to Australia, where his father worked for an oil company. Paul tells us his story.

> My first year of school in Australia was horrible. I learned that Americans weren't very popular because of a nuclear base they'd set up near Sydney. People protested against the "ugly Americans" all the time. I felt other students assigned me guilt by association just because I was a U.S. citizen. Looking back, I realize the only kids who were good to me didn't fit in either.
>
> By the end of the first year, I'd developed an Australian accent and learned to dress and act like my Australian counterparts. Then I changed schools so I could start over and no one knew I was American. I was a chameleon.

As a hidden immigrant, Paul made a choice an obviously foreign TCK could never make. Until he chose to reveal his true identity, no one had to know that he was not Australian. Theoretically, some might argue that he made a poor choice, but from Paul's perspective as a child, blending in to this degree gave him the opportunity to not only be accepted by others but also to more fully participate in school and social events while he remained in Australia.

Challenge: Defining the Differences

While Paul chose to hide his identity, Nicola and Krista are TCKs who reacted in an opposite way. Because they looked like those around them, they felt they would lose their true identity if they didn't find some way to shout, "But I'm *not* like you." This is how each of them proclaimed their differences.

> Nicola, a British TCK, was born in Malaysia while her dad served with the Royal Air Force. He retired from the service when Nicola was four years old. The family moved to Scotland, where Nicola's dad took a job flying airplanes off the coast of Scotland for a major oil company.
>
> At first, Nicola tried to hide her English roots, even adopting a thick Scottish brogue. In spite of that, by secondary school she realized something inside her would never fit in with these classmates who had never left this small town. She looked like them, but when she didn't act like them, they teased her unmercifully for every small transgression. It seemed the more she tried to be like them, the more she was having to deny who she really was inside.
>
> Finally, Nicola decided to openly—rather defiantly, in fact—espouse her English identity. She changed her accent to a proper British one and talked of England as home. She informed her classmates that she couldn't wait to leave Scotland to attend university in England. When Nicola arrived in Southampton on her way to university, she literally kissed the ground when she alighted from the train.
>
> Krista is an American business TCK raised in England from age six to sixteen. She attended a British

school for six months before attending the local American school. We were surprised to hear her tell of how fiercely anti-British she and her fellow class-mates in the American school became. In spite of the prevailing culture, they steadfastly refused to speak "British." They decried Britain for not having Ameri-can-style shopping malls and bought all their clothes at American stores like The Gap and The Limited during their summer leave in the States. And why did every-one insist on queuing so carefully anyway? It looked so prim and silly. She couldn't wait to return to the U.S. permanently, where everything would be "normal."

The difficulty for Nicola and Krista, however, is that in trying to proclaim what they consider their true identity, they ultimately form an "anti-identity"—be that in clothes, speech, or behavior. Unfortu-nately, this also tends to cut them off from the many benefits they could be experiencing in friendships and cultural exchange with those around them from the local community. In addition, as TCKs scream to others, "I'm not like you," people around soon avoid them and they are left with a deep loneliness—although it might take them a long time to admit such a thing.

Prejudice: Less versus More

Benefit: Less Prejudice

The opportunity to know people from diverse backgrounds as friends—not merely as acquaintances—and within the context of their own cultural milieu is another gift TCKs receive. They have been members of groups that include a striking collection of cultur-ally and ethnically diverse people, and most have the ability to truly enjoy such diversity and to believe that people of all backgrounds can be full and equal participants in any given situation. Sometimes their unconscious, underlying assumptions that people of all back-grounds are still just that—people—can surprise others, and the TCKs in turn are surprised that such acceptance isn't necessarily "normal" for everyone else.

> One white ATCK living in suburban U.S.A. had an African American repairman arrive to fix a leaky faucet. As the repairman prepared to leave, he said, "I can tell you've been around black people a lot, haven't you?" Since the ATCK had grown up in Africa, she had to agree, but asked, "Why do you say that?" He replied, "Because you're comfortable with me being here. A lot of white people aren't." And she was surprised, because she hadn't been thinking about racial relationships at all. To her, they had simply been talking about fixing faucets and paying the bill.

TCKs who use their experiences well learn there is always a reason behind anyone's behavior—no matter how mystifying it appears—and may be more patient than others might be in a particular situation.

> When ATCK Anne-Marie returned to Mali as a United Nations worker, she heard other expatriates complaining that the Malians who worked in the local government hospital never planned ahead. The medicine, oxygen, or other vital commodities were always completely gone before anyone reported that it was time to reorder. This had caused endless frustration for the UN workers.
>
> While listening to the usual grumbling during morning tea one day soon after she arrived, Anne-Marie interrupted the flow of complaints. "I understand your annoyance," she said, "but did it ever occur to you what it's like to be so poor you can only worry about each particular day's needs? If you haven't got enough money for today, you certainly aren't worrying about storing up for tomorrow."

Of all the gifts we hear TCKs say they have received from their backgrounds, the richness and breadth of diversity among those they truly count as friends is one they consistently mention as among the greatest.

Challenge: More Prejudice

Unfortunately, however, there are a few TCKs who appear to become *more* prejudiced rather than less. Perhaps it is because historically many TCKs' parents are part of what others consider a special, elite group (such as diplomats or high-ranking military personnel) in the host country and their positions often bring special deference. Their standard of living is usually well above the mean for that particular country, and their lifestyle may include servants, drivers, and other special privileges such as extensive travel.

> The movie *Empire of the Sun* gives a clear picture of what this privileged lifestyle has been for some TCKs. The story opens with the scene of a young British lad being driven home from school in the back seat of a chauffeured limousine while he stares uncaringly out the windows at starving Chinese children on the streets. As he enters his home, the young man begins to order the Chinese servants around as if they were his slaves.
>
> One day all is changed. When the British boy tries to tell the maid what to do, she runs up and slaps him. The revolution has come, and years of suppressed bitterness at his treatment of her erupt. It takes World War II and several years of incarceration in a concentration camp before this TCK finally understands that the world is not completely under his control.

While this may seem like an exaggeration, when adults from any expatriate community constantly speak poorly of the host culture residents in their presence, TCKs can pick up the same disdain and thereby waste one of the richest parts of their heritage.

Decisiveness: The Importance of Now versus the Delusion of Choice

Benefit: The Importance of Now

Because their lifestyle is transitory, many TCKs have a sense of urgency that life is to be lived *now*. They may not stop to deliberate long on any particular decision because the chance to climb Mt. Kilimanjaro will be gone if new orders to move come through. Do it now. Seize the day! Sushi is on the menu at the shop around the corner today. Better try it while you can. Some may fault them for impulsiveness, but TCKs do get a lot of living done while others are still deciding what they do or don't want to do.

Challenge: The Delusion of Choice

Ironically, for the same reason that some TCKs seize every opportunity, other TCKs seem to have difficulty in making or feeling excited about plans at all. So often in the past, their desires and intentions to do such things as act in a school play, run for class office, or be captain of the soccer team were denied when Dad or Mom came home one day and said, "Well, I just received orders today; we are shipping out to Portsmouth in two weeks." No matter how much the TCKs thought they had a choice to do things they wanted to do at school or in the neighborhood, it turned out they had no choice at all. They weren't going to be there for the next school year or the next soccer season after all. Off they went, their dreams vanishing. In Portsmouth, or wherever their next post was, the TCKs asked themselves, "Why even make plans for what I want to do? I'll just have to leave again."

These preempted plans can lead to what some mental health professionals call a "delusion of choice." In other words, a choice to act is offered ("Would you like to run for class president next year?"), but circumstances or the intervention of others arbitrarily eliminates that choice ("Pack your bags, we're leaving tomorrow"). In reality, the person has no choice at all. The achievement of a goal, the development of a relationship, or the completion of a project can all be cut short by some unexpected event or the decision of a personnel director.

For some TCKs, decision making has an almost superstitious dimension. "If I allow myself to make a decision and start taking the necessary steps to see it through, something will happen to stop what I want." For others, this delusion of choice is wrapped in a theological dimension. "If God finds out what I really want, he'll take it away from me." Rather than be disappointed, they refuse to acknowledge to themselves, let alone to others or to God, what they would like to do.

Other TCKs and ATCKs have difficulty in making a choice that involves a significant time commitment because they know a new and more desirable possibility may always appear. Signing a contract to teach in Middleville might be a wise economic move, but what if a job opportunity opens in Surabaya next week? It's hard to choose one thing before knowing all the choices. Experience has taught that life not only offers multiple options, but these options can appear suddenly and need to be acted on quickly or they are gone—yet the very fact that one choice might preclude another keeps some TCKs and ATCKs from making any choice at all.

Chronically waiting until the last minute to plan rather than risk disappointment or having to change plans can be particularly frustrating for spouses or children waiting for decisions to be made that will affect the entire family. Adult TCKs may also miss significant school, job, or career opportunities. It becomes such a habit to wait, they never follow through on leads or fill out necessary forms by the deadline.

Of course, many TCKs have parents who have given them significant opportunities for meaningful choices—even within what appeared to be "no choice" situations—and they have developed the ability to look for possible options and ramifications of those possible choices in any circumstances and make solid decisions based on those facts.

Relation to Authority:
Appreciative versus Mistrustful

Benefit: Appreciative of Authority

For some TCKs, living within the friendly confines of a strong organizational system is a strong and happy fact of their lives. Relationships with adults in their community are basically positive and nurturing. There may be almost a cocoon atmosphere on their military
base or at their embassy, business, or mission compound. The
struggles of others in the world can be shut out, at least for some
period of time, and perks such as generators, special stores, and paid
vacations are all part of a wonderful package deal. As adults, they
look back on their TCK childhoods and those who supervised their
lives with nothing but great fondness.

Challenge: Mistrustful of Authority

Other ATCKs and TCKs feel quite different. For all the reasons (and
maybe more) mentioned under "The Delusion of Choice," they begin to mistrust the authority figures in their lives, easily blaming
virtually all of their problems in life on parents or organizational
administrators who made autocratic decisions about where and when
they would move with little regard for their needs or the needs of
their family. One of them told us:

> My parents finally got divorced when Mom said she
> wouldn't make one more move. The company had
> moved my dad to a new position every two years.
> Each time, we went to a different place, even a
> different country—sometimes in the middle of the
> school year, sometimes not. My mom could see how it
> was affecting us children as well as herself. We would
> finally start to find our own places within the new
> group, when it was time to move again. Mom asked
> Dad to talk to the managers of his company and
> request they leave us in one place while we went

through high school at least. They said they couldn't do it; they were amalgamating their headquarters and the office in our town was being phased out. Dad didn't want to find a new job, and Mom wouldn't move, so they got divorced. I've always been angry about both my dad's decision and the company's.

In the end, some TCKs who have had their life unhappily affected because of decisions made by others tell us they will starve before risking the possibility that the direction of their lives will be so profoundly changed once more by the decision of someone in authority over them.

Arrogance: Real versus Perceived

Sometimes the very richness of their background creates a new problem for TCKs. Once, after a seminar, a woman came up to Dave Pollock and said, "There's one issue you failed to talk about tonight and it's the very thing that almost ruined my life. It was my arrogance."

Unfortunately, arrogance isn't an uncommon word when people describe TCKs or ATCKs. It seems the very awareness which helps TCKs view a situation from multiple perspectives can also make TCKs impatient or arrogant with others who only see things from their own perspective—particularly people from their home culture. This may happen for several reasons.

1. A cross-cultural lifestyle is so normal that TCKs themselves don't always understand how much it has shaped their view of the world. They easily forget it's their life experiences that have been different from others', not their brain cells, and they may consider themselves much more cosmopolitan and just plain smarter than others.

2. This impatience or judgmentalism can sometimes serve as a point of identity with other TCKs. It becomes one of the markers of "us" versus "them." It's often easy for a get-together of

TCKs to quickly degenerate into bashing the stupidity of non-TCKs. The irony is that the TCKs are then doing unto others what they don't like having done unto themselves—equating ignorance with stupidity.

Sometimes TCKs and ATCKs appear arrogant because they have chosen a permanent identity as being "different" from others.

> Todd, an ATCK, was angry. His parents could do no right. His sponsoring organization had stupid policies, and his American peers ranked among the dumbest souls who had ever been born. Todd castigated everyone and everything. Mark, his good friend, finally got tired of the tirades and pointed out the pride and arrogance coming out in his words.
>
> "You know, Todd," Mark said, "it's your experiences that have been different—not your humanity. I think if you try, you might discover you are not as different from the rest of the world as you seem to feel. You know, you're a normal person."
>
> At that, Todd fairly jumped out of his chair. "The last thing I want to be is 'normal.' That idea is nauseating to me."

This "I'm different from you" type of identity is often a defense mechanism to protect against unconscious feelings of insecurity or inferiority. But a "different from" identity has a certain arrogance attached to it. TCKs who put other people down often do so as a way to set themselves apart or boost their sense of self-worth. "I don't care if you don't accept me, because you could never understand me anyway." TCKs chalk up any rejection they feel or interpersonal problems they have to being different rather than taking a look to see if they themselves might have added to this particular problem.

At other times, however, what is labeled as arrogance in TCKs is simply an attempt to share their normal life experiences. People who don't understand their background may feel the TCKs are bragging or name-dropping when they speak of places they have been or people they have met. Non-TCK friends don't realize TCKs have no other stories to tell.

And sometimes there may be a mix of both real and perceived arrogance. The conviction or passion with which TCKs speak because of what they have seen and/or experienced makes them seem dogmatic and overly sure of their opinions. Is that arrogance? It's hard to know.

While these are some of the general personal characteristics we have repeatedly seen among TCKs, there are others McCaig also referred to that can develop into true life skills. We look at them in chapter 7.

Endnote

1   Norma M. McCaig, "Understanding Global Nomads," *Strangers at Home* (New York: Aletheia Press, 1996), 101.

7

Practical Skills

> One day I poured out my bitter complaints to a senior
> missionary. I could not understand why the mission
> imported thirty Canadian and U.S. young people to do
> famine work, when not one of the more than fifteen
> resident MKs [missionary kids]—experienced in
> language and culture—had been asked to help. He told
> me to quit complaining and sign on. I did.[1]
>
> —Andrew Atkins

The feelings Andrew expresses reflect the fact that growing up as a TCK not only increases an inner awareness of our culturally diverse world, but the experience also helps in the development of useful personal skills for interacting with and in it. Some of these skills are acquired so naturally they aren't recognized, acknowledged, or effectively used—either by ATCKs or others—as the special gifts they are. At the same time, some of these skills also have a flip side, where a skill becomes a liability, as we will see in the discussion of social and linguistic skills below.

Cross-Cultural Skills

As TCKs have the opportunity not only to observe a great variety of cultural practices but also to learn what some of the underlying assumptions are behind them, they often develop strong cross-cultural skills. More significant than the ease with which they can change from chopsticks to forks for eating or from bowing to shaking hands while greeting is their ability to be sensitive to the more hidden aspects or deeper levels of culture and to work successfully in these areas. For ATCKs who go into international or intercultural careers, this ability to be a bridge between different groups of people can be useful in helping their company or organization speak with a more human voice in the local community and be more sensitive to the dynamics of potentially stressful situations in the work environment.

> ATCK Jamal became a prime negotiator for his company during tense negotiations between executives from the home office in the United States and members of the host country who oversaw daily operations in the company's branch overseas. He told us: "Everyone gets mad at me because I can see both sides in the discussions." But ultimately he played a key role in bringing resolution when he pointed out to both sides that much of the impasse related to different cultural styles of negotiation rather than a difference in what each side wanted. The executives from the home office presumed frank, confrontational discussions were most useful, while host culture members believed that saving face was more important. To them, confrontation meant openly shaming another person—a cardinal offense in that particular culture. Once Jamal helped them understand their different outlooks, both sides were able to step back and consider each other's views more objectively and work to a mutually satisfactory conclusion.

Because of their experience in very different cultures and places around the world, ATCKs often find themselves particularly qualified when it comes to jobs or situations such as teaching or mentoring. For those who choose teaching as a career, the fact that most TCKs have themselves attended schools with a wide variety of cultural learning and teaching styles helps them understand and be sensitive to their students' struggles with language, spelling, and conceptual differences. They have every potential of being particularly effective in cross-cultural educational processes—even if it is only with one child in their classroom who has recently immigrated to the area from another country or culture. ATCKs, of all people, should be willing to allow for some differences in writing as well as thinking and learning styles.

ATCKs may also be particularly effective teachers because they have many firsthand stories to augment the facts recorded in geography or social studies textbooks. They may be able to bring life to the textbook's chapter on how the Netherlands reclaimed its land from the sea because they have walked on those dikes. Maybe they have seen the cells in the Philippines where American and Filipino POWs were held during World War II. Whatever countries they have lived or traveled in, they can, one hopes, bring their students fresh ways of looking at the world.

Children who grow up playing and going to school with children of other races and cultures naturally learn that friendship and respect have nothing to do with skin color or cultural differences. Those who have moved often and been the new kid on the block several times over also realize how painful it can be if no one reaches out to a newcomer or, conversely, how wonderful it is when someone does.

Because of their own experience, TCKs and ATCKs can be effective mentors for new students coming to their school or community from different countries or cultures or even from different parts of their own country. They already know some of the hazards of this process and can effectively help others settle in more quickly—and less traumatically—than might happen otherwise.

Sometimes TCKs can be connectors or mediators between groups that are stereotypically prejudiced against one another.

> Francisco is a black Panamanian TCK. At age six, he
> moved to the States while his stepfather pursued a

military career. Initially, Francisco lived in the predominantly white culture in the community surrounding the army base. Here he learned firsthand the shock of being the target of racist slurs and attacks. Later, his parents moved and he went to a more racially diverse high school where he became a chameleon who apparently fit perfectly into the African American community. Eventually most of his friends saw him as Francisco and forgot, if they ever knew, that his roots were not the same as theirs.

One day, however, a heated discussion erupted among his black friends about why "foreigners" shouldn't be allowed into the country. Finally, Francisco spoke up and said, "You know, guys, what you're saying about them, you're saying about me. I'm not a citizen either. But foreigners have flesh and blood like me—and like you." Then Francisco pointed out how this kind of group stereotyping was why he and they as black people had known prejudice. Francisco reminded them that he—their personal friend, a foreigner—was living proof that people of all backgrounds, races, colors, and nationalities were just that—people, not statistics or embodiments of other people's stereotypes.

Observational Skills

TCKs may well develop certain skills because of the basic human instinct for survival. Sometimes through rather painful means, they have learned that particularly in cross-cultural situations it pays to be a careful observer of what's going on around them and then try to understand the reasons for what they are seeing.

One TCK received the "nerd for life" award when, on his first day of school "at home," he carried his books in a brand-new briefcase—just like his dad's. The briefcase served a most utilitarian purpose—keeping

books together in an easily transportable manner. But
in this new school, a backpack slung over one shoulder
(and one shoulder only) served the same purpose in a
far more socially acceptable manner.

Through such experiences, TCKs learn firsthand that in any culture
these unwritten rules govern everyone's acceptance or rejection in a
new setting. In addition, they have seen how behavior unnoticed in
one place may cause deep offense in another. Something as seemingly insignificant as raising a middle finger or pointing at another
person has distinctly different meanings depending on the culture.
Mistakes in conscious and unconscious social rules—whether eating style, greetings, or methods of carrying schoolbooks—often send
an unwanted message to people in the new culture. Observing carefully and learning to ask "How does life work here?" before barging
ahead are other skills TCKs can use to help themselves or others
relate more effectively in different cultures.

Mariella, a German ATCK who had grown up in India,
took a job working for an NGO hospital in Ghana. It
wasn't long before she heard complaints from the
expatriate staff that the patients often threw their
prescriptions away immediately after exiting the
doctor's office. That seemed odd to her as well, so
Mariella began investigating.

She soon noticed that when the new doctor from
Germany dispensed these prescriptions, he always sat
sideways at the desk. The patients were on the
doctor's left side as he wrote notes on their charts
using his right hand. Whenever the doctor finished
writing the prescription, he would pick it up with his
free left hand and give it to the patient.

This process probably would not have caused a
second thought in Germany, but Mariella knew from
her childhood in India that there the left hand is
considered unclean by many because it is the one used
for dirty tasks. Giving someone anything with that hand

is both an insult and a statement that the object being offered is worthless. She wondered if that might be the case in Ghana as well and asked her new Ghanaian friends if the way a person handed something to another person made a difference in their culture. When their replies confirmed her suspicion that using the left hand in Ghana had the same connotation as she remembered from her childhood in India, Mariella understood why the patients didn't fill the prescriptions! She suggested the doctor turn his desk around so all the patients sat at his right and that way he would naturally give out the prescriptions in a culturally appropriate manner. He followed her advice and the problem disappeared.

Social Skills

In certain ways, learning to live with the chronic change which often characterizes their lifestyle gives many TCKs a great sense of inner confidence and strong feelings of self-reliance. While not always liking change—sometimes even hating it—TCKs do expect to cope with new situations. They generally approach upheavals with some degree of confidence because past experience has taught them that given enough time, they will make more friends and learn the new culture's ways. This sense that they'll be able to manage new situations—even when they can't always count on others to be physically present to help in a crisis—often gives them the security to take risks others might not take. A Belgian ATCK, Helga, planned to go alone on a five-week trip to Australia and New Zealand. Some friends were shocked.

"Do you know anyone there?" they asked.

"Not yet," she replied.

"Well, how can you just go? Aren't you scared? How will you find your way? What kind of food will you eat?"

Actually, she hadn't thought of it. She'd just pre-

sumed one way or another it would all work out. As a
teenager and university student, she'd often traveled
halfway around the world alone to see her parents
each school vacation. Customs and language barriers
were no longer intimidating. Lost luggage could be
dealt with. She had a great time.

But there is a flip side to this type of confidence as well. While
TCKs develop feelings of confidence in many areas of life, there are
other times or situations in which they may be so fearful of making
mistakes they are almost paralyzed. Paul, an American TCK who
grew up in Australia, moved once more as a teenager. Here's what
he said about that move.

I changed worlds once more at age fourteen when my
dad's company moved him from Australia to Indonesia.
But the consequence of switching worlds at that age is
you can't participate in the social scene. Everyone else
seems to know the rules except you. You stand at the
edge, and you shut up and listen, mostly to learn, but
you can't participate. You only sort of participate—not
as an initiator, but as a weak supporter in whatever
goes on—hoping that whatever you do is right and flies
okay. You're always double-checking and making sure.

Just as true chameleons move slowly while constantly checking
which color they should be to blend into each new environment, so
TCKs can appear to be socially slow while trying to figure out the
operative rules in their new situations. To avoid looking foolish or
stupid, they retreat from these situations in such ways as overem-
phasizing academics, belittling the new culture, or withdrawing in
extreme shyness. Even those who have been extremely social in one
setting may refuse to join group activities in the next place because
they have no idea how to do what everyone else already can. Maybe
they have returned home to Sweden from a tropical climate, never
having learned to ice skate, toboggan, or ski. They would rather not
participate at all than let anyone know of their incompetence.

Insecurity in a new environment can make TCKs withdraw even

in areas where they have knowledge or talent. It's one thing to join the choir in a relatively small international school overseas. It's quite another to volunteer when you are suddenly in a school of three thousand students. Who knows what might be expected? Who knows how many others are better than you? And so the TCK holds back to wait and watch, even when it might be possible to be involved.

While TCKs are trying to figure out the new rules and if or where they might jump in, people around them wonder why they are holding back. If the TCKs do jump into the fray, it's easy for them to make dumb mistakes and be quickly labeled as social misfits. This can lead to another problem. Because TCKs often don't feel a sense of belonging, they, as did both Paul and Ginny, can quickly identify with others who don't fit in. Unfortunately, this is often the group that is in trouble with the school administration or one in which scholastic achievement is disdained. Later, if the TCKs want to change and make friends with those more interested in academic success, it may be difficult because they have already been labeled as part of the other group.

Linguistic Skills

Acquiring fluency in more than one language is potentially one of the most useful life skills a cross-cultural upbringing can give TCKs. Children who learn two or more languages early in life, and use these languages on a day-to-day basis, develop a facility and ease with language unlike those who learn a second language for the first time as teenagers or adults.

Bilingualism and multilingualism have advantages in addition to the obvious one of communicating with different groups of people. For instance, Dr. Jeannine Heny, an English professor, believes learning different languages early in life can sharpen thinking skills in general and can actually help children achieve academically above their grade level.[2] Learning the grammar of one language can strengthen grammatical understanding in the next one.

Strong linguistic skills also have practical advantages as the TCK

becomes an adult. Some careers are available only to people fluent
in two or more languages. One American ATCK works for a large
international company as a Japanese/ English translator. She learned
Japanese while growing up and attending local schools in a small
town in Japan. Another American ATCK works as an international
broadcaster using the Hausa he learned as a child in Nigeria.

Even if a career isn't directly involved with language, opportunities to take jobs in certain countries may require language acquisition. There's no doubt that a job applicant who can already speak
the country's language will see his or her resume land a lot closer to
the top of the pile than those who will have to spend a year in language school along the way. And if the language required doesn't
happen to be the one the ATCK already knows, the fact that he or
she can obviously learn more than one language improves job opportunities as well.

When we first learn a new language as an adult, the thinking
process of our mother language often superimposes itself on the second language and makes learning the new language more difficult.
It also inhibits us from fully understanding the thinking patterns of
those who use that language. When children learn languages, they
instinctively pick up the differing nuances of how people in that
culture think and relate to one another. Adults often translate word
for word and never understand that the same word can have a different meaning in another language. Ironically, however, learning the
nuances for certain words in their adopted language can sometimes
keep TCKs from fully understanding the nuances of the translation
of that same word in their own mother tongue. This happened to
JoAnna.

> For years, ATCK JoAnna's American friends told her
> she was the most guilt-ridden person they'd ever met.
> No matter what happened—if a glass fell out of
> someone's hand, a friend lost her notebook, or
> someone bit his lip—JoAnna always said "Sorry."
> The instantaneous answer always came back.

"What are you sorry for? You didn't do anything."

JoAnna's equally instantaneous reply was also always the same. "I know I didn't do anything. I'm just sorry."

It was a point of significant frustration for both JoAnna and her friends for years. She couldn't get out of the habit of saying sorry and her friends couldn't get over being irritated by it. None of them understood the impasse.

In her forties, JoAnna went to live in Kenya for a year. During a hike in the woods with Pamela, another American, Pamela said, "I'll be glad when I get back to America where everyone doesn't say sorry all the time."

JoAnna wondered why that was a problem.

"It drives me crazy," Pamela said. "No matter what happens, everyone rushes around and says *Pole, pole sana* (which means 'Sorry, very sorry'). But most of the time there's nothing to apologize for."

For the first time, JoAnna understood her lifelong problem with the word *sorry*. For Pamela, an American, *sorry* was only an apology. She had never realized in this African context that people were expressing sympathy and empathy rather than apologizing when they used that word. For JoAnna, in the African language she had learned as a child and in the two she had learned as an adult, sorry was used as both an apology and as an expression of sympathy. It had never occurred to her it was only an apology word in American English. No wonder she and her American friends had misunderstood each other. They weren't speaking the same language!

Although the linguistic gifts for TCKs are primarily positive ones, there are a few pitfalls to be aware of. These include being limited in any one language, becoming a "creative speller," and losing fluency and depth in the child's native language. As we saw earlier with Ilpo, no matter how bright the child is, the specialized terminology needed for studying medicine (or fixing cars, discussing computers, studying science, etc.) may be missing if someone is working in many languages. Ultimately, he or she may never have time to learn the more specialized meanings and usage of each. JoAnna's story above demonstrates how idiomatic expressions or nonliteral meanings of common words can also cause confusion in such situations.

Interestingly enough, it's not simply those who work or study in entirely different languages that may find themselves linguistically challenged. Perhaps for the very reason it seems so minor, TCKs who speak and write English find it very difficult to keep American and English spelling straight. Is it *color* or *colour? Behavior* or *behaviour? Pediatrician* or *paediatrician?* Even worse, how do you remember if it's *criticise* or *criticize* when criticism is spelled the same everywhere? While this may seem a minor irritation, it can become a major issue when, for example, a British student transfers to a school in the United States (or an American-based school in another country), where teachers may not be sensitive to this issue.

These differences in spelling provide a special challenge to schools everywhere that have a mix of nationalitics among their students. Many solve the problem by keeping both an English and American dictionary available to check on the variations that come in on assigned papers. With a sense of humor, an understanding teacher, or a spell checker appropriate for the current country, most TCKs weather this particular challenge successfully.

The most serious problem related to learning multiple languages at an early age is that some people never become proficient in their supposed mother tongue—the language of their family roots and personal history. Among TCKs, this occurs most often among those who come from non-English-speaking countries but attend international schools overseas where classes are predominantly taught in English. When that is a boarding school with little home (and thus language) contact for months at a time, language can become a major issue when the TCK returns to his or her parents, with the supposed mother tongue becoming almost a foreign language. Families whose members lack fluency in a common language by which they can express emotions and profound ideas lose one critical tool for developing close, intimate relationships.

> Kwabena is a Ghanaian TCK who faced the problem of never gaining fluency in his parents' languages. His father was from the Ga tribe, his mother from the Anum tribe. Kwabena was born in predominantly English-speaking Liberia, where his father worked for several years. Eventually, the family moved to Mali, where French was the official language. The family could only make occasional visits back to the parents' villages in Ghana, where his grandparents spoke only the local languages. By the time Kwabena reached his teens, he sadly realized he could never talk to his grandparents and ask for the family stories all children love to hear, because he couldn't speak enough of any of their languages and they couldn't speak the English, French, or Malian languages he knew.

Most TCKs we know, however, would count the benefits of having facility in two or more languages another of their greatest practical blessings. What is more, it's just plain fun to watch a group of ATCKs at an international school reunion suddenly break into the greetings or farewells of the language they all learned in some faraway land during their youth. At that moment, language becomes one more marker of all they have shared in the world that now may seem invisible to them.

Endnotes

[1] Andrew Atkins, "Behavioral Strings to Which MKs Dance," *Evangelical Missions Quarterly* (July 1989): 239–43.

[2] Jeannine Heny, "Learning and Using a Second Language," in *Language: Introductory Readings,* 5th ed., edited by Virginia Clark, Paul A. Eschholz, and Alfred F. Rosa (New York: St Martin's Press, 1994), 186.

8

Rootlessness and Restlessness

> Being a TCK has given me a view of the world as my
> home and a confidence in facing new situations and
> people, particularly of other countries and cultures.
> However, it has its negative side [because] Americans
> and foreigners have a problem relating to me, for I am
> not a typical American! The hardest question still to
> answer is where I am from. What is my place of origin?[1]
> —Response to ATCK Survey

While this writer obviously enjoyed the type of confidence a TCK childhood can foster, he or she also brings up two very common characteristics TCKs often share—a deep sense of rootlessness and restlessness. These are such key aspects of the TCK Profile that they deserve a chapter of their own.

Rootlessness

There are several questions many TCKs have learned to dread. Among them are these two: "Where are you from?" and "Where is home?"

Where Are You From?

Why should anyone dread such a simple question? Consider Erika again.

Like most other TCKs, when someone asks Erika that question, her internal computer starts the search mode. *What does this person mean by "from"? Is he asking my nationality? Or maybe it's "Where were you born?" Does he mean "Where are you living now?" or "Where did you come from today?" Or does he mean "Where do your parents live now?" or "Where did you grow up?" Actually, does he even understand what a complicated question he asked me, or care? Is he simply asking a polite "Let's make conversation about something while we stand here with shrimp on our plates" question, or is he really interested?*

Erika decides what to answer by how she perceives the person who asked or what she does and doesn't feel like talking about. If the new acquaintance seems more polite than interested or if Erika doesn't want a lengthy conversation, she gives the "safe" answer. During college she simply said, "Wisconsin." Now she replies, "Dayton." It's the "where I'm living now" answer.

If Erika does want to extend the conversation slightly or test out the questioner's true interest, she throws out the next higher-level answer: "New York"—still a fairly safe answer. It's where she visited during each home leave and where her family roots are.

If the person responds with more than a polite "Oh" and asks another question such as, "Then when did you leave New York?" Erika might elevate her reply to a still higher level, "Well, I'm not really from New York, but my parents are." Now the gauntlet is thrown down. If the potential new friend picks up on this and asks, "Well, where are *you* from then?" the conversation begins and Erika's fascinating life history begins to unfold. Of course, if the newcomer doesn't follow up that clue and lets the comment go, Erika knows for sure she or he wasn't really interested anyway and moves the conversation on to other topics—or simply drops it altogether.

On days when Erika feels like talking more or wants to make herself stand out from among the crowd, however, she answers the question "Where are you from?" quite differently. "What time in my life are you referring to?" she asks. At this point the other person has virtually no choice but to ask Erika where she has lived during her life and then hear all the very interesting details Erika has to tell!

Where Is Home?

While this question at first seems to be the same as "Where are you from?" it is not. In some cases, TCKs have a great sense of "at-homeness" in their host culture. As long as Erika's parents remained in Singapore, "Where's your home?" was an easier question to answer than "Where are you from?" She simply said, "Singapore." Both her emotional and physical sense of home were the same.

Other TCKs who have lived in one city or house during each leave or furlough may have a strong sense of that place being home. In January 1987 the U.S. ambassador to Ecuador spoke at a conference about TCKs in Quito and said, "I think every expatriate family should buy a home before going abroad so their children will have the same base for every home assignment. My kids feel very strongly that Virginia is home even though they've lived outside the States over half their lives." This is undoubtedly an excellent idea, and one to be seriously considered when at all possible.

When, for various reasons, buying a house in the home country isn't a viable option, some TCKs still develop a strong sense of "home" in other ways. Often those whose parents move every two years rarely consider geography as the determining factor in what they consider home. Instead, home is defined by relationships.

When Dave Pollock asked Ben, a TCK from the diplomatic community, "Where's your home?" Ben replied, "Egypt." Dave was somewhat surprised as he

had not previously heard Ben talk about Egypt, so
Dave asked how long he had lived there.

"Well," Ben replied, "actually, I haven't been to
Egypt yet, but that's where my parents are posted
now. They moved there from Mozambique right after I
left for university, so when I go home for Christmas
vacation, that's where I'll go."

For some TCKS, however, "Where is home?" is the hardest question of all. *Home* connotes an emotional place—somewhere you truly belong. There simply is no real answer to that question for many TCKs. They may have moved so many times, lived in so many different residences, and attended so many different schools that they never had time to become attached to any. Their parents may be divorced and living in two different countries. Some TCKs have spent years in boarding schools and no longer feel a close attachment to their parents. In fact, they may feel more emotionally at home at boarding school than when thinking of their parents' home. Paul Seaman writes,

"Home" might refer to the school dormitory or to the
house where we stayed during the summer, to our
family's home where our parents worked, or, more
broadly, to the country of our citizenship. And while
we might have some sense of belonging to all of these
places, we felt fully at home in none of them. Boarding
life seemed to have the most consistency, but there we
were separated from our siblings and shared one
"parent" with other kids. As it grew colder, we could
look forward to going home for the holidays. We were
always eager to be reunited with our families, but after
three months of separation from our friends, we were
just as eager to go back. Every time we got on the
train, we experienced both abandonment and communion.[2]

No matter how home is defined, the day comes for many TCKs when they realize it is irretrievably gone. For whatever reasons, they, like Erika, can never "go home." Now when someone asks Erika where her home is, she simply says, "Everywhere and nowhere." She has no other answer.

Restlessness—The Migratory Instinct

In the end, many TCKs develop a *migratory instinct* that controls their lives. Along with their chronic rootlessness is a feeling of restlessness: "Here, where I am today, is temporary. But as soon as I finish my schooling, get a job, or purchase a home, I'll settle down." Somehow the settling down never quite happens. The present is never enough—something always seems lacking. An unrealistic attachment to the past, or a persistent expectation that the next place will finally be home, can lead to this inner restlessness that keeps the TCK always moving.

> Inika had waited for what seemed like forever to return to her host country, Guatemala. She finally found a job which offered her the prospect of staying there for many years, possibly even until she retired. Two weeks after arriving, however, Inika felt a wave of panic. For the first time in her life, there was no defined end point. Now she had to be involved with the good and bad of whatever happened in this community. She wondered why she felt like this so soon after reaching her goal. Then she realized that throughout her life no matter where she had lived, any time things got messy (relationships with a neighbor, zoning fights in the town, conflicts at church), internally she had leapfrogged over them. There was always an end point ahead when she knew she would be gone—the end of school, the end of home leave, or something. Suddenly, that safety net had disappeared. For the first time in her life Inika either had to engage completely in the world around her or start forming another plan to leave.

Obviously, it is good to be ready to move when a career choice mandates it, but to move simply from restlessness alone can have disastrous effects on an ATCK's academic life, career, and family.

Without question there are legitimate reasons to change colleges or universities. Sometimes TCKs who live a continent away must enroll in university without having the opportunity to visit beforehand. After arriving, they discover that that school doesn't offer the particular courses or majors they want. Perhaps they change their interest in a career they want to pursue and this school doesn't offer concentrated studies in that field. In such situations, there is no choice but to change. Some TCKs, however, switch schools just because of their inner migratory instinct. Their roommates aren't quite right; the professors are boring; the weather in this place is too hot or too cold. They keep moving on, chronically hoping to find the ideal college or university experience. Unfortunately, frequent transfers can limit what TCKs learn and inhibit the development of their social relationships.

Once through with school (or after dropping out), a TCK who has moved often and regularly may feel it's time to move even when it's not. Some ATCKs can't stay at one job long enough to build any sort of career. Just as they are anticipating a position of new responsibility and growth, that old rolling-stone instinct kicks in. They submit their letters of resignation, and off they go—again always thinking the next place will be "it."

> Sylvia raced through life. In the ten years following her university graduation, she acquired two master's degrees, had seven career changes, and lived in four countries. One day it struck her that while she had a vast amount of broad knowledge and experience, her career was going nowhere. And she wasn't sure she still wanted, or knew how, to settle down.

Some feel almost an obligation to be far from their parents, siblings, or even their own children. When it is possible to live closer, these adult TCKs choose not to. They have spent so much time separated from family that they don't know how to live in physical proximity, or don't want to. Others, like Bernie, have learned to deal with interpersonal conflict—including family conflict—by separating from the situation. He said, "I loved growing up with high mobility. Every time there was a problem, all I had to do was wait and either the people causing the problem left or I left. I have handled all of my life's conflicts the same way." Peggy is another example of how this restlessness works.

> Peggy, a foreign service ATCK, attended twelve
> schools in sixteen years all around the globe. Now,
> every two years, an internal clock goes off that says,
> "This assignment is up. Time to move." She has either
> changed jobs, houses, cities, and—twice—husbands in
> response to that message.
>
> Unfortunately, her migratory instinct has affected
> Peggy's children. Although she has noticed their
> insecurities developing as she perpetually uproots
> them, Peggy appears powerless to settle down. The
> overt reason for change always seems clear. "I don't
> like the neighborhood we're in," or "My boss simply
> doesn't understand me," or "I have a nasty landlord." It
> never occurs to her that she is replaying a very old
> tape that says, "No place can ever become permanent.
> Don't get too attached" or "If you have a problem, just
> leave." Nor does she realize it might be possible to
> replace the old tape with a new one that plays a
> message that could serve her better.

Some TCKs have an opposite response to their highly mobile background. They have moved so many times, in so many ways, and to so many places, they swear they will find a place to call their own, put up the white picket fence, and never, ever move again. Lorna, a non-TCK married to an ATCK, told us,

> When I met Dwight, I think I fell in love with his
> passport as much as I did with him. I was intrigued
> with all the places he had been and everything he had

seen. I envisioned a life of worldwide travel and living in all sorts of exotic places. Unfortunately, I assumed wrong. When my father surprised us with an old farmhouse for our wedding present, Dwight was thrilled. That was the first time he shared with me how he had always dreamed of finding a place to call his own and settle down. This was it. So I'm still reading my travel magazines and dreaming.

Now we take a further look at how the TCKs' experience, including this rootlessness and restlessness, shapes the patterns of their relationships.

Endnotes

[1] From Ruth E. Van Reken, unpublished original research on ATCKs, 1986.

[2] Seaman, *Paper Airplanes in the Himalayas*, 8.

9

Relational Patterns

Multiple separations tended to cause me to develop
deeper relationships quicker. Also, when I was with
family or friends, we tended to talk about things that
matter spiritually, emotionally, and so on. I still become
impatient with [what I see as] superficiality.[1]
                                    —Response to ATCK Survey

Because TCKs often cope with high mobility by defining their sense
of rootedness in terms of relationships rather than geography, many
TCKs will go to greater lengths than some people might consider
normal to nurture relational ties with others—be they family members, friends with whom the TCKs have shared boarding school years,
or other important members of their third culture community. Unfortunately, that same mobility can result in relationships being a
source of great conflict and pain as well. The cycle of frequent good-
byes inherent in a highly mobile lifestyle not only creates strains on
specific relationships—such as parents and children, when it's time
for the kids to fly an ocean away for school—but it can also lead to
patterns of protecting themselves against the further pain of good-
byes that affect relationships throughout their lives. Here, within the
context of relationships, is another example of both the gifts and
challenges of the TCK experience. Through relational patterns we

can see even more why the TCK life can be a rich source of meeting our basic human need for relationships for many, while making it very difficult for others.

Large Numbers of Relationships

TCKs usually develop a wide range of relationships as they or people around them habitually come and go. New friends enter their lives, while old friends become another entry in their burgeoning address books.

"I could travel to almost any country in the world and stay with a friend," Tom bragged after one transition seminar. This may sound like an exaggeration, but for many adult TCKs it's the truth. With friends from their childhood now in countless places, TCKs build a rich international network that is useful for all sorts of things—from finding cheap room and board while traveling to setting up business connections later in life.

The problem with having this many relationships, however, is that eventually they simply can't all be maintained. Renee learned this the hard way.

> ATCK Renee's personal address list grew to over eight hundred names. No matter how hard she tried to keep up with her correspondence, she couldn't. The stack of letters to answer always exceeded the time available—especially since many of those missives came from friends whom she thought deserved long letters in reply. Eventually, Renee had to resort to a yearly Christmas form letter, but it still took a month of constant work, as she always added personal notes before mailing them off. One year Renee was simply short of time. Presuming her friends would under-stand, and hoping they would rather have some news than none at all, she mailed the letters with no personal notes.
>
> Four months later she attended a wedding and met an African friend from her five years in Malawi. When

Renee rushed to greet him warmly, his response was exceedingly cool.

"Seems like you've forgotten us," he said.

Renee was dumbfounded. "How can you say that?"

"Well, you haven't called for months, and when you sent out your Christmas letter there wasn't even a personal note on it. My wife and I have been wondering what we've done to offend you."

Renee finally had to accept the sad reality that she wasn't going to be able to keep up with every wonderful person she had ever met.

Deep and Valued Relationships

Relationships everywhere move through various levels of communication as people get to know each other. While this happens in different ways in various cultures, here is one common pattern for how relationships are established.

1. *Superficial level:* This involves conversation generally referred to as "small talk"—How are you? Where are you from? The weather or today's headlines.

2. *"Still safe" level:* This is an exchange of no-risk facts. Where did you go on vacation last year? What sights did you see?

3. *Judgmental level:* Here, we begin to risk a few statements about our opinions on politics, religion, or other matters about which our new friend might disagree with us.

4. *Emotional level:* We begin sharing how we feel about life, ourselves, and others (e.g., that we're sad, happy, worried, or depressed).

5. *Disclosure level:* We reveal our most private thoughts and feelings to another person, confessing secret dreams as well as painful failures. This stage involves an honesty and vulnerability that lead to true intimacy. Most of us only have a few people in our lives with whom we share at this level. Some people have no one to share such a place.

One common complaint from at least Canadian and U.S. American TCKs is that they feel people in their home cultures are "shallow." Conversations with peers seem boring, and the TCKs long for the good old days with their international friends. Why is this such a common complaint? It has to do with these levels of relationships. People in different cultures not only enter but move through the various levels at different paces. Some cultures jump past the small talk quickly and treat strangers like long-lost cousins, inviting them to stay the night, eat what they want, and come as often as they wish. In other cultures nobody bothers to go next door to say hello to the family that just moved in from who knows where.

For various reasons, TCKs seem prone to passing quickly through levels one and two and moving immediately into topics that fall into level three. In other words, while others are still at the polite stages, TCKs are offering opinions on and asking what others think about such topics as how the president's term is going, what the government should do on its immigration policy, or whether the United Nations should intervene in some new world crisis. When others either don't seem to care about such things, or don't want to express their opinions, TCKs deem them shallow—and who knows what these others think of the TCKs?

Why do TCKs often jump into these at least supposedly deeper levels of communication faster than others? There are a number of reasons. One of these is cultural habit. On an Internet list serve for TCKs, this matter of relational levels became a hot topic of discussion. An interesting response came from a Dutch ATCK, Ard A. Louis, who grew up in Gabon and now lives in New York.

> At least among educated Europeans it's very common to discuss politics or other potentially divisive topics upon a first encounter. In fact, sometimes we look for something to argue about on purpose. Part of being "educated" is being able to talk about art, philosophy, politics, and so on.... and argue your points if need be.
>
> This is very different with Americans, who seem always to look for points of common interest. For

example, how often when you meet someone do they
ask where you're from and then try to find some point
of commonality like "I've been there" or "Do you
know so and so?"

Another very common topic of discussion is pop
culture, especially movies/TV shows most people have
seen. (Pop culture is the great unifying factor in the
U.S.—and being well versed in its history helps
tremendously in fitting in.) Thus, a very common first
impression of Europeans arriving in the U.S. is that
Americans are superficial because they seem to have
no opinions about even their own political situation, let
alone what's happening in the rest of the world.[2]

Ard's point is that the methods and styles of relating to one another
differ from culture to culture according to cultural habit. When we
discuss entering relationships at a "deeper level," perhaps this is
only in comparison to particular cultures, as in the case above—
U.S. culture. In reality, discussing politics in some cultures may be
no closer to true intimacy than talking about the weather in other
cultures. This, of course, calls into question the universality of how
the levels themselves are defined.

Another ATCK recounted how this mix-up of culturally appropriate relationship levels and styles caught her unaware:

I'd never met this Israeli businessman before that
evening, but during supper I asked him how the
political situation in Israel was doing.... Another
American eating with us almost spit out his food and
instantly changed the subject of conversation. When
we finished that new topic and I went back to my
original question, the American had the same reaction.
Afterwards he told me how horribly rude I'd been to
ask such a question of someone I barely knew. Frankly,
I was stunned. Here was a guy with lots of information
about key world issues and this American thought I
shouldn't talk about it. So I asked him why. He told me
in his family you were never allowed to talk about

> religion or politics because that always caused trouble.
> Until I heard about these different levels of communi-
> cation and personal relationships, I couldn't understand
> why I shouldn't start with political questions.[3]

There are three other reasons TCKs may jump more quickly than others into what we are calling deeper levels of relationship.

1. *Practice:* Many TCKs know how to get into relationships fairly quickly simply because they have had to start so many. They have learned to observe the dynamics of a situation, ask questions that can help open a door, hopefully be sensitive to cultural cues of what is or is not appropriate for this group, and respond appropriately when others approach them.

2. *Content:* The store of knowledge and experience they have acquired feeds into many different topics, so they often think they have something relevant to say. Because of their parents' careers, TCKs often grow up in homes where discussions on a current political crisis, starving children, religious views, or solutions to the economic woes of the country are standard fare. To express opinions on these topics is normal, and people around seem interested because the TCK's firsthand insights may help others understand the complexity of issues in the newspaper or on television that are happening a world away.

3. *Sense of urgency:* TCKs may also jump into deeper levels of communication quickly because there is little time to develop a particular relationship. They understand that if something doesn't happen now, perhaps it never will. TCKs routinely meet people of incredible diversity who can teach them so much about their part of the world. Why waste time in small talk? In one sense, almost everyone can be an instant friend. Because they have connected at a relatively deep level, many of these quick relationships do become long-term friendships—or at least part of that bulging address book for occasional telephone calls and yearly letters.

In *Military Brats*, Mary Edwards Wertsch talks about the "forced extroversion" the military lifestyle fosters because time is too short to wait to make friends. She says one technique she used to break in to new groups was the "confessional impulse." In quickly spilling family secrets (a level 4 or 5 disclosure), she sent a message that she wanted to invest in a new friendship. Often her confession was met by a mutual confession from the new friend. Wertsch also says that military kids might be more willing to be open than their civilian counterparts because they probably won't be around to deal with any negative consequences from these confessions.[4]

Non-TCKs, who are used to staying at the first or second level of relationship for relatively long periods, may misread TCKs who jump in at a deeper level. This type of confusion happened at a camp where Dave Pollock served as a seminar leader.

> Several days after camp started, a group of tearful, non-TCK young women sought Dave out. They felt completely confused by actions of the TCK males. A young man would engage one of these young women in, to them, deep and meaningful conversation, and she would think he was interested in her. But the next day he would do the same with someone else. After three days the young women were confused, angry with each other, and angry at the young men.
>
> When Dave spoke to the guys, they were shocked that these girls thought they had even considered anything more than a friendship for this week at camp. The TCK young men said they had no romantic presuppositions whatsoever. They just wanted to get to know these young women, find out what they thought about life, the world, their faith, and other assorted interesting topics. It seemed like a perfect chance to understand more about Americans. But the seriousness of the conversation communicated a level of warmth and relationship that meant something quite different to the young women.

TCKs usually place a high value on their relationships—especially those from their TCK world. Often the style and intensity of friendship within the international third culture are quite different from the types of friendship they have in their home country. Most expatriate families live far from relatives and tend to reach out to one another as surrogate families in times of need. When there is a coup, for example, it's the friends in this international community who band together in the fear, the wondering, the packing, and the leaving. Without doubt, a great deal of bonding that lasts a lifetime takes place at such times.

Relationships—both with friends and family at home as well as with friends from their third culture world—are also valued because they give the TCKs a sense of connectedness. These relationships offer the one place where TCKs can say, "Do you remember when...?" and someone actually does!

> A TCK's wedding is usually quite a sight. When Robin married Kevin, her high school sweetheart from boarding school, you would have thought you were in Africa rather than in New York. Papier-mâché palm trees framing a painted mural of a tropical beach decorated the reception hall. Kevin and his groomsmen all wore flowing robes from Sierra Leone. Robin's dad wore a country-cloth chief's robe as he walked her down the aisle. Friends came from far and near, filling the pews with equally colorful attire. The wedding had turned into a minireunion. Watching these TCKs chatter unceasingly throughout the reception was like watching long-lost family members reunite. There was no question about how they viewed their relationships from the past.

Effects of Cycles of Multiple Losses on Relationships

While many TCKs jump into relationships with both feet, others approach any new relationship with caution. In a 1986 survey of three hundred ATCKs, 40 percent of the respondents said they struggled with a fear of intimacy because of the fear of loss.[5] Too many close friends have moved away. Frequent, painful good-byes make some TCKs unwilling to risk emotional involvement again.

Often these TCKs are labeled as quiet or shy. They never take available opportunities to be deeply engaged in their schools or communities. Even TCKs who are regarded as gregarious, open, and friendly because of their skill at jumping into the second and third levels of communication often refuse to move on to the fourth and fifth levels of true intimacy. They manage to erect walls, usually without realizing it, to keep out anyone trying to come closer.

> When Karen became engaged to Jack, she couldn't believe that someone would actually be with her for the rest of her life, so she prepared for what seemed the inevitable loss by presuming Jack would have a fatal car wreck before their marriage. When that didn't happen, she feared it would happen on their honeymoon. After safely returning from their honeymoon, Karen worried whenever Jack was a few minutes late coming home from work. On their first anniversary, he was over two hours late due to an electrical failure in the mass transportation system. By the time he got home, she had started crying with an "I knew it would happen" despair, had begun to plan his funeral, and was wondering how long you had to be married before you didn't need to return the wedding gifts.

> Although Jack is living to this day, for a long time after the wedding, Karen couldn't understand why she always seemed to fuss over insignificant details—like whose turn it was to take out the garbage—just when she and Jack felt especially close. She finally realized that deep inside such closeness terrified her because she still feared losing it. Fussing was her way to keep up a wall of safety. Karen had been losing people she loved dearly since first separating from her parents at

> age six, when she left for boarding school, and it took a
> long time for her to let her guard down and dare to
> believe Jack would be staying.

As we saw in our discussion on the stages of transition, people try to protect themselves from the pain of losing a precious, or at least valued, relationship in various ways. TCKs are no different. Some try to limit their vulnerability to impending grief by refusing to acknowledge they care for anyone or anything. In the end, however, they know a pain of loneliness far greater than the one they are running from. The independence they have been so proud of turns into a profound isolation, which keeps them prisoner until the day they become willing to once more feel the pain of loss in order to know the joy of closeness.

A second common response for people trying to avoid the pain of losing a relationship is called the "quick release." When friends are about to leave, or when TCKs think they themselves might be leaving, their response is frequently to let go too soon. Friends quit calling each other and don't visit, play together, or go out for lunch. Each wonders what he or she did to upset the other one. A "quick release" also happens at points where some kind of temporary separation is about to occur. Many ATCKs talk of how easily they have an argument with a spouse the night before one of them is leaving for a short business trip the next day, in an unconscious attempt to let go.

Some ATCKs who have commonly used anger themselves (or had it used by those they were separating from) as a shield against future pain may see any type of anger as a precursor to separation and emotionally detach at the first sign of it.

> Garth and his new bride had their first argument. He
> told us later, "I knew right then she was going to leave
> me." Inside, he went stone-cold toward her. Let her
> leave. I don't care. I don't know why I married her
> anyway, he thought. When he finally realized his wife
> had no intention of leaving, he began to think through

his reaction and what had happened. He remembered
frequent arguments with his parents just before he left
for boarding school, probably each of them unconsciously trying to make the leaving easier. Garth began
to realize that because of that previous pattern, he
made automatic assumptions that any conflict meant
the impending loss of a relationship.

Refusing to feel the pain is a third common response of TCKs to the
multiple losses due to the high mobility of their lives. Even when
TCKs feel intensely about leaving a friend or relative, some refuse
to acknowledge the hurt to others or to themselves. They say they
don't like messy good-byes and, in fact, refuse to say them. Becky
and Mary Ann were two ATCKs caught in this pattern.

Becky and Mary Ann met at a Global Nomads International conference. For both of them, this was the first
time they had consciously reflected on how their pasts
as TCKs had affected them. Each had basked in the joy
of discovering another person who understood her
deep, inner, secret places. They had laughed together,
cried together, and talked incessantly. Suddenly the
conference was over, and that inevitable moment of
saying good-bye had come.

Becky and Mary Ann stood by the elevator as Mary
Ann prepared to leave for the airport. Chances were
great they would never see each other again; they
lived an ocean apart. As they looked at one another,
each knew she had let the other into a space usually
kept off-limits. What did they do now?

After a brief, uncomfortable stare, both broke into
wry smiles of understanding.

"So what do we say?" Becky asked first.

"I guess there's not much to say but the usual," and
Mary Ann paused, bent her right arm up so the palm of
her hand faced Becky. Like a windshield wiper making
one sweep across the windscreen, Mary Ann moved

> her forearm from left to right while saying, *"Byyeee."*
>   "I guess you're right, Mary Ann. So *Byyeee,"* and
> Becky mirrored the perfunctory farewell wave Mary
> Ann had just made.
>   Then they laughed. For some, this might have
> seemed an incredibly cold way to say good-bye after
> they had shared their lives so intensely. For them,
> however, it was a moment of recognition, of under-
> standing how each had learned to avoid painful
> farewells. They simply didn't acknowledge them! But
> in another way, it also represented the sum of all they
> had shared that needed no verbal explanation.

Unfortunately, however, not all who exercise the protective mechanism of emotional flattening realize it as poignantly as Mary Ann
and Becky did at the moment of farewell. Even more unfortunately,
this flat emotional response can be transferred from avoiding the
pain of farewells to all areas of life. Sometimes what is praised as
confidence and independence among TCKs may actually be a form
of detachment. In his book *Your Inner Child of the Past,* psychiatrist
Hugh Missildine cites the work of John Bowlby and says that whenever there is a prolonged loss of relationship between parent and
child, for *whatever* reason, children go through grief, despair, and
finally, detachment in trying to cope with that loss.[6] Certainly, many
TCKs have known profound separation from their parents at an early
age. But in addition to that, some have separated so repeatedly from
friends and other relatives, they simply refuse to let themselves care
about or need anyone again. The sad thing is, when pain is shut
down, so is the capacity to feel or express joy.

This response can be devastating in a marriage. The ATCK's
partner feels rejected because there are too few external demonstra-
tions of love from the ATCK. Conversely, no matter how many romantic gestures are offered to the ATCK, nothing seems to spark a
warm response.

It can be equally painful for the child of such an ATCK. Some
ATCK parents seem genuinely unable to delight openly in the pure

joy of having a child, of watching that child grow, of playing games together, or of reading stories at bedtime. Not only do the children miss the warmth and approval they long for, but the ATCK parent also loses out on one of the richest relationships possible in life.

On the other hand, however, we have seen how TCKs who learn to deal in healthy ways with the cycle of relationships they face become richer for it. They do, in fact, have a wealth of experiences to share and rich diversity among those they have met, and they have every possibility for making truly deep friendships that last across the years and miles. As TCKS become skilled at going through the process of transition in healthy ways, they can learn to enjoy each relationship they have, whether it be a long- or short-term friendship. Because all people lose relationships at one time or another, they can share the transitional skills they've learned for themselves to help others cope during their life transitions as well.

Endnotes

1   From Ruth E. Van Reken, unpublished original research on ATCKs, 1986.

2   Ard A. Louis, e-mail letter on MK-Issues, August 1996, used by permission.

3   E-mail letter from MK-Issues, August 1996, used with permission of author.

4   Wertsch, *Military Brats,* 263–65.

5   Van Reken, original research.

6   Hugh Missildine, *Your Inner Child of the Past* (New York: Simon and Schuster, 1963), 245–46.

10

Developmental Issues

Sometimes I think the cement of my being was taken from one cultural mould before it cured and forced into other moulds, one after the other, retaining bits of the form of each but producing a finished sculpture that fit into none. At other times I think of myself like the fish we caught [while we were] snorkelling off Wewak. My basic shape camouflages itself in the colours of whatever surroundings I find myself in. I am adept at playing the appropriate roles. But do I have a colour of my own apart from those I appropriate? If I cease to play any role would I be transparent? To mix metaphors, if I peeled away the layers of the roles I adopt would I find nothing at the centre? Am I after all an onion—nothing but the sum of my layers?[1]

—Sophia Morton

In her powerful essay, "Let Us Possess One World," Sophia is reflecting on the basic question we have been talking about that TCKs (and all others) must ultimately answer, Who am I? What does it mean to be human, and what does it mean to be *this* human—me?

Developing Personal Identity

In 1984 Sharon Willmer, an ATCK and therapist for TCKs, spoke at a conference about TCK issues and said that one of the greatest challenges she faced among her clients was that few of them had any idea what it meant to be a person. In particular, they had little sense of their own personal identity. During her talk, Sharon explained how every person—regardless of race, nationality, background, economic status, educational experience or lack thereof—has been created with specific, legitimate needs.[2] These include the need for strong relationships; a sense of belonging, of being nurtured and cared for, of internal unity, of significance; and a feeling of knowing ourselves and being known by others. Every human also has the need to express in one way or another the emotional, creative, intellectual, volitional, and spiritual aspects of his or her being. These needs are what define us as human, and to deny any of them is to deny something precious and important about ourselves as human beings. Furthermore, it is the specific mix and manner in which we meet or express these universal needs that lead to our sense of unique, personal identity.

So why is that such a particular problem for TCKs? Obviously, this is an important issue for non-TCKs as well. At first glance, it may seem that finding a sense of identity is difficult for TCKs simply because of all the cultural or national confusion we've talked about: "Am I an Austrian or a Brazilian?" "Do I fit better in a village setting or a city?" they ask themselves. But having a strong sense of who we are is more than just knowing our nationality or culture, though that is part of it. It's a matter of answering these questions: What is a person? Who am I as *this* person? What are my gifts, my strengths, my weaknesses? Where do I fit or belong? We seek answers to these questions in any culture.

How does that relate to TCKs any differently than non-TCKs? Throughout the preceding chapters and as we complete our look at the TCK Profile in the next chapter, it is becoming clear that the

TCK lifestyle itself affects how TCKs meet these fundamental needs that help them develop a strong sense of personal identity. In the formation of a sense of personhood and identity, the TCK experience has the same paradoxical potential, as we have been discussing, to be either a source of rich blessing or a place of real struggle. Often it is both. Many ATCKs tell us they have felt very nurtured and cared for—by biological parents, dorm parents, other expatriates, their friends among the host nationals, and friends and relatives at home. An Indian TCK raised in the United States said she felt more nurtured than most of her American peers because all the gatherings at the local Indian community center included the children as well as adults, while few American parents included their children in the same way for their social activities. Other TCKs, however, use the word *abandonment* when they reflect on their childhood. For whatever reason, the sense that parents were too busy for them, or were physically or emotionally absent, has left a chronic feeling of emptiness. Nothing and no one else seems to be able to fill this need.

For now, however, we want to look at the first two personal needs we mentioned above—a need for strong relationships and a sense of belonging—and see how the TCK experience presents special challenges as well as opportunities for fulfilling those needs.

Each of us has a strong need to be in relationship with other human beings. "No man is an island" is more than a trite phrase by some ancient poet. Babies who are left alone without human touch will die, no matter how often they are fed. Solitary confinement is considered the worst punishment next to death for a convicted criminal. In relationships we can share and begin to discover many aspects of ourselves. It is also where we receive the love and support we need as the foundation for living a life that is rich and meaningful. But for those things to happen, we must have lasting relationships in our lives, ones in which we don't need to constantly re-explain ourselves and our history. When a person moves continually, however, it's not easy to establish the ongoing relationships that fill this basic human need.

A sense of belonging is the second need we must all have filled to live fully. That can mean belonging to a family, a group of people, a culture, and/or a nation. Certainly it is an extension of our need for relationships, but it's also feeling secure in knowing how a place and people work and how and where we fit into the larger picture. This sense of belonging gives us the freedom we need to continue developing rather than having to repeat the basics constantly. Without that security, it seems we almost go in circles, continually repeating the same lessons of life rather than moving on to new ones.

Now that we know more about the need for relationship and belonging, we can focus a bit more closely on particular developmental issues TCKs may face while they are continuing to sort out their personal identity—a pattern of uneven maturity and delayed adolescence.

Uneven Maturity

People often tell TCKs, "I can't believe you're only fourteen (or whatever). You seem much older." Equally often (and probably behind their backs), these same people marvel at the TCKs' lack of sophistication or social skills. TCKs feel this discrepancy too and soon begin to wonder which person they really are: the competent, capable, mature self or the bungling, insecure, immature self? That's part of the problem in trying to figure out who they are: in many ways they're both.

Early Maturity

It's not only others who see TCKs as "more mature." They often feel more comfortable with older students than with fellow classmates when they begin college or university back in their home countries, probably for several reasons. Among them:

1. *Broad base of knowledge*. TCKs often have an "advanced-for-their-years" knowledge of geography, global events, and poli-

tics in other countries and are interested in topics not usually discussed by younger people in their home cultures. Many have learned unusual practical skills at a very young age as well—such as how to set up solar energy panels to keep computers going for translation work in the Amazon jungle.

2. *Relationship to adults.* TCKs generally feel quite comfortable with adults because they have had lots of experience with them. Generations usually mix much more in third culture communities than often takes place in the home country. Why? Because, at least traditionally, international expatriate communities are often small and quite communal—that is, most of the kids attend the same school; parents appear at the same international or organizational functions; many may go to the only international church in town; and people bump into each other in the one or two grocery stores that carry foods imported from their particular homeland. Since the children may already be friends from school, families visit as families rather than as adults only. In certain situations, some spend more time with adults than other children and almost come across as "mini-adults."

3. *Communication skills.* Children who speak two or more languages fluently also seem like mini-adults. How could they have learned to speak like this so soon in life? Multilingual TCKs generally feel at ease using their languages to communicate with quite diverse groups. In fact, TCKs often serve as translators for their parents—again, a task usually reserved for adults. All this continues to increase their exposure to, participation in, and comfort with a world of culturally diverse adults as well as other children and gives them an unusual air of maturity.

4. *Early autonomy.* In certain ways, many TCKs have an earlier sense of autonomy than peers at home. By their early teenage years, they literally know how to get around in this world and enjoy functioning in quite diverse ways and places. This may be a result of traveling alone to boarding school or having the

opportunity as young children to explore their surroundings freely by trikes, bikes, and hikes. A reliable, safe public transportation system in some countries adds to that sense of autonomy. Many TCKs in Japan take the train to school for two hours each way, every day in early elementary grades. When Paul lived in Australia, he took a ferry and bus by himself to school every day at age eleven, while his friends back in the States were going to the corner of their street and waiting for the school bus to pick them up.

Delayed Adolescence

Ironically, while there are many ways TCKs seem advanced for their years, there are also many ways they seem to lag far behind. In a survey of nearly seven hundred ATCKs, Dr. Ruth Hill Useem and Ann Baker Cottrell observed that it wasn't unusual for TCKs to go through a delayed adolescence, often between the ages of twenty-two and twenty-four, and sometimes even later.[3] TCKs who have never heard the expression "delayed adolescence" have still sensed that they are definitely out of sync with their peers but can't figure out why.

The first question then is—What does *delayed adolescence* mean? The second is—Why is it a characteristic of many TCKs?

Every person must go through certain stages of life successfully in order to function as an independent adult. At least in Western culture, it is during the teenage years that several of these critical developmental steps take place. Each of these tasks relates to a core need of human beings, and going through this process properly is one of the major ways we form a clear picture of who we are—that is, our identity. Below are some of these critical developmental tasks.

1. *Establishing a personal sense of identity.* This is what we talked about earlier in this chapter: the need to figure out—Who am I? What makes me *me*? Where do I fit in my family and group?

2. *Establishing and maintaining strong relationships.* Young children may be bonded to their immediate families, but the teenage years are when relationships with the larger world of peers become critical.

3. *Developing competence in decision making.* Competent decision making is based on the assumption that the world is predictable and that we have some measure of control. In an ideal situation, adolescents learn to make decisions under the protection of the family and then move on to making their own choices.

4. *Achieving independence.* When we have the stability of knowing what the rules of family and culture are and have learned to make competent decisions, we can begin moving toward the independence of adulthood. We realize that not only can we make choices for ourselves, but we are also now accountable for the consequences of our decisions. We—not someone else—become responsible for whether or not we accomplish our goals.

For TCKs, this developmental process may be delayed for a number of reasons. The first one relates back to why cross-cultural transitions and high mobility *during developmental years* are so significant. If establishing a personal sense of identity is a major task of adolescence, how do we do it? One critical way is by taking the cultural rules learned during our childhood and testing them out during adolescence. Often this involves the type of direct challenges teenagers' parents around the world know only too well: Why do I have to be in by midnight? Who says I can't wear my hair like this? After the testing is a period of integrating the cultural practices and values we decide (often unconsciously) to keep. We then use these to make decisions about how we will live as autonomous adults rather than continuing to live as children guided by external, parental rules alone.

When the cultural rules are always changing, however, what happens to this process? This is, again, why the issues of cultural balance and mobility—and the age or ages when they occur—become very important. Often, at the very time TCKs should be testing and internalizing the customs and values of whatever culture they've grown up in, that whole world, its familiar culture, and their relationship to it can change overnight with one plane ride. While peers in their new (and old) community are internalizing the rules of culture and beginning to move out with budding confidence, TCKs are still trying to figure out what the rules are. They aren't free to explore their personal gifts and talents because they're still preoccupied with what is or isn't appropriate behavior. Children who have to learn to juggle many sets of cultural rules at the same time have a different developmental experience from children growing up in one basically permanent, dominant culture that they regard as their own.

Some TCKs experience delayed development because of an extended compliance to cultural rules. In certain situations, TCKs are not as free as peers at home might be to test cultural rules during their teenage years. For instance, some TCKs need to comply with the status quo in a given situation for their own safety and acceptance. Instead of freedom to hang out with friends in shopping malls or on the street corners, many TCKs find themselves restricted, perhaps for safety reasons, to the military base or missionary compound. If they don't want to be kidnapped or robbed, they must obey regulations that might not be necessary in the home country. Also, some TCKs belong to organizations with fairly rigid rules of what its members (and their families) may and may not do. An embassy kid doing drugs or a missionary daughter who gets pregnant can result in a quick repatriation for the family. In such cases not only might the parents lose their jobs, but the TCKs might also lose what they consider to be home. This adds pressure to follow community standards longer than they might otherwise. When TCKs aren't as free as their friends in the home country might be to make some of the decisions about where they will go and what they will do, they must often wait to begin the normal adolescent process of testing parental and societal rules until a later period in life than usual—often to the shock of their parents.

As we saw with "The Delusion of Choice," the fact that life is often unpredictable makes it hard for many TCKs to make decisions. It's hard to make a competent decision if the basis used to decide something is always changing. Also as mentioned before, a TCK's lifestyle in many third culture communities is frequently dictated by the sponsoring agency. If the U.S. Navy assigns a parent for a six-month deployment, it doesn't matter what the TCK does or doesn't decide about it—that parent will be going. For these reasons and probably more, some TCKs don't learn to take responsibility for the direction of their lives. They are more prone to just "letting it happen."

TCKs who are separated from their parents during adolescence may not have the normal opportunity of challenging and testing parental values and choices as others do. Those who were separated from their parents in early years find themselves wanting to cling to parental nurturing to make up for early losses. They don't want to move into adulthood yet. Still others who have spent years away from home may idealize their parents in almost fantasy form. To challenge anything about their parents would call that dream into question. In situations such as these above, we've seen many TCKs delay the normal adolescent process of differentiating their identity from that of their parents until their late twenties, or even into their thirties.

Incompatible educational and social factors also contribute to at least the appearance of delayed adolescence. The Danish TCK who graduates from an American-based international school may return to Denmark and discover that she must do two more years at the secondary level before moving on to university. Suddenly she is grouped with those younger than herself and treated as their peer. This is especially traumatic if she's become accustomed to being seen as older than her years.

The social slowness discussed earlier can contribute to delayed adolescence by severely impeding the normal developmental task of establishing and maintaining strong relationships—particularly with peers and members of the opposite sex. Judith Gjoen, a Dutch

ATCK who grew up in Indonesia and is now a clinical counselor in Norway, wrote about the difficulties Europeans face on their return home after attending a predominantly international school.

> Dating is very American. Scandinavian ways of interrelating between the sexes are much more informal. There is much more flexibility in the sex roles. All boys learn to knit, all girls learn carpentry. Furthermore, a young person's identity is not so strongly connected to "dating status." From a Scandinavian perspective, the American way can be slightly overdone and hysterical. You are not prepared for the European way of being together [males and females] when you are socialized into an American system.[4]

The development of other social skills may also be delayed by not knowing the unwritten rules in the TCK's age group back home or in the new culture. How loud do you play music? How long do you talk on the phone? When do you engage in chitchat and when in deeper conversations? How do you behave with a friend of the opposite sex? When the rules around them have changed, TCKs sometimes retreat into isolation from others rather than try to cope.

Sometimes the very maturity noted earlier coupled with the sometimes more hidden delayed adolescence may lead to unforeseen problems. The initial attraction of a young TCK to older, more mature people may result in the choosing of an older marriage partner. Unfortunately, while the "early maturity" of the TCK may make such a match seem like a good idea, the deeper delay in development may scuttle the relationship later on. Sometimes the TCK isn't as ready for the responsibility or partnership of marriage as he or she appeared to be because the issues of personal identity, good decision making, and ability to build strong relationships haven't been resolved. Other times, as in any marriage, when the younger partner goes on to develop a deeper, truer maturity, the older spouse doesn't always continue to grow at the same rate. This can leave the younger partner disappointed, disillusioned, or dissatisfied.

Uneven maturity offers almost paradoxical benefits and challenges, as do all other TCK characteristics. The very reasons for some of the delays in adolescence are rooted in the greatest benefits of the third culture experience. Once they are aware of and understand the process, however, TCKs and/or their parents can guard against a certain smugness or sense of elitism they sometimes exhibit about how "mature" they are, while at the same time not panicking about areas where they still need to catch up. Given time, the maturity process will sort itself out into a more even flow as they, like others, move on through adolescence—delayed or not—into adulthood.

Delayed Adolescent Rebellion

A delayed adolescence is painful enough for the TCK who keeps wondering why he or she can't be like others, but even more painful—not only for TCKs but for their families as well—is a delayed adolescent rebellion, a time when the normal testing of rules either starts unexpectedly late or becomes exaggerated in an all-out, open defiance of nearly every possible convention the family and/or community holds dear and extends far beyond the adolescent years. Obviously, this type of rebellion also occurs in families that don't live abroad, but we want to look at some specific reasons for a delayed rebellion in some TCKs and then at why it often continues later than the normal teenage years.

1. *Extension of delayed adolescence.* In any journey to adulthood, there are always those who, in the process of testing the rules of their upbringing, decide they will avoid adults' expectations, no matter what. For whatever reasons, they assume an "anti-identity." This process of rebellion is often an offshoot of normal adolescent testing of cultural norms. When the time for that normal process is delayed for all the reasons mentioned above, the rebellion that often comes during that time will also be delayed.

2. *End of the need for compliance.* Sometimes it seems that young people who have been forced to comply with a fairly rigorous system throughout their teenage years decide to try everything they couldn't do before, once they are finally free from those external restraints. Rather than the usual process of testing rules a few at a time while still under a parent's watchful eye, they go off to university and seemingly "go off the deep end."

This form of rebellion may actually be a positive—though slightly misguided—move toward independence. In these situations, parents and others may need to understand the reason for the behavior and be patient in the process, while also pointing out (when possible) that some of this behavior may be counterproductive to the goal of independence they seek.

3. *Loneliness.* Sometimes the rebellion is a plea for help. We have met many TCKs who have tried to express to their parents that they need a home base; that they feel desperately lonely when vacation time comes and everyone else goes home and they stay in the dorm because their parents are still overseas and relatives in the home country seem like strangers; or that they are struggling in school and want to quit. But the parents never seem to hear. Instead, they send e-mail messages with platitudes like "Cheer up," "It will get better," or "Trust God"; or they explain once more why they need to stay in the job they're in.

Eventually, some TCKs finally scream, through their behavior, the message they have not been able to communicate verbally: "I need you to come *home*—to be near me." When they get arrested for drugs, or get pregnant, or try to commit suicide, they know their parents will come—at least for a short period. Unfortunately, the parents who didn't hear the earlier verbal or nonverbal messages often don't understand, even at this point of major rebellion, the deep loneliness and longing their child is experiencing. They judge the rebellion without understanding the reason, and a deeper wedge than ever is driven between parent and child.

At that point, the TCK's behavior may become more extreme than before, and whatever form the rebellion takes—drugs, alcohol, workaholism, some esoteric cause—becomes a way in itself to numb the pain of longing for some type of security and home base. The sad thing is that until the loneliness and longing are addressed, the TCK will stay walled off, often in very destructive behavior, fulfilling the worst prophecies made about him or her.

4. *Anger.* One of the common manifestations of unresolved grief, anger, may erupt in this time of rebellion and intensify it. The anger may be directed at parents, the system they've grown up in, their home country, God, or other targets. Unfortunately, once again people don't always stop to find out what's behind the explosion. The judgment and rejection of the TCK's experience increases the pain and leads to further anger and rebellion.

There is another situation that may be the cause of anger. TCKs who have spent many years physically apart from their parents may, as we said, unrealistically idealize them. As young adults, these TCKs begin to discover their own imperfections, realize their parents aren't perfect either, and not only become angry at the loss of their fantasy but also begin to blame their parents for the lack of perfection in *themselves*. "If I'd just lived a normal life or had better parents, I wouldn't be struggling the way I am now." While anger against parents for imperfections in ourselves is probably a normal part of the developmental process for everyone, TCK or not, when parents remain overseas, working through it can be difficult for all concerned.

The bottom line is that no matter what the reason for the anger, it's often turned against the parents and may be expressed in an almost punitive rebellion—the TCKs want to hurt those whom they feel hurt them.

A major problem with delayed adolescent rebellion, however, is that rebellion in the mid to late twenties may have a destructive effect far beyond that of teenage rebellion.

> Pierre was a diplomat's son from Switzerland, who grew up in four different South American countries. During his early twenties, when friends asked how he had liked his nomadic lifestyle, he always replied, "Oh, I loved it! It never bothered me to pack up and move. We always knew there was something very exciting ahead. I've lived in nine different countries."
>
> After marriage and three children, however, the story changed. Certain job situations didn't work out. He became tired of trying to find ways to support his wife and children. In the end, he became totally disenchanted with family life and the attendant responsibilities and simply walked away from everything he'd apparently valued before. "I've spent my life," he replied to those who questioned him, "doing what everyone else wanted me to do and I'm tired of it. Now I'm finally going to do whatever I want to do."

We stress that this type of rebellion is neither desirable nor necessary. The TCK as well as parents, family, and friends are all wounded in this process. Being aware of some of the reasons delayed rebellion occurs may sometimes prevent it, or it may help the family deal with delayed adolescence in its early stages, so they aren't held prisoners to destructive behavior. Perhaps the best preventive measure parents and other adults can take against this type of rebellion is to make sure, even in situations where their TCKs are raised in a strong organizational (or family) system, that there are opportunities for the children to make real choices in matters that don't compromise their safety or the agency's effectiveness. Most important, TCKs and ATCKs who read these lines and recognize themselves need to know they have the choice to take responsibility for their own actions and find help for their behavior rather than continuing to blame others for how awful their lives have been or become. (See chapter 18 for further help in this area.)

Identity in a "System"

TCKs who grow up in the subculture of the parents' sponsoring organization have a few extra factors to deal with in this process of establishing a sense of identity. Although in reality these issues are extensions of what we have already talked about, it's important to understand how growing up in what is often a fairly structured community can be one more factor in a TCK's developmental process.

There can be many strong benefits to living in a carefully defined system. In many situations, the whole system of the sponsoring organization serves to some extent as both family and community. It provides materially as a good parent might, with air travel paid for, housing provided, and perhaps special stores made available. In many cases, as mentioned earlier, it also provides specific guidance or regulations for behavior.

An organizational system is one of the places where the need for belonging can truly be fulfilled because there are clear demarcations of who does and doesn't belong. Some TCKs have a deeper sense of belonging to that community than they will ever have with any other group and feel secure within the well-ordered structure of their particular system.

Other TCKs, however, feel stifled by the organizational system in which they grew up. They may be straining at the bit to get out of what they see as the rigid policies of the system. They realize that they have had almost no choice in countless matters that have deeply affected their lives—such as when and where their parents moved, where they could go to school, how to behave in certain common circumstances, or how they could express their inner passions. They see their organization as an uncaring nemesis and they feel intense rage at a system that requires conformity to rules and regulations regardless of individual preferences. Some blame the system for ruining their lives.

Certainly anyone who grows up in a clearly defined system is very much aware of how the group expects its members to behave. Failure to conform brings great shame on the TCK or the whole family. In many cases, the rules of these systems are a higher priority than the rules of the family, superseding decisions parents would normally make for their own children—such as when and where the children go to school.

What might make the difference in how or why an organizational system seems so positive for one person and restrictive for another?

At the risk of oversimplifying, and recognizing that there are many differences in how each agency may be run, we have identified four basic ways TCKs relate to the system in which they grew up—from the perspective of their own personal makeup, gifts, and personality. Understanding this picture can help us answer the above question.

1. *A TCK who fits the system.* Feeling comfortable is relatively easy for those whose personality and interests fit pretty well within the structure or rules of the system under which they have grown up. It might be an easygoing military kid who never seems to question authority, a pragmatic missionary kid who doesn't see the point of the fancy accessories in a Lexus, or a diplomat's kid who is an extrovert and thrives on meeting new people. They can go along with how life works in this system, and it doesn't conflict with how they think, what they like to do, what they want to be, or, most important, who they are by their very nature. There is room in this system to express who they are. It's a pretty good match.

2. *A TCK who doesn't fit the system but attempts to conform.* Other children don't match the system as well. Secretly, they prefer rap, while others around are denouncing it as junk. They long for color and beautiful decor but live in a plain, brown, adobe-type home within a system that feels it isn't spiritual to focus on worldly beauty. They find crowds of new people frightening, but they paste on a smile and act cordial to the dignitaries at never-ending receptions. They have learned not to reveal their feelings or desires because they learned early on that it was

wrong to feel or think that way. Instead of being able to explore the mystery of their own personality and set of gifts, they feel ashamed of this secret longing and try harder and harder to be what they perceive the system says they should be.

The major problem for members of this second group is that their sense of identity comes almost totally from an external system rather than from who they are deep within. If this type of conformity doesn't change at some point, people in this group may become more and more rigid over the years in adhering to the system that now defines them. They fear that if they let any part of it go, they will lose themselves because they don't know who they are without this structure to hold them together.

3. *A person who doesn't completely fit the system but doesn't realize (or at least doesn't seem to mind) it.* People in this group go ahead and listen to rap—not to be rebellious but because they like it. It doesn't occur to them—or worry them—that others might disapprove. If told that others might disapprove, they would likely respond, "That's O.K. If they do, I'll use my earphones." They stay in their rooms and read—not because they're rejecting the social scene, but because they love to read. They make decisions that don't quite match those of everyone else—not for the sake of being different but simply because they prefer the way they've chosen. They don't feel compelled to be exactly like everyone else but are happy to join with others when they do share an interest. Perhaps they have the inner security to be independent because many of their foundational needs for relationship and belonging have been well met in early years within their family. Maybe it just happens to be one of the attributes of their personality. Either way, they are discovering and operating from who they are inside rather than letting their environment define them.

4. *A person who doesn't fit the system, knows it, and spends his or her life proving it.* People in this fourth group like to think of themselves as members of the group just discussed, but they're

not. For whatever reasons, they learned early on that at least parts of them didn't fit the system. Perhaps they cried their first night at boarding school and were told to be brave—but they couldn't stop crying. Maybe they honestly wanted to know why things should be done one way rather than another but were given the unsatisfactory reply, "Because I said so." Still, the burning question inside wouldn't go away. Unfortunately, as they keep bumping into something that doesn't fit them inside, some TCKs finally decide—consciously or unconsciously—to throw out everything the system stands for. They'll be anything *but* that system.

The irony is that these outwardly rebellious TCKs actually get their identity from the very system they're rejecting. People who are determined to prove who they are *not* rarely go on to discover who they *are*.

It's important to remember that it's not wrong to be part of a strong organizational system. An organization is an efficient and necessary way of forming a community into functional groups, usually for the purpose of accomplishing a common goal. We can relate to it; be part of it; and even have some of our core needs of belonging met by it. But it's not, by itself, who we are.

Once that's understood, TCKs and ATCKs can take a better look at their group and determine which parts of the system do or don't fit with who they are, keeping in mind that they don't have to reject or retain an entire system.

By the time we sort through these many challenges, it's easy to wonder once again how any TCK can survive. Dirk, a German TCK who grew up in Taiwan and went to university in the United States, has learned to live with the challenge of many cultures and places by living fully in whichever one he is currently in while not denying the others are also part of his life. He uses a computer metaphor to describe this phenomenon.

I just build windows. When I'm in America, I activate
the American window. When I'm in Germany, I
activate the German window and the American
window goes on the back burner—and so do the
people in it.

In summary, when thinking about TCKs' identity and development issues, don't forget the interweaving of challenges with great benefits. TCKs find in their experience numerous opportunities for fulfilling their basic human needs in the most profound ways of all, and they often emerge with a very secure self-identity. We have seen that TCKs who dare to wrestle through the hard questions of life can develop a deep and solid sense of purpose and values that go deeper than those who are not forced to sort through such questions to the same degree. In addition, the exposure to philosophical, political, and social matters which are almost part and parcel of the TCK experience means there is every potential for substantive intellectual development. By its diversity alone, a TCK's world creates questions to ponder. This is one aspect of personhood that has every potential of being filled to overflowing for TCKs. Of all the TCKs we have met or worked with, very few would ever exchange the richness of their lives to avoid the inevitable challenges they have faced along the way.

Endnotes

1   Sophia Morton, "Let Us Possess One World," see Appendix B.

2   Sharon Willmer, "Personhood, Forgiveness, and Comfort," in *Compendium of the ICMK: New Directions in Mission: Implications for MKs*, edited by Beth Tetzel and Patricia Mortenson (West Brattleboro, VT: ICMK): 103–18.

3   Ruth Hill Useem and Ann Baker Cottrell, "TCKs Experience Prolonged Adolescence," *Newslinks* 13, no. 1 (September 1993): 1.

4   Judith Gjoen, personal letter to David C. Pollock, November 1995.

11

Unresolved Grief

There was no funeral.
No flowers.
No ceremony.
No one had died.
No weeping or wailing.
Just in my heart.
I can't...
But I did anyway,
and nobody knew I couldn't.
I don't want to...
But nobody else said they didn't.
So I put down my panic
and picked up my luggage
and got on the plane.
There was no funeral.[1]

—"Mock Funeral"
by Alex Graham James

Next to sorting out their sense of personal identity, unresolved grief ranks as the second greatest challenge TCKs face. "But what do TCKs have to grieve about?" people often ask. "They've had such exciting lives."

Yes, many have. For that very reason, some TCKs refuse to accept the idea that unresolved grief could possibly be an issue for them. They agree they've had wonderful, interesting lives. Who else has seen the world, traveled to all sorts of fascinating places where few others have been, speaks exotic languages, and enjoys different foods the way they have? What is there to grieve for?

While there is no single reason unresolved grief is a major—and often unrecognized—factor for countless TCKs, many of them experience this grief *because* of the very richness of their lives. We only grieve when we lose people or things we love or that matter greatly to us, and most TCKs have much they love in their childhoods. Much of what they love—and then lose—however, are intangible parts of their world (e.g., the sights, sounds, and smell of market day or the call of a particular bird each morning). Other losses, such as never seeing a best friend again, are more tangible and certainly happen to non-TCKs as well, but as we have seen, for most TCKs the collection of significant losses and separations before the end of adolescence is often more than most people experience in a lifetime. Still, while we may agree that all losses (whether recognized or not and no matter how small or how big) set in motion a grief reaction, the question remains: why do a significant number of TCKs struggle with *unresolved* grief? Some of the reasons we suggest in this chapter—followed by ways TCKs express unresolved grief—may seem obvious now that we better understand the totality of their experience. However, because this unresolved grief is such a major and potentially crippling issue for TCKs if not dealt with, we want to collect the many possible causes of it—both tangible and intangible— that have been touched on throughout our discussion of the TCK Profile and bring them all into direct focus. With a clearer definition of the problem, we hope to prepare the reader for the discussion in the ensuing chapters on how to make the most of the TCK experience.

Reasons for Unresolved Grief

Fear of Denying the Good

It seems some TCKs believe that acknowledging any pain in their past will negate the many joys they have known. To admit how sad it was to leave Grandma in the home country feels like a denial of how glad they were to return to their friends in the host country. To say it was hard to leave the village they grew up in might mean they don't appreciate all the effort relatives in the home country have gone to in preparing for their return. Until these TCKs can acknowledge that proper mourning for the inevitable losses in their lives is an affirmation of the richness of the past rather than a negation of the present, they will continue to deny any grief they have felt.

Hidden Losses

Many intangible losses are tucked in amid the many benefits of a TCK's life, creating a special problem for dealing with the grief related to each loss. Because these losses are hidden, they are most often unnoticed. Because they are unrecognized, the TCK's grief for them is also unrecognized—and thus unresolved. We call them the "hidden losses."

Many of these hidden losses are also recurring ones. The exact loss may not repeat itself, but the same *types* of losses happen again and again, and the unresolved grief accumulates. What are some of these hidden losses?

Loss of their world. With one plane ride a TCK's whole world can die. Every place that's been important, every tree they've climbed, every pet they've had, and virtually every close friend they've made are gone with the closing of the airplane door. TCKs don't lose one thing at a time; they lose everything, but there's no funeral. In fact, there's no time or space to grieve, because tomorrow they'll be in Bangkok to see the sights, then fly to four other exciting places before getting to Grandma's house and seeing the relatives who are eagerly awaiting their return. How could they be sad? As they continue to move from one world to another, this type of loss occurs over and over.

Loss of status. With that plane ride also comes a loss of status. Whether in their home or host country, many TCKs have settled in enough to establish a place of significance for themselves. They know where they belong in the current scene and are recognized for who they are and what they can contribute. All at once, not only their world but their place in it is gone. As they travel back and forth between home and host country, this loss is also repeated.

Loss of lifestyle. Whether it's biking down rutty paths to the open-air market, taking a ferry to school, buying favorite goodies at the commissary or PX, or having dependable access to electricity and water—that too can change overnight. Suddenly, there's too much traffic for bike riding, stuffy buses carry everyone to school, local stores don't have what you want, or electricity and water supplies can go off for three days at a time. All the patterns of daily living are gone and with it the sense of security and competency that are so vital to us all. Indeed, these are major losses.

Loss of possessions. This loss doesn't refer to possessions of monetary value but to the loss of things that connect TCKs to their past and, again, their security. Because of weight limits on airplanes, favorite toys are sold. Tree houses remain nested in the foliage waiting for the next attaché's family. Evacuations during political crises mean nothing can be taken along. And so it goes.

At one conference, TCKs were asked to name some of their hidden losses. All sorts of answers popped up:

"My country" (meaning the host country).

"Separation from my siblings because of boarding school."

"My dog."

"My history."

"My tree."

"My place in the community."

"Our dishes."

Dishes? Why that?

"We'd lived in Venezuela the whole eighteen years since I'd been born. I felt so sad as I watched my parents sell our furniture. But when we got back to England and my mom unpacked, I suddenly realized she hadn't even brought our dishes. I said, 'Mum, how could you do that? Why didn't you bring them?' She replied, 'They were cracked, and it's easier to buy new ones here.' She didn't understand those were the dishes we'd used whenever my friends came over, for our family meals, for everything. They were not replaceable because they held our family history."

The lack of opportunity to take most personal possessions from one place to another is one of the differences in international mobility compared with mobility within a particular country. If someone moves from Amsterdam to Rotterdam, usually a mover comes, loads up the furniture and dishes along with everything else, and drives the truck to the new home. Although the house and city may be different, at least familiar pictures can go up on the wall, the favorite recliner can be placed in the living room, and some sense of connectedness to the past remains.

In international and intercontinental moves, shipping the entire household is often impossible. Shipping costs a lot more than the furniture is worth. Instructions come from the organization or business (or parents) to keep only those possessions that can fit into a suitcase. Many things are too big or bulky to pack. It seems simpler to start over again at the next place with new things.

Loss of relationships. Not only do many people constantly come and go in the TCKs' world, but among these chronically disrupted relationships are the core relationships of life—the ones between parent and child, siblings, grandparents, aunts, uncles, cousins, and close friends. Dad or Mom may go to sea for six months. Grandparents and other extended family members aren't merely a town or state away, they're an ocean away. Education choices such as boarding school or staying in the home country for high school can create major patterns of separation for families when the children are still young. Many TCKs who return to their home countries for secondary school grow up as strangers to their brothers and sisters, who remain in the host country with their parents during those same years.

> Until Ruth Van Reken was thirty-nine and started writing the journal that turned into *Letters Never Sent* (the story of her own TCK journey), she had no idea that the day her parents and siblings left her in the States and returned to Nigeria for four years was the day her family, as she had always known it, died. Never again did all six children live with two parents as a family unit for any extended period of time. As she wrote, Ruth allowed herself to experience for the first time the grief of that moment twenty-six years before—a grief almost as deep as if she had just had a phone call that her family had been killed in a car wreck.

> In another case, Courtney stayed with grandparents in the States for high school, while her folks were in Saudi Arabia. She says, "I didn't feel nearly so much that I was always going somewhere as that I was always being left. I felt abandoned."

Loss of role model. In the same way we "catch" culture almost instinctively from those around us, we also learn what to expect at upcoming stages of life by observing and interacting with people already in those stages.

In a gathering of older ATCKs, we again asked the question, "What are your hidden losses?" One gentleman answered, "Role models." He had only recently realized that during his twelve years in a boarding school from ages six to eighteen, he had not had a model for a father who was involved in his family's life. Although a successful businessman, he had been married and divorced four times and remained estranged from his adult children.

From our role models, we decide what and who we want to be like when we are adults. We also believe that another potential factor in some TCKs' delayed adolescent response is that while living overseas as teenagers, they aren't around peers from their home culture in the age group just ahead of them—the university or beginning career age group—and so they are deprived of role models for young adulthood.

Loss of system identity. As mentioned before, many TCKs grow up within the friendly (a few might say unfriendly) confines of a strong sponsoring organizational structure, which becomes part of their identity. They have instant recognition as a member of this group. Then at age twenty-one the commissary card is cut up, the support for education stops, invitations to organizational functions cease, and they are on their own as "adults." TCKs understand this mentally and probably maintain personal friends within the original system, but their sense of loss that they are no longer part of that system is real. In fact, some have told us it feels like they were disowned by their own families.

Loss of the past that wasn't. Some TCKs feel deep grief over what they see as the irretrievable losses of their childhood. They remember the graduation ceremony parents couldn't attend because they were a continent away and know the chance will never come again. They wish they could have gone to school where they could have studied in their native language. Some regret that they had to return to their home country when their parents did; they wanted to stay in the host country.

> Chris, a Finnish TCK, returned to Helsinki after a childhood in Namibia. While living there, separation from extended family seemed normal. All the other TCKs she knew had done the same. But that hadn't been the experience of her Finnish relatives. One evening, just after Christmas, Chris listened to her cousins reminisce about their childhood in Finland. They talked of family Christmas traditions, summer

vacations at the family cottage on the lake, birthday
celebrations and weddings when the family gathered.
Suddenly, Chris felt overwhelmed by what she had
missed growing up. Later, in a gathering of TCKs from
various countries, Chris spoke of how living overseas
had robbed her of knowing the closeness of her
extended family back home.

Loss of the past that was. While some TCKs grieve for experiences they missed, other TCKs grieve for the past no longer available to them. People who live as adults in the same country where they grew up can usually go back and revisit their old house, school, playground, and church. In spite of inevitable changes, they can still reminisce "on site," but a highly mobile TCK often lacks this opportunity.

****

In any of the types of hidden losses we've just mentioned, the main issue again is not the grief, per se. The problem is that in these types of losses, no one actually died or was divorced, nothing was physically stolen. Contrary to obvious losses, there are no markers, no rites of passage recognizing them as they occur—no recognized way to mourn. Yet, each hidden loss relates to the major human needs of belonging, of feeling we are significant to others, and of being understood. The majority of TCKs are adults before they acknowledge and come to terms with the depth of their grief over any or all of these areas of hidden loss.

Hidden losses aren't the only reason for unresolved grief, however. Even when losses are recognized, other factors may prevent a healthy resolution of grief.

Lack of Permission to Grieve

ATCK Harry wrote the alumni magazine of his school
in response to earlier letters in which various ATCKs
had talked about painful issues from their childhood.
"Stop fussing," he wrote. "Don't you think any kid in

the Harlem ghetto would trade places with you in a
second?"

Sometimes TCKs receive a very direct message that lets them know it's not okay to express their fears or grief. Many are asked to be "brave soldiers," perhaps particularly in the military and missionary context. Colonialists' offspring were encouraged to "keep a stiff upper lip." In *Military Brats,* Mary Wertsch writes of a girl who came down the stairs one morning and asked her mom, "What would happen if Dad got shot in Vietnam?" The mother's instant reply was "Don't—you—*ever*—say—that!"[2]

Also, when parents are doing such noble things—saving the country from war or representing the government on delicate negotiations or preaching salvation to a lost world—how can a child admit grief or fear? The child would feel too much shame for being selfish, wrong, or not spiritual or patriotic enough if she or he acknowledged how much it hurt to leave or be left. In such situations, TCKs may easily learn that negative feelings of almost any kind, including grief, aren't allowed. They begin to wear a mask to cover those feelings but conform to the expectations and socially approved behavior of the community.

TCKs who grow up in a missionary community may face an added burden. Some mission people see an admission of painful feelings as weakness or, worse, a lack of faith. TCKs who want to keep their faith often feel they can't acknowledge any pain they have experienced. Conversely, other TCKs from such communities take the opposite tack; they believe that in order to deal with their grief, they must deny the faith they've been taught. They, too, have forgotten the paradoxical nature of the TCK experience.

Lack of Time to Process

Unresolved grief can also be the result of insufficient time to process the losses. Any person who experiences loss needs a period of time to face the pain, mourn and accept the loss, come to closure, and move on. In the era when most international travelers went overseas by ship, the trip could take weeks, providing a built-in transition period that allowed time for the grieving process. In today's world of jet travel, however, there is literally no transition, no time or space to deal properly with the inevitable grief of losing what has been left behind.

Lack of Comfort

The presence or lack of comfort is another huge factor in whether grief is resolved. In 1984 Sharon Willmer first identified this as a key issue when she wrote Dave Pollock, "If someone were to ask me, 'From your experience as a therapist and friend of [TCKs], what do you see as the [TCKs'] greatest need?' I would reply, beyond the shadow of a doubt...that they need to be comforted and helped to understand what it means to be a person."[3] We've already looked at the issues relating to personal identity, but to understand why we need comfort and why it's often missing for TCKs, we must first look at what comfort is and isn't and how it differs from encouragement.

Merriam-Webster's Collegiate Dictionary defines *comfort* as "consolation in time of trouble or worry."[4] Comfort doesn't change the situation itself, nor can it take away the pain, but it relays the message that someone cares and understands. Comfort validates grief and gives permission for the grieving process to take place. For example, when a person walks up to a widow standing by her husband's casket and puts an arm around her shoulder, that gesture, with or without words, is comforting. It can't bring the husband back to life or stop the tears or the pain, but it lets the widow know her grief is accepted and understood. She's not alone in her sorrow.

Unfortunately, in their very efforts to help another person "feel better," people often confuse comfort with encouragement and end up giving neither. Encouragement is a person's attempt to change the griever's perspective. It may be a reminder to look at the bright side of a situation instead of the loss or to think about a past success and presume this present situation will turn out just as successfully.

Obviously there's a time for both comfort and encouragement, but what happens if the two are confused? When the grieving widow is told that it's a good thing her husband at least had a substantial life insurance policy, how does she feel? Neither comforted nor encouraged! When encouragement is given before comfort, the subtle or not so subtle message is "Buck up, you *shouldn't* feel so low." It becomes a shame message rather than encouragement.

Perhaps because a TCK's losses are often far less visible than the widow's, it's this mix-up between comfort and encouragement that can sometimes keep TCKs from being comforted. There are several ways people may unknowingly try to encourage rather than comfort TCKs and thus do neither.

Discounting grief. As TCKs and their families prepare to board the plane, Mom and Dad admonish them not to cry, and say, "Don't worry. You'll make new friends quickly once we get there." In not acknowledging the pain involved in the good-bye, they communicate the hidden message that their son or daughter *shouldn't* be so sad. What's the big deal about saying good-bye to these friends when they can be so easily replaced? Somehow, though, the TCKs still feel sad and end up thinking something must be wrong with *them.* After a while there is nothing to do but bury the pain.

Comparing grief to a higher good. When TCKs express sadness at an approaching move or loss, adults may try to cheer them up with the reminder that the reasons behind this lifestyle—and thus the losses involved—are of such importance (defending or representing the country, saving the world, earning enough money to pay for the child's later educational bills) that the TCKs *shouldn't* complain about a few hardships along the way. Unfortunately, this is not comforting. Often, TCKs already understand—and often agree with—the reason why their parents have a particular career and lifestyle. Most TCKs aren't asking their parents to change. All they're trying to say is that, in spite of what they *know*, it still hurts to leave friends and a place they love dearly. When that opportunity to express sadness is denied, some TCKs begin to develop a sense of shame regarding their feelings.

Denying grief. It's not only TCKs who may deny their grief. Adults around them often do the same. To comfort another person, to say "I understand," is to admit there's a reason for grieving. Adults who busily mask their own sense of loss by denial can't afford to admit they understand the sad TCK. If they did, their own internal protective structures might tumble down and leave them quite unprotected. One therapist asked us if anyone had ever done a study on how parents react when they know they must send those kids away to school at age six. Bowlby[5] and others have written about how early separations between parents and children affect a child's ability to later attach to those parents or others, but we know of no official study regarding how parents cope in such situations. We have heard, however, from ATCKs who speak of how their parents stopped hugging them in their early years so they wouldn't "miss it" when they left for school at age six.

Again, the losses TCKs encounter—recognized or unrecognized—and the grief that follows aren't, in themselves, the biggest problems. They are natural and when we can grieve openly for what we have lost, it's "good grief"—a productive way to deal with the pain. The problem is *unresolved* grief, and because it isn't dealt with directly, it emerges in other forms—forms that are destructive and that can last a lifetime. That's "bad grief."

Expressions of Unresolved Grief

Unresolved grief will always express itself somehow. Often it will be in ways that appear completely unrelated to feelings of grief. The following are some typical reactions to unresolved grief.

Denial

Some TCKs refuse to admit to themselves the amount of sadness they have felt. "It didn't bother me to leave my parents for boarding school when I was six. I was so excited to go that once I got on the train, I didn't even think about them anymore." While this may be their conscious recollection of events, they forget that if a six-year-old *doesn't* miss Mommy and Daddy when he or she leaves for months at a time, something must be fundamentally wrong with that relationship—or they have already disconnected. Grief is normal when separating from those we love.

Others admit these separations were painful but claim to have gotten over them. Yet, as we've already seen, they continue to live lives that wall out close relationships to others—including spouses and children.

Anger

The most common responses triggered by unresolved grief are defensiveness and a quick, flashing anger at seemingly small circumstances. These types of responses can have devastating consequences in every context: marriage, work, social relationships, and parenting. For some, the anger is sublimated and eventually finds expression when TCKs take up a "righteous cause." They can defend the need for justice, environmental matters, civil rights, political reform, or religious practices with adamancy and vigor because no one can argue with their sense of outrage on such matters. Those who try will, of course, be seen as fools. This is not to say TCKs and others shouldn't be involved with such issues, but there is often a level of intensity which seems to go beyond the cause itself.

In any of these situations, people complain about how difficult the angry TCK is to live, work, or deal with, but few try to understand the pain behind the anger. Somewhere along the way, the TCK decided the pain was simply too much to bear and replaced grieving with anger as anesthesia for the pain. Unfortunately, anger ultimately increases the pain as the TCK's world becomes more isolated and lonely; no one wants to be near such an angry person.

Depression

Depression is another manifestation of unresolved grief. When there's no opportunity to acknowledge their feelings externally, people often turn those feelings inward. When too much grief gets bottled up for too long, depression can set in. Of course, depression (as well as denial, anger, and withdrawal) is a normal stage of any grieving process and must be respected as such. The problem, however, is getting stuck in this stage, because they have never been able to name the grief and mourn the loss.

Withdrawal

Grief can also be expressed through withdrawal. For parents, a child's withdrawal can be painful. How many parents have been deeply hurt by only sporadic letters from their child? by phone calls that are erratic and monosyllabic at best? by only superficial conversation during infrequent reunions? They don't realize withdrawal is a way to protect from pain. This withdrawal may also be a conscious or unconscious way to strike out at parents and hurt them for "dragging me away from the place I love"—be it home or host country.

We've heard story after story from parents of TCKs whose adult children were in the midst of a life crisis but told their parents, "Don't come. You can't do anything." Parents are often confused, not knowing what to do. They fail to recognize that their children might well deny their need for support rather than risk being disappointed once more that no one will be physically or emotionally present in their times of crisis.

Rebellion

If the normal anger felt in any grief situation isn't dealt with, it can easily take the form of extreme rebellion. For some, rebellion takes an inward, silent form; for others, it's blatant and loud. Either way, rebellion becomes the nearly impenetrable shield behind which the pain is deeply hidden. Each time a new circumstance comes that threatens to break through the fragile protection and expose the pain, it's like something inside the TCK metaphorically grabs a trowel and plaster to reinforce the shield. Until he or she is willing to let the protection be gently removed so the wound can be exposed to light and air, however, healing cannot begin.

Vicarious Grief

Transferring the focus from personal grief to that of others is another way to express unresolved grief. A TCK might sit at an airport weeping as he or she watches total strangers say good-bye. Some TCKs go into professions where this vicarious grief finds a more active, long-term expression.

As a child, ATCK Joan spent twelve years in boarding schools. On a conscious level, she remembered the fun of game nights, the senior banquet, and the lifelong friends she had made. She denied any particular sadness from these years of family separation, outside of the initial tears of farewell in first and second grades.

After university, however, Joan found herself working in a day-care center. She explained her choice of career by saying, "I just want to help kids whose parents must work not to feel lonely. I like to sit and hug them all day so they know they're wanted and loved. Kids need to be nurtured."

Joan realized after several years that she was excessively involved with every child under her care, trying to protect each one from emotional pain. Her anger sparked against parents who forgot to bring their child's favorite teddy bear. She fought with other workers if they sharply reprimanded a child.

Finally, Joan began to recognize that her deep involvement with these children reflected more than a normal concern for them. It stemmed from the extreme loneliness she had felt when separated from her own parents during her years at boarding school, which began when she was six. Instead of directly dealing with the loss of day-to-day parenting she had experienced, Joan had unconsciously tried to deal with her own grief by making sure no child under her care would feel that same pain.

Even ATCKs who don't express their grief through a profession often become the "rescuers" of the community. For whatever reasons, they are the unofficial dorm counselors, the ones who befriend lonely people, who may take in the homeless. All of these can, in fact, be noble and positive gestures, but if their activities substitute for working out their own grief, eventually their behavior will become counterproductive. They may be so involved in rescuing others that they never rescue themselves.

Delayed Grief

TCKs may go through life without showing or consciously feeling any particular sadness and suddenly find to their great surprise that a seemingly small incident triggers a huge reaction.

> For ATCK Dan, it was the first day his son, Tommy, went off to kindergarten. Dan should have been happy that Tommy was starting this new phase of life. School was only one block away, so Dan walked Tommy right to the door, said good-bye, turned around to walk away—and found himself unable to see the sidewalk for the tears that filled his eyes. Once back home, his body sagged against the door as he sobbed uncontrollably. His wife couldn't imagine what had happened. "Is everything all right? Is Tommy O.K.?" Dan could only shake his head as his body continued to shudder with pain.

> Dan was experiencing delayed grief. As he left his son at school, he suddenly had a flashback of his own departure for first grade. But the picture was different from how his son was beginning school. For Dan, the new picture put him inside a small, one-engine plane with four other schoolkids as it took off from a grassy airstrip. He could still see his parents standing on the edge of the forest waving to him. The memory of what he had felt while returning their farewell wave hit like an engulfing tide as he turned away from Tommy that morning.

Often the people most surprised by the delayed grief are those feeling it. What amazes so many ATCKs is that the grief from losses they have never consciously defined seems to hit them hardest between the ages of twenty-five and forty. Often the first glimmerings of their unrecognized grief begin when they have their own children. Sometimes that's when they first ask themselves, "If my parents loved me as much as I love this baby, how could they have ever let me go away?" Or they must face the fact they aren't the perfect parents they were expecting to be. Even without children, many begin to realize there's a good chance that the rootlessness, withdrawal from close relationships, or whatever they're experiencing isn't going to change no matter how much they change their circumstances. At that point, it's easy for ATCKs to think that if they had lived a "normal" life, they wouldn't have problems. They begin to blame others; then family and friends are shocked that this ATCK who "never had any problems" seems suddenly to be conjuring up all sorts of fantastic painful experiences. Finally, most ATCKs begin to face the fact that some answers for their reactions to life reside inside themselves rather than in outside events and situations. This is the time many finally examine some of this unresolved grief, work through it, and move on in productive, adult ways from having gone through the grieving process.

****

Now that we have looked in detail at the TCK experience itself, we will move on to specific, constructive ways we all—TCK, ATCK, parents, relatives, friends, and sponsors alike—can be involved in maximizing the great potential benefits of this third culture life and dealing with the challenges in healthy ways so that the drawbacks, too, become part of the TCK's strength and gifts.

Endnotes

[1] Unpublished poem by ATCK Alex Graham James, used with permission.

[2] Wertsch, *Military Brats*, 44.

[3] Sharon Willmer (personal letter to David C. Pollock, 1984).

[4] *Merriam-Webster's Collegiate Dictionary,* 10th ed., *s.v.* "comfort."

[5] John Bowlby, cited in Terry M. Levy and Michael Orlans, "Intensive Short-term Therapy with Attachment-Disordered Children," in *Innovations in Clinical Practice: A Source Book*, Vol. 14, edited by L. VandeCreek, S. Knapp, and T. L. Jackson (Sarasota, FL: Professional Resource Press, 1995).

Section Two
Maximizing the Benefits

12

Building a Strong Foundation

Wise cross-cultural parenting doesn't just happen. Moving to a new culture far from familiar support systems causes new stress for everyone, and parents often need to learn new parenting skills and practices. Below are some questions parents should consider before committing their family to such a major move.

1. *What are family needs that require attention regardless of location?* A child's age and level in school can be especially important factors to consider. For example, the last two years of secondary school aren't usually a good time to uproot teenagers. Not only will they miss graduating with their friends, but they probably won't be able to plan for what they want to do after they graduate. If they decide to further their education they won't have the opportunity to visit different universities and evaluate which would be the best one to attend the following year. Does any child have a learning or physical disability or a chronic medical condition that requires special care? If so, parents must make sure those needs can be met in the new location. Will home schooling or tutoring be sufficient if special education programs aren't available in the regular school? Will medical facilities be adequate?

2. *What are the policies of the sending agency?* Does the agency look carefully at family and educational needs when moving its personnel? Parents need to read the stated policies, but more important, perhaps, they need to talk with others who work for the organization and have already faced similar situations. This will give a much clearer picture of the reality of these policies.

3. *How will existing family patterns and relationships be affected by the move?* In the home culture, parents generally have a support system of extended family, friends, and people from school and church to help raise their kids. A cross-cultural move radically disrupts that support system.

> A Nigerian man told of the surprise he'd felt when he and his wife first moved to the States so he could pursue a graduate program. In Nigeria their family had lived in proximity to grandparents, aunts, and uncles, who often functioned as surrogate parents for their children. Finding a baby-sitter was never a problem. In the States, they were on their own. No one offered to take their children when they needed to go to class or to the store. The special nurturing that comes from living in an extended family had disappeared, and the couple had to develop completely new patterns of parenting.

4. *Do both spouses favor the move?* This is a key question. If both spouses aren't fully committed to a cross-cultural move, the experience often ends in disaster. A reluctance on the part of one spouse easily turns to resentment and hostility under the pressure of adjusting to the cross-cultural assignment. That unwilling spouse often uses extremely damaging passive-aggressive methods (e.g., emotional withdrawal, drug or alcohol addiction, generalized hostility, or destructive levels of personal criticism) to sabotage the experience for the entire family. One military spouse refused to hang curtains or pictures in the house and kept all the household possessions in boxes as a daily re-

minder to her husband and children that she was only waiting to leave.

5. *How does the family—and the individuals in it—handle stress?* It's important for parents to realize that not only they but also their children will experience the new stresses of a cross-cultural move. Stress is part of everyone's life, causing all sorts of reactions including depression, anger, and withdrawal. But sometimes specific individuals or families seem to have a particularly hard time handling stressful conditions. If someone in the family, or the family as a whole, becomes seriously depressed or reacts in an extreme way to stress in general, parents would be wise to seek outside counsel before planning a cross-cultural move.

6. *If the family does decide to move, how will it take advantage of the cross-cultural opportunities ahead?* It's a sad waste for families to live in another country and culture and not be enriched by the experience. When families don't think ahead about how they want to explore their new world, they often never do it. Soon after moving, life becomes as filled with daily routines as it was in the home country, and the vast resources for learning—whether it be about the history of this new country or the geographical and cultural differences they see around them—are unthinkingly ignored. During her college years, one TCK chided her mother, "Mom, we lived in the middle of a tropical rain forest, and you never taught me a thing about it." The truth was that Mom had never *thought* a thing about it. She had lived there a long time and considered the trees and plants around them in their host country the same way she had those in their home country—simply as part of their environment to be lived in, not a rain forest to be studied or explored.

7. *What educational options are available in the new setting?* This is a crucial matter to consider before accepting any particular assignment. Will children be required to go to boarding school?

Are parents expected to home school them? If so, how will this affect family dynamics? What are the local school options? Are international schools available? What are some of the pros and cons of each choice? The matter of education is so critical, in fact, we've devoted all of chapter 14 to it.

8. *How will the family prepare to leave?* Once parents have decided to make the move, there's a lot they can do to help their children through the transition process (see chapter 13). Closure is as important to a child as it is to an adult. It's important that parents make specific plans to help their children settle relationships and think about what's ahead. Leaving well has as profound an impact on the ability of children to enter and adjust successfully as it does on adults.

There are always trade-offs and sacrifices in making a cross-cultural move, but parents must never sacrifice their children. When considering such an assignment, parents need to make use not only of their own good sense and faith but also that of others, such as school guidance counselors, successful cross-cultural sojourners, and family and friends who know them well, to make the best decision possible. Cross-cultural living can be a wonderful experience in countless ways, but it is far better when it begins with clear thinking and good planning rather than with naive visions of a romantic adventure.

Foundation Blocks for Healthy TCKs

When parents make the decision to take their family into a cross-cultural situation, they are also deciding that they will be raising TCKs. Fortunately, this isn't a malady they inflict on their children. In fact, in most situations it's a great gift. Nevertheless, as we've noted at length, some TCKs do well, while others don't. What can parents do to help their kids maximize the great benefits of this experience and deal most effectively with the challenges?

Unfortunately, there's no perfect formula for "how to raise TCKs 100 percent successfully." But there are specific principles parents can follow to build a foundation strong enough to support their children while they try out the options and opportunities of a TCK lifestyle. It's great to watch countless TCKs build on such foundations as they use the gifts of their background and grow from the challenges rather than being hurt or overwhelmed by them.

The following four foundation blocks are important to all children, but for TCKs, whose world is in continual flux, they are critical.

Parent-to-Parent Relationship

We realize not all third culture families have two biological parents in the home. Some families are blended through marriage or adoption; other TCKs are raised in single-parent families. When there is a two-parent household, however, the relationship between parents is of vital importance. If a poor parental relationship is added to all the other challenges TCKs face, the consequences can be devastating. There are three critical areas parents must examine.

1. *Commitment to each other. Commitment* is an unfashionable word these days, but any lasting relationship must begin with it. Commitment is what gets us through those days when we wonder if the struggle makes it worth sticking around. Commitment forces us to work out our differences rather than throwing in the towel. It's how we grow. When approaching a change as major and as stressful as a cross-cultural move, it's especially important for both parents to decide if they are sufficiently committed to one another, their relationship, and their family to make the necessary personal sacrifices to achieve their common goals.

2. *Respect and support for one another.* These go hand in hand with commitment. When kids know their parents' relationship is solid, they feel secure. They also need to see that their parents *like* each other. Small signs of affection—pecks on the cheek while passing or holding hands while watching TV—may not seem very important, but for children, these types of actions

assure them that all is well with Mom and Dad. That's one area they don't have to worry about.

3. *Willingness to nurture the relationship.* A new cultural environment can severely hamper a couple's traditional ways of nurturing their relationship. Elegant restaurants aren't available for a lovely anniversary meal. Servants or nannies restrict the opportunities for quiet, private conversations. Visitors pop in unannounced any time of day or night. Couples in cross-cultural settings often have to look hard for new and creative ways to carve out enough uninterrupted time to help their relationship not only survive but thrive.

Parent-to-Child Relationship

Parents are the most important caregivers in any child's life. The relationship between parent and child must be as consciously nurtured as the one between parents. Research indicates that this relationship is the single most significant factor in determining how TCKs (or any kids) ultimately fare.[1] It is here that the most basic human needs for meaningful relationship, for a true sense of belonging, and for a feeling of significance are met in early, foundational years.

But cross-cultural living introduces new challenges to parenting. In this section, we will look at ways third culture parents can specifically help meet those needs.

Children need to be valued. Having a sense that we are valued—that what we think and feel makes a difference to those around us—is part of feeling significant as a human being. But for that to happen, someone must know us well enough to be sensitive to and supportive of our thoughts and feelings. And that's what parents do for children. Parents of TCKs communicate that they value their children in all the usual ways parents normally do—by listening when children talk, by asking good questions, by seeking clarification when a child talks or acts in a way parents don't quite understand, or by giving a quiet hug.

Perhaps one of the special challenges for parents in a third culture experience is that their children are growing up in a different world from the one in which they themselves grew up. Because of this, they may not realize that some cross-cultural situations can become far more stressful to children than they had thought. Some ATCKs have told us of their extreme fear when they tried to do such normal things as go to market, because they were the targets of constant attention and rude remarks simply because they were foreigners. Others have known tremendous stress because of the political climate in the new country. For all these reasons, parents need to listen carefully and not brush off their child's concern or behavior as silly until they understand the reason for it.

> International businessman Byron and his family survived a coup, seemingly unscathed in spite of machine-gun fire in their front yard one night. Shortly after the coup, however, one daughter became panicked when the family car developed a flat tire and they stopped by the side of the road to fix it. After a second flat tire the very next day, this daughter refused to take any more car trips with the family.
>
> But why should a simple flat tire cause her so much panic? When questioned, she said something about the "soldiers"; when she was questioned further, however, the cause of her panic finally became apparent: the first tire went flat near an army barracks, where soldiers walked around with guns prominently displayed. Their daughter had panicked, afraid that if the soldiers came after them or started to shoot, there would be no way for the family to escape because of the flat tire. With soldiers present throughout the city, she didn't want to risk being caught in such a situation again.

It's particularly important for parents to listen not only to the words their children say but also to what lies behind the words when they're discussing upcoming transitions. Sometimes parents try to protect their children and keep them from worrying by not telling them about an impending move until just before it happens. Of course, kids don't usually have the final say in their parents' career choices, but if they are included early on in discussions and preparations, they will get the all-important message that their needs are respected. They will know they are valued members of the family.

This list of questions from cross-cultural educator Shirley Torstrick helps parents assess how well they have been listening to their child.

> What makes your child really angry?
>
> Who is your child's best friend?
>
> What color would your child like his or her room to be?
>
> Who is your child's hero?
>
> What embarrasses your child most?
>
> What is your child's biggest fear?
>
> What is your child's favorite subject in school?
>
> What is the subject your child dislikes most?
>
> What is your child's favorite book?
>
> What gift from you does your child cherish most?
>
> What person outside your family has most influenced your child?
>
> What is your child's favorite music?
>
> What is your child's biggest complaint about the family?
>
> Of what accomplishment is your child proudest?
>
> Does your child feel too big or too small for his or her age?
>
> If you could buy your child anything in the world, what would be his or her first choice?
>
> What has the biggest disappointment in your child's life been?
>
> What does your child most like to do as a family?
>
> When does your child prefer to do her or his home-work?
>
> What makes your child sad?
>
> What does your child want to be as an adult?[2]

It's likely the more of these the parents can answer, the more their kids will feel valued.

Children need to be special. There's no greater gift parents can give children than to let them know beyond any doubt that there is at least one place in this world where they will always belong and are so special that no one else could ever replace them. That place is here in this family.

For many TCKs, however, the need to feel special is an area of particular vulnerability. So many parents are involved in important, high-energy, people-oriented jobs that it's easy for TCKs to feel they are less important than the people their parents work with. This is an issue that often surfaces in ATCKs years after the fact, and it surprises parents who thought their children didn't mind their busy lifestyle. To help prevent the sense of being orphaned or abandoned that we've heard some TCKs express, parents need to make sure that amid all the busyness of their schedules, there are spaces reserved for their family to spend that time together we mentioned above—no matter what other apparently urgent matters arise.

Children need to be protected. Children need to know beyond all doubt that their parents love them enough to protect them from unnecessary hurt or harm and that Mom and Dad will be available to comfort and console them when painful times are unavoidable. All of us—including children—feel especially vulnerable in a new setting, and we require a sense of safety before we can take the risks needed to adjust.

Protecting their children can become more complicated than parents expect, however, when they move to a place with different rules not only for what is acceptable, but also for what is safe. For example, an important parental job in every culture is to provide physical and emotional protection for children while still encouraging a healthy independence. But what does that mean in different places or cultures? Walking alone to the store might be safe in one environment and risky in another. Since cultural rules and practices often change rapidly for third culture families, parents must find a balance between protection and independence. Otherwise, it's easy to move from guiding and maintaining boundaries to smothering. When that happens, children either want to break out of what they see as excessive restraints, or they wind up with a lot of unnecessary fears themselves.

We stress the importance of protection, because some of the deep expressions of pain we have heard come from TCKs who have felt unprotected by parents or other caregivers. Sometimes they felt pushed out on their own too soon into a new school or community, especially when they didn't know the language yet. It has also happened on leave, when the TCKs felt they were put on display against their will for church congregations or relatives.

The worst stories, however, are from those who were left with a caregiver—whether a domestic worker or fellow expat in the host country, a friend or relative in the home country, or a dorm parent at boarding school—and were emotionally, physically, or sexually abused by the very person parents trusted to take care of them. The trauma was intensified, of course, if the parents refused to believe what was happening, sometimes sending their child back to that very situation. The fact that their parents put these abusers in charge made the children assume at some probably unconscious level that the parents themselves sanctioned the abuse. This is one reason it often takes years before the child (now an adult) will tell the parents what really happened. Most parents weren't trying to hurt their kids, but they just didn't think about how vulnerable their children might feel or actually be in such situations, or perhaps they simply didn't listen well enough when the child tried to tell them at the time.

Parents can help children not only feel but also *be* protected. If the kids have to attend school in a new language, parents can arrange for tutoring before landing on the doorstep of the school. TCKs who express resistance at being "little missionaries" or "little ambassadors" shouldn't be forced into that role. Children are persons in their own right, and *not merely extensions of their parents*. They need to be respected as such.

Parents must make sure that anytime they are separated from their children, clear, open lines of communication are established. Children must have access to their parents with no one else able to intercept or divert the messages.

If a young child must live away from home, it's extremely important to teach and frequently reinforce concepts of personal safety and private body zones. Children need to be reminded that their parents will always believe them and protect them—no matter what anyone else might say. And then, if the child *does* report some potential or actual infringement, parents must be prepared to intervene on their child's behalf—even if doing so may put their career at risk.

Children need to be comforted. We talked extensively about comfort in chapter 11. Being comforted communicates that parents care enough to understand and be sensitive to their children's feelings, even if the situation can't be changed. Parents should remember, particularly in any transition experience, that the quietest, most compliant child may be grieving and may need comforting the most.

TCKs' Perception of Parents' Work

Nietzsche once said, "I can endure any *how* if I have a *why*." The resilience of human beings is often related to whether or not they have a reason to be resilient; hence, the third foundation block is how TCKs view their parents' work. TCKs will be able to tolerate the most difficult adjustment challenges if the reasons are good enough.

For many, seeing their parents' work as significant and life-changing is a great asset of the TCK experience. They feel pride that their parents are involved in a career that can make at least a small difference in the world. They feel a sense of ownership in that work—and thus a sense of significance themselves—because their family has traveled the globe together to do the job. The challenges of their upbringing are insignificant compared with the sense of what is being accomplished.

Other TCKs, however, express great bitterness toward parents who are involved in these types of international careers. What makes the difference? Certainly the parents' attitude toward the job, the host country and culture, and the sincerity of the political or religious beliefs that have motivated them to go abroad in the first place are critical factors. Parents who feel and act positively toward their situation and the host country people with whom they are working communicate that attitude to their children.

On the other hand, the parent who shows disrespect for the people or culture of the host country can make the young TCK observer wonder why the family is there at all. When the going gets tough, the question can quickly change from "Why are we here?" to "Why don't we go home?"

Once that question is raised, TCKs often begin acting out. International business kids may conclude that money isn't a good enough motivation for living abroad; they end up breaking local laws, hoping their parents will be expelled. Foreign service kids may become so disillusioned with what they perceive as the hypocrisy of governmental politics that they start covering the embassy walls with graffiti. Missionary kids who see a major discrepancy between what their parents preach and what they practice at home can feel that spreading such an apparently ineffective faith isn't worth the cost. They blatantly smoke, drink, use drugs, or get pregnant, hoping the mission will send the family home. Military kids who see their government's presence in a particular conflict as a matter of economic advantage rather than principle may join an antiwar demonstration.

A particular irony sometimes results when parents who have done a good job of convincing their children how important their overseas assignment is decide to return home. How could they think of leaving, the TCK wonders, if it's as important as they said it was? They question whether the parents ever really valued the work they were doing, casting a retrospective doubt on their whole experience. In such cases, as always, parents need to have an open discussion of the upcoming move and make sure their children understand the true reasons for it—even if the children have difficulty listening.

Positive Spiritual Core

The fourth foundation block is the child's awareness that there is a stable spiritual core in their parents' lives and in the life of the family as a whole.

In a world where moral values and practices can be radically different from one place to another, this block is the key to true stability throughout life. When TCKs have a core personal faith and a stable set of values, they will be equipped to remain on a steady course no matter which culture or cultures they live in.

Endnotes

[1] Leslie Andrews, "The Measurement of Adult MKs' Well-Being," *Evangelical Missions Quarterly* (October 1995): 418–26.

[2] Shirley Torstrick, (seminar handout, used with permission).

13

Dealing with Transition

It's vital that highly mobile families learn to deal well with the entire process of transition. Earlier we discussed the common characteristics of the five stages in any transition experience: involvement, leaving, transition, entering, and reinvolvement. Here, then, are some concrete ways to not only survive but also grow while moving through each stage.

From Involvement through Leaving

The time has finally come. After carefully thinking through the pros and cons, the decision is made: the family will be moving to a new place and, for many TCKs, a new world. With that decision, each member of the family moves from the comfortable stage of involvement they have hopefully been in to the leaving stage. Whether this move is between countries or even to new locations in the same country, leaving is a critical stage for everyone to navigate well.

Since denials—our own or those of friends around us—and moments of special recognition such as graduation or farewell ceremonies don't change the ultimate reality of our leave-taking, it's essential that we face and deal with the normal grief inherent in leaving a place and people we love. Doing this rather than running away from it will allow a healthy transition process to continue. We also need to look ahead realistically and optimistically. How can we do both—face our approaching losses squarely while still looking forward with hope? The best way is by making sure we go through proper closure during this leaving stage. Without that, the rest of the transition process can be very bumpy indeed, and settling on the other side will be much more difficult. Leaving right is a key to entering right.

Building a "RAFT"

The easiest way to remember what's needed for healthy closure is to imagine building a raft. By lashing four basic "logs" together, we will be able to keep the raft afloat and get safely to the other side.

> **R**econciliation
> **A**ffirmation
> **F**arewells
> **T**hink Destination

Reconciliation. Any time we face a move from one place to another, it's easy to deal with tensions in relationships by ignoring them. We think, "In two weeks I'll be gone and never see that friend again anyway. Why bother trying to work out this misunderstanding?"

Unfortunately, when we refuse to resolve interpersonal conflicts, two things can happen. First, we are so focused on how good it will be to get away from this problem that we not only skip over the reconciliation needed for good closure but also ignore the total process of closure and don't move on to building the rest of the RAFT. Second, the difficulties don't go away when we move. Instead, as we leave, we carry with us our mental baggage of unresolved problems. This is a poor choice for three reasons: bitterness is never healthy for anyone; the old discontentment can interfere with starting new relationships; and if we ever move back to this same place and have to face these people again, it will be much harder to resolve the issues then.

Reconciliation includes both the need to forgive and to be forgiven. How that happens may vary among cultures. In one culture, it might mean going directly to the person with whom we have a conflict and addressing the issues. In another culture, it may mean using an intermediary. Obviously, true reconciliation depends on the cooperation and response of the other party as well, but we at least need to do all we can to reconcile any broken relationships before leaving.

Affirmation. Relationships are built and maintained through affirmation—the acknowledgment that each person in the relationship matters. Again, styles or customs of affirmation vary from culture to culture, but in every culture we must let others know we respect and appreciate them. Here are four ways to do so:

1. Take the time to tell coworkers you have enjoyed working with them.

2. Tell friends how important their friendship has been, perhaps leaving them some memento of a special time you have shared.

3. Send a note with a small gift to your neighbors to let them know what you've learned about kindness, faith, love, or perseverance through your interactions with them.

4. Reassure parents, siblings, and close friends of your love and respect and that you don't leave them lightly. A bouquet of flowers might be ordered for delivery the day after you leave.

Affirming others helps us as well as those we affirm. It not only solidifies our relationships for future contact, but in expressing what they have meant to us, we are also reminded of what we have gained from living in this place. Part of good closure is acknowledging our blessings—both to rejoice in them and to properly mourn their passing.

Farewells. Saying good-bye to people, places, pets, and possessions in culturally appropriate ways is important if we don't want to have deep regrets later. We need to schedule time for these farewells during the last few weeks and days.

> One woman forgot to take into account that everyone
> comes to the departing friend's house on the last day
> to bid a final farewell. In order not to offend the
> countless people who streamed in all day long, she
> visited with each one in turn. By the end of the day,
> her bags still weren't packed and she missed her flight!

Here are some suggestions for saying good-bye in four key areas, all of which just happen to begin with *p:* people, places, pets, possessions.

Farewells to significant people in our lives are crucial. Parents should take special care to help their children say good-bye to people with whom they have had meaningful relationships in the past as well as the present. Helping kids say good-bye may include writing a note or baking cookies together for that special person—anything that acknowledges the importance of that relationship and says "Thank you for being a special person in my life. I will miss you."

Everyone has places that evoke an emotional response. It may be a spot tied to a special moment in our lives (our engagement, for instance) or where we go when we are upset or where certain events always occur. These are the places we come back to visit, either alone or to show our children years later. Part of healthy closure includes visiting such sites to reminisce and say farewell. This is particularly important for TCKs who may be losing their whole world with next week's plane ride. Many TCKs we have talked to mourn for the favorite tree they used to climb years after they have left the land of their childhood.

People say good-bye to places in different ways. Some plant a tree that will grow long after they are gone, symbolizing a living, ongoing connection to this part of their lives. Others leave a hidden secret message or "treasure" to look for in case they should return. No matter how it is done, openly acknowledging this time as a true good-bye is important, as is recognizing that this stage in life and all that these places represent to us are passing.

Pets aren't equally important in every culture, but they can be significant when it comes to good-byes. TCKs need to know how their pets will be cared for, who will love them. If the pet must be put to sleep, everyone who cares for that pet, particularly children, should say good-bye. Some TCKs tell us how devastated they were after parents promised their pet would be happy in a new home, only to find out months or years later that the dog was euthanized or the chicken given to someone for food.

One problem (some might say blessing!) international sojourners face is that they can rarely take all their possessions with them when they move. Parents may delight in the chance to throw out a child's rock collection, never realizing how precious those rocks were to their child. Certainly, we realize part of life is letting go, but parents should talk with their children about what to take and what to leave as they pack. Everyone in the family needs to carry some treasured items to the new location. These become part of the collection of *sacred objects* that help connect one part of a global nomad's life to the next.

But sometimes even treasures must be left behind. When that happens, it's important to part with them consciously. Placing a precious object in the hands of someone else as a gift or taking photographs of it are two ways to say good-bye to an inanimate but important old friend.

The celebratory rituals of farewell commonly associated with certain types of transitions (e.g., graduations, retirement parties, etc.) are another important part of building this RAFT. Taking the time for "rites of passage" gives us markers for remembering meaningful places and people and directly addressing the fact that we are saying farewell. Many international families permanently return to their home country after the oldest child graduates from secondary school abroad. The graduating TCK goes through the rites of passage—the graduation ceremony, the "wailing wall" afterward, where all line up and say good-bye to one another. However, the needs of the younger children for the same types of closure when they leave for home are often overlooked. This can later add greatly to the younger child's sense of "unfinished business," while the older TCK in the same family is off and running once he or she gets to the homeland. Remember, *every* member of the family needs to build the RAFT during any leaving process.

Thinking destination. Even as we are saying the good-byes and processing the sad reality of those good-byes, we need to think realistically about our destination: Where are we going? What are some of the positives and negatives we can expect to find once we get there? Will we have electricity and running water? How will we learn to drive on the other side of the road? Do we need to take a transformer with us to keep our 110-volt appliances from burning out on a 220-volt electrical system?

This is also the time to look at our external (e.g., finances, family support structure) and internal (e.g., ability to deal with stress or change) resources for coping with problems we might find. What resources will we find in the new location and what will we need to take with us? Who can help us adjust to the new culture when we get there? This is the best time to find out from the sponsoring agency who will meet us at the airport, where we will stay until housing is located, and what that housing will be.

If we don't think through some of these issues, our adjustment may be rockier once we arrive at the new destination. If we are expecting too much, we'll be disappointed. If we don't expect enough, we may not use the resources available, thereby making life more complicated than necessary. Of course, we can never have a perfect picture of what life in the new place will be like, but doing our best to prepare beforehand can prevent a lot of problems later on.

After all of this thorough preparation in the leaving stage, it's time to move on into the transition stage itself.

Maintaining Stability through the Transition Stage

When people ask how they can avoid the chaos and confusion of the transition process, we have to say they can't. They can, though, keep in mind that it's normal and will pass if they hang on long enough. Also, there are a few steps we can take to help us maintain some sense of equilibrium and connectedness with the past and to smooth the way for the future stages of entry and reinvolvement.

One way is through sacred objects—those mementos we mentioned earlier that specifically reflect a certain place or moment of our lives. That's why the choice of which possessions to keep and which to give away is so important during the leaving stage. A favorite teddy bear pulled out of the suitcase each night during the travels from one place to another reminds the child that there is one stable thing in his or her life amidst the general chaos. At the same time Mom or Dad may be reading a treasured book they brought along, which reminds them of other times and places where they have read those same inspiring or comforting words. Other sacred objects are worn. Did you ever look around a group of TCKs or their parents and see how many were wearing some article of clothing or jewelry that connected them with their past? It might be a Taureg cross hanging on a gold chain or a V-ring on a finger. Perhaps they're wearing a sari instead of a sweater. Often an ATCK's home is quite a sight to behold—with artifacts gathered from around the world, all proving that "I was there! It's part of my history." Each sacred object serves as a good reminder that the current moment or scene is part of a bigger story of that person's life.

Pictures are another way we connect with special moments and memories in our past. One ambassador asked each staff member to list what he or she would put in the one bag allowed for an emergency evacuation. Photographs headed the list for every person, far above things with much more intrinsic worth. Why? Because each picture reminds us of some relationship, an experience we have had, a place we have visited. Pictures add a value to our lives that money alone can't buy. A small picture album of photographs representing significant highlights of our past life and location gives us a lovely place to visit when we need a few reflective moments in the middle of this sometimes turbulent stage. Pictures can also be helpful for letting people in the new place know something more of our history.

Of course, we recognize that everyone we would like to show these pictures and sacred objects to may not see the same value in them that we do. (And often it's vice versa when they try to show us theirs!) Why don't most people particularly enjoy another person's slide or video show? Because friends who weren't there can't see anything interesting in a skinny cow walking down the middle of a road; it seems rather bizarre to them. And they certainly don't want to hear a twenty-minute story about the man with the shaved head in the back row. For the person who was there, though, that picture or video segment brings back a flood of memories, and every detail is fascinating. That's why globally nomadic people should make a pact to look at each other's slides or home videos. It's how they can affirm their experiences!

Even if we built our RAFT perfectly in the leaving stage, transition is usually the stage where we begin to mourn most acutely the loss of things and people left behind. We feel unbearable emptiness when we realize we can't call our best friend to meet us for a cup of coffee. We miss the comfort of knowing everyone in our factory or office by name. The permanence of the move and the irretrievability of the past stare us in the face and we wonder if we have made a terrible mistake. During the leaving stage we knew these losses were coming, but now they are here. This is a critical moment and one which can affect us for years to come: we must decide what we will do with the grief. Will we deal with it or try to pack it away, out of sight, out of mind? Sometimes the chaos of the moment is so great we simply can't afford to deal fully with the reality of what we are losing, and our only choice to survive seems to be to ignore those feelings. This is a common means of getting through this transition stage, but if we feel we must shut out our feelings for simple survival's sake, we need to make an agreement with ourselves that we will go back and work through these feelings fully as soon as life stabilizes a bit more. And then we need to keep that agreement. Too many people get through transition by packing away these painful feelings of loss and never taking them out consciously at a later stage.

Years later they continue to exhibit the patterns of behavior we have already talked about.

Other people, of course, seem to be able to deal more easily with the losses as they are happening. Whenever we choose to deal with the inevitable losses in our move—during this stage itself or later—there are some specific ways we can help ourselves and those we love come through this normal process in a healthy way. A professor of philosophy, Jim Gould, says that loss always produces grief, conscious or unconscious, and it will come out one way or another, whether the person intends it to or not.[1] Mourning is the conscious acknowledgment of loss, and by finding ways and rituals that will help us recognize and mourn our loss, we will not only survive this painful period but also be ready to move on to the challenges of our new location unencumbered by a heavy burden of grief.

Mourning the Losses

Any healthy mourning process requires permission, people, and process time. The first of these, permission, includes the internal permission we must give ourselves to recognize that it's not immature, unspiritual, or childish to grieve our losses. In fact, it's most appropriate to mourn the loss of a home, friends, pets, or status. We also need other people who will give us this same permission by letting us express our feelings without judging us. Being willing to acknowledge their own grief is one important way parents and other adults let children know it's okay to be sad for what they themselves are about to lose. We hope the days are gone when parents, as well as children, are told—either by a voice inside or from others around—not to cry.

During this time, we not only need permission to mourn, we also need people who can provide support while we do so. A good comforter helps us maintain balance during our grieving process by being available to help with physical needs and to express empathy, both verbally and in other ways. Listening quietly, asking appropriate questions, reminiscing, and allowing us to be silent are ways people can help us to move through the process of grief.

Even with permission and people to help in the process, however, grief is not dispelled in a moment. It takes time to move from shock through pain, anger, and guilt until there is a return to the normal flow of life. How long it takes people to go through each stage varies from person to person. Few people move smoothly through the grief process. Usually we go forward and then backward several times between various stages as we move on toward a final sense of acceptance. Healthy mourning acknowledges that we need time to sort through these many conflicting emotions before we can get on with the rest of life. Rushing this process only transforms normal grief into unresolved grief.

The grieving stage, however, isn't only about looking at our losses. It also includes the need to plan for the future—immediate and long-range. Such planning can be something as simple as deciding to make a long-distance phone call for Grandma's birthday next week to say "Happy Birthday" and to let her know we miss her, or it can be figuring out what subjects we will study in the new school we are about to attend. Planning ahead in such ways is realistic; it also helps us move through the grieving process by reminding us and our children that life does go on in spite of great loss.

The good news is that with a proper foundation during the leaving stage, and by using these few tips to survive the transition, we can move on to making a positive entry and finding our way in this new world.

Entering Right

Physical arrival alone doesn't mean we have begun the entering stage. Sometimes the chaos of the transition stage remains for some days or weeks after our initial arrival. The more we have thought ahead about this time, however, and the more we are consciously aware of what we and our family will need to make a positive entry, the sooner and smoother we can begin to positively move into our new life. It's important that we recognize that we don't have to wait helplessly for the new community to reach out and receive us; there are many ways we can proactively help ourselves in this process. So how, then, can we (and the new community) move from the desire to establish ourselves in our new community to actually accomplishing it?

Choosing and Using Mentors

The key to successfully negotiating the entry stage is to find a *mentor*—someone who answers questions and introduces the new community to us and us to it. These mentors function as "bridges" and can smooth our way in, significantly shorten the time it takes for us to get acclimated to the new surroundings, and help us make the right contacts.

The problem, of course, lies in finding the *right* mentor. After all, the mentor is the person who determines the group of people we will meet, the attitude we will absorb about this new place, and from whom we learn the acceptable behavioral patterns. Ultimately, the mentor not only affects our long-term relationship to this new community but often determines our effectiveness in it as well. If we find the right one, we're in great shape. The wrong mentor, however, can be a disaster. If our mentor is negative about the place, its people, or our organization, we begin to doubt whether we should have come and become afraid to try new things. If this mentor has a bad reputation in the community, others may put us in the same category and avoid us too.

How can we as newcomers know who is or isn't trustworthy? Often people who themselves are on the fringes of the receiving community will be the first to introduce themselves to a newcomer. We, of course, are so happy *someone* has reached out to us that we can easily jump into this new relationship before we understand what the ramifications of such a relationship might be. How can we make a wise decision at this point?

Our suggestion is to be appreciative and warm to all who reach out a helping hand during this entry time, but inwardly you need to be cautious about making a wholehearted commitment to this relationship by asking yourself a few questions: Is this person one who fits into the local community or is he or she definitely marginalized in one way or another? Does this person exhibit the positive, encouraging attitudes we would like to foster in ourselves or make negative remarks and display hostile attitudes about almost everything?

When we take a little time to evaluate a potential mentor, we may discover that this person who greeted us so warmly is, in fact, one of those wonderful people who belong to the heart of any organization and have the great gift of making newcomers feel almost instantly at home. That person could well go on to be the best possible mentor and a great friend. If, however, we find out that this person who is so eager to be our friend is a marginal member of the community, then we must ask the next question: why does she or he want to befriend us?

Some are marginal simply because they, like us, are relative newcomers and are still looking to establish new friendships. While they may not yet be members of the inner circle, they have learned the basics of how life is lived in this place and can be most helpful. In fact, they often have more time to spend orienting newcomers than those whose plates are already full with well-defined roles and relationships. Relationships that start like this often turn into lifelong friendships.

If, however, we find out that the first person who approaches us so invitingly has been intentionally marginalized from the community, we need to be cautious about adopting this person as our mentor. Such people are often in some kind of trouble within the community. Perhaps they rebel against the accepted standards of behavior, break laws, or defy teachers, and they often want to recruit naive newcomers for their own agenda.

Besides using our common sense in situations such as we have just described, how else can we find good mentors? Some groups have active mentoring programs already in place. Other agencies set up "matching families" for those coming to their community. Many international schools have set up a "big brother/big sister" program, with good mentors already identified, to help new students through their first few weeks at school. One potential problem is that an agency may have a mentoring program for the adults in the family, but the children's need for a mentor is forgotten. In such cases, parents can ask advice from other adults already in the community. They usually know who would and wouldn't be a positive mentor for their children.

How else can or does the community deal with this entry stage? In communities with chronically high mobility, we have noticed two interesting, though rather opposite, responses to newcomers. Some have a regular routine to help new members get oriented. There are maps of the town with the key places to shop marked and instruction guides for dealing with the local host culture—all tucked in a basket of goodies. One person is specifically assigned to take the new family around, and the whole system of orientation goes like clockwork because it has happened so many times. Members of other highly mobile communities, however, are so tired of seeing people come and go they basically don't do much at all for the newcomer. Their thought process goes like this: "What's the use? These people will just be gone again," or "Why bother getting to know them? I've only got three months left here myself."

Most of our discussion on this entry stage applies to any kind of move. But there are extra stresses recognized by experts around the world for those trying to enter a completely new culture. Lisa and Leighton Chinn, a couple who work with international students, have outlined four stages of cultural stress that occur during this phase: fun, flight, fight, and fit. It's important to acknowledge them for a moment because they often happen in spite of all we have done right to prepare for our move and can make us feel that none of our other preparations mattered. The process can go something like this.

As we have looked ahead, we have developed a sense of anticipation and excitement for our new assignment. We decide it will be fun to explore the new environment, learn its history, and enrich our lives through meeting new people. The first few days after arrival, we busily engage with all we meet, feel excitement that we can actually answer the greetings in this new language we tried to study before we came, and all seems well. We think, "What fun!" A few more days pass, however, and things aren't quite as exciting. We don't like not knowing how to get to the store on our own because we haven't learned yet how to drive on the "wrong" side of the road, we're tired of not being understood past simple greetings by those around us, and we wish we could go "home"—back to where we knew how to function and where we fit. This is the flight stage.

Soon, however, we get tired of feeling so useless or out of place and begin to get angry. After all, we used to fit. We were competent individuals in our last home, so it can't be our fault that we feel so lost and insecure, so we begin to blame everything and everyone in this new location for our discomfort. If they would only do things "right" (meaning the way we are used to doing them), everything would be fine. Internally, and sometimes externally, we begin to fight with the way things are being done here—perhaps even becoming angry at our mentor who is doing his or her best to teach us these new ways.

Knowing that these reactions might happen doesn't necessarily stop them, but, again, knowledge helps us at least make more appropriate choices. In this case we might choose not to be quite so vocal about all we despise in our new situation.

These are the moments we need to remind ourselves that entry also takes time, to remember that six months from now we can presume that somehow we will have learned to drive here, discovered where the stores are for the things we want to buy, and most likely made new friends by then.

Reinvolvement Stage

The light at the end of the proverbial tunnel is that in any transition, cross-cultural or not, a final, recognized stage of reinvolvement is possible. We settle into our new surroundings, accepting the people and places for who and what they are. This doesn't always mean that we like everything about the situation, but at least we can start to see *why* people do what they do, rather than only *what* it is they do. We've learned the new ways and know our position in this community. Other members of the group see us as one of them, or at least they know where we fit. We have a sense of intimacy, a feeling that our presence matters to this group, and once more we begin to feel secure. Time again feels present and permanent as we focus on the here and now rather than hoping for the future or constantly reminiscing about the past.

In all transitions, we gain as well as lose. Perhaps one more paradox of the TCK experience is that learning to deal in healthy ways with the losses of transition can become a great asset in a TCK's life. When TCKs learn these lessons well, they no longer have to shut down their emotions or shut out relationships. Instead, they can risk the pain of another loss for the sake of the gain that goes with it. Learning to live with this kind of openness affects all areas of life in a positive way and can help TCKs become good listeners to friends dealing with loss for other reasons as well.

Endnote

[1] Personal conversation with Ruth E. Van Reken, July 1997.

14

Meeting Educational Needs

Dave and Betty Lou Pollock will never forget that warm September morning in Old Bridge, New Jersey, U.S.A., when they sent their oldest child, Danny, to his first day of school. After outfitting him with new clothes, Dave took his five-year-old son's hand and together they walked to the John Glenn Elementary school.

Although Dave and Betty Lou experienced the nostalgic emotions many parents feel when their offspring take that first step away from home, the decision about where and when to send Danny to school hadn't been a difficult one. Schooling patterns for children in Old Bridge followed a predictable cycle that had gone on for generations. Every September each five-year-old in town headed for the neighborhood school to begin his or her academic career.

Years later, however, when Dave and Betty Lou's daughter, Michelle, turned seven, things were different. By then the Pollocks lived in Kenya and suddenly the simple, routine formulas for "how to do school" were gone. No familiar John Glenn Elementary School down the road, nor Timothy Christian School reached

by carpooling with others. The Pollocks faced many
choices, as did their colleagues. Would they teach
Michelle and her three older brothers at home, send
them to a local national school or to an international
day school? Would it be necessary to consider a
boarding school? Dave and Betty Lou discovered that
the issues of schooling in a cross-cultural world aren't
nearly as straightforward as at home.

Third culture families face a variety of choices when it comes to deciding how to educate their children, and every option has distinct advantages and disadvantages. How can parents know which one is best for each particular child?

Unfortunately, parents often face this major decision with little or no awareness of the different types of opportunities available for schooling in a cross-cultural setting, let alone the pros and cons accompanying each method. Yet, for many TCKs, their experiences in school dramatically shape how they view their childhood and whether they look back on it with joy or regret. Because making the right choice for schooling is so crucial for TCKs, we want to look at this issue in depth.

As we mentioned earlier, before parents accept any cross-cultural assignment, it's important that they ask the sponsoring organization about its current educational opportunities and policies. These can vary greatly from one group to another: Are families required to send children away to a boarding school? Are parents expected to home school the children? Are all children required to attend the local international school?

Once parents know the answers to these questions, they must decide whether the organization's policies will or won't accommodate their children's educational needs. If a family feels that an agency's policy won't work well for them, they are generally better off to seek another sponsor than try to force the organization to change its policy—or perhaps worse, to compromise the family's needs.

If parents discover an organization gives complete freedom of choice to its employees regarding their children's schooling, there are still important questions to ask: What, in fact, are the available options? What language and curriculum do local national schools use? What language and curriculum does the local international school use? Who will pay for the extra costs of schooling (including vacation travel for secondary school or university students left at home to join the rest of the family), since some options are very expensive?

Under the stress of raising kids in settings markedly different from their own upbringings, parents often go to extremes. On one hand, because they want to make sure their children have the best education possible, some parents become supervigilant and overly critical of both the school personnel and programs. Nothing is done right or as it would have been at home. On the other hand, well-meaning parents may place a child in an educational setting, especially a boarding school, expecting that the school will fully substitute for the parents. Neither works.

Making the Best Choice

Through the years, we have come to realize that there is no perfect schooling formula that guarantees a happy outcome for all TCKs. There are, though, some underlying principles about the educational process that can help parents make the best choices possible.

Some parents fear taking their children into a cross-cultural setting at all because they believe their children will miss out on too many educational opportunities offered in the home country. But the educational process for any child includes more than school; it includes *all* learning, in every dimension of a person's life. Everyone acquires information and masters skills by a variety of formal and informal means.

One great advantage TCKs have is the wealth of learning opportunities available to them from their travels, cross-cultural interactions, and the third culture experience itself. When TCKs move through the *suk* in Sanaa, eat in an Indian friend's home in Bombay, or watch the murky brown river flow through the greenery of the Brazilian or Vietnam jungle, they are learning in the most dynamic way of all—through the five senses. This hands-on education in geography, history, basic anthropology, social studies, and language acquisition is a great benefit of the TCK experience and more than replaces some of the deficits in equipment or facilities that might be present in an overseas school.

Parents must also remember that in terms of preparing their children for life, they themselves are the primary educators. Schools can't substitute for the home in building values, developing healthy attitudes, and motivating children in positive directions.

Dr. Brian Hill, professor of education at Murdoch University in Australia, suggests seven basic outcomes parents in cross-cultural settings should look for from their children's educational experience. The experience should enable them to maintain a stable and positive self-image while learning new things; acquire survival skills appropriate to their own culture; identify and develop their personal creative gifts; gain access to the major fields of human thought and experience; become aware of the dominant worldviews and value orientations influencing their social world; develop the capacity to think critically and choose responsibly; and develop empathy, respect, and a capacity for dialogue with other persons, including those whose primary beliefs differ from their own.[1] Any specific choice for schooling should be measured in terms of how well it will help meet these larger goals of the educational process.

Educational Philosophies Differ among Cultures

Parents must examine the total approach to education in any system of schooling, not merely the academics. Styles of discipline, teaching, and grading can vary widely from one culture to another. These differences can have an enormous impact on children. Those who always make straight As and a few Bs in one system are devastated when they bring home mostly Cs with only one or two Bs when they switch. In Britain, 50 percent is passing, 70s and 80s are considered great, and scores in the 90s are practically unheard-of. In the United States, 50 percent is failure, but As are given to those with 94 percent and higher. An American child going to a British school can panic when she sees these lower marks. She knows if her transcript is filled with 70s and 80s and is sent to universities in the States without interpretation, she may never be admitted.

Corporal punishment is a common practice in certain places, while it would be unthinkable in others. Some school systems stress learning by rote. Others use only problem-based learning, where students must personally seek out the answers to each assignment. In some cultures discussion and other forms of student participation are encouraged, or even required. In others, this type of behavior is considered disrespectful.

Ways of motivating students vary from culture to culture too. In some places, external methods are emphasized. Homework is assigned and graded each day. Every six weeks parents are notified of their child's progress, or lack thereof. Instant rewards and punishments are the major means of encouraging students in these systems. Other school systems rely far more on internal motivation. Students are assumed to be responsible for their own learning, daily homework is neither assigned nor checked, and class attendance is optional. Only the final exam matters.

We have seen this one difference between motivational philosophies cause great consternation for TCKs and their families. When a student who is used to homework assignments every night goes to a school with no daily assignments, he or she often has trouble knowing how to organize the study time necessary to cover the assigned work before the end of the semester. Parents may wonder why their child seems to go out and socialize with little regard for schoolwork, but since no reports come home to tell them otherwise, they presume all is well. Only when the final exam comes and the TCK fails does anyone know something is wrong.

Conversely, a student who is used to working independently may see no reason to do the daily homework assignments; they seem trivial. Perhaps he or she also sees no reason to attend class regularly; studying in the library seems more important. Only when the first reports come home with failing grades does it become clear that things like homework and class attendance matter in this new setting.

In considering a particular school, parents must ask for an explanation of its philosophy of education, its methods of teaching, and its policy toward discipline and then decide if this school is a good match for their child. Even when an educational option seems like a good one from the parents' view or has been great for other children in the same family, some of these differences in the philosophical or psychological approaches to education can cause enough stress for a particular TCK that a change to a school with a different method of teaching is justified.

School Teaches More than Academic Subjects

As we said in an earlier chapter, school is one of the principal means whereby one generation communicates its culture and its values to the next. As long as everyone comes from the same culture, we hardly notice this process and what's taught is accepted as "right."

In international schools the transmission of cultural values and expectations takes place as it does in any other school, because there is no such thing as value-free education. The difference is that teachers and peers who come from many countries and cultures, along with the curriculum itself, may represent value systems that vary markedly from that of the parents of any given TCK. Parents who forget this are often surprised to discover that the cultural values and behaviors of their children's teachers and peers have influenced their children far more or in different ways than expected.

> One Korean father told us how shocked he was during an exchange with his son. The son had attended an American-oriented school in an Asian country. As the

Korean community in that country grew, they started their own school. The Korean parents believed the American school wasn't preparing their children to take the exams necessary for them to continue school in Korea. They also felt their children were forgetting Korean culture.

When the father told his son he would soon be changing schools, the son refused. "No, I'm not. I've attended the American school all my life, my friends are there, and I'm going to graduate from there."

This conversation distressed the father—not because his son refused the improved educational opportunity but because he dared to disobey. "When I was my son's age, I would never have considered resisting my father," he said. "No matter what I felt, I would have obeyed without question."

For good or ill, educating this Korean student in a school based on the American values of independence, free speech, and individualism had deeply affected a family's cultural heritage.*

Schooling Should Not Make It Impossible for the Child to Return to the Home Country

Attending school in what may almost amount to a "third or fourth culture" can make it extremely difficult—or even impossible—for some TCKs to return to the system in their home country. But it isn't only the difference in school systems or curriculum that can pose problems.

Judith Gjoen, a Dutch TCK from Indonesia, was educated in American schools in Malaysia and now lives with her Norwegian husband in Oslo. She is a practicing counselor who has expressed particular

---

* Many international schools are now attempting to address such issues of identity and cultural mixing their students may face. Wise parents might want to ask about such opportunities when considering whether to send a child to one school or another.

concern about TCKs who return to their passport
culture wanting to continue their education but lacking
proficiency or confidence in using their mother tongue.
A young woman from a Nordic country observed that
her speaking, reading, and writing ability in her mother
tongue was fine for home and social use, but her
school language was English, the language of her high
school education. She finally had to pursue her
university education in the United States. This, of
course, further alienated her from her home country.

Parents, educators, and agency administrators have a responsibility to provide the opportunity for TCKs to learn their native language so that they have the option of returning to their passport country for further formal education and settling down there, if that's what they choose.

However, there's another potential barrier to TCKs acquiring fluency in their own language. Sometimes the TCKs themselves resist. For a child, nothing may seem more important than being like his or her peers. If everyone else around is speaking French (or in the case above, English), why take more time away from socializing or be labeled as different, just to learn another language? School-age children are not able to look ahead to long-term consequences. Most don't think about life after secondary school. Parents and educators need to be sensitive to this possibility and try to help their TCKs see how learning their own language is an expansion of their world rather than a limitation.

Different Schooling Choices Are Available

Having said all of this, one fact remains: school is, in fact, important; it's the place where we learn things that can't be assimilated by pure observation. The only questions are where and when.

To help parents make wise choices, let's look at specific options generally available to third culture families. Although the variety may seem a little confusing at first, these choices give parents the necessary flexibility to help meet the needs of each individual child. The most common methods for formally educating TCKs include the following: home and correspondence schooling, satellite schools, local national schools, local international schools, overseas boarding schools, and preuniversity schooling in home country. Here are some of the specific pros and cons of each choice.

Home and Correspondence Schooling

Pros	Cons
Child lives with parents	Lack of parental teaching skills
Individual instruction	Parent-child stress
Moral and spiritual values of parents taught	Lack of peer contact
Parent- and home-centered	Lack of healthy competition
Child can continue schooling in home country without interruption	
Can use curriculum of choice	

An increasing number of internationally mobile families use various methods of home schooling, particularly for younger TCKs. Some parents create their own curriculum. During home leave, one mother went to the local public grade school in Chicago, found out what textbooks they used, ordered those books directly from the publisher, and made her own lesson plans from them for each of her four school-age children.

Other parents combine materials offered by several home-schooling groups to design their own curriculum. Still others use a syllabus offered by a specific correspondence school, including videos. In some of these cases, the lessons are monitored by the parents but graded by teachers back home.

Some parents have gone a step further and successfully put together a smorgasbord of educational options by combining modified home schooling and correspondence courses with national schools. A few have worked this out under the supervision of school counselors from their home country or from the nearest international school.

For this, or any type of home schooling or correspondence plan, parents must have access to educational tools and resources in order to do a good job. They must also have the testing apparatus necessary to be certain of proper progress and development for their TCK, and they must be sure that the content and sequencing of the curriculum will be compatible with the next step in the education of the child. It's fine to use these options of home schooling or correspondence school as long as steps are taken to ensure the children can maintain the standards that would be required of them in a more structured school setting.

The obvious main benefit of home schooling is that kids remain with their parents, thereby decreasing some of the disadvantages of separation. Another benefit—especially to those with erratic home leave or frequent relocations—is that the children can maintain continuity in school without having to jump from one system to another in the middle of the year.

Home schooling, however, isn't always the best option—even in its most creative form. First, TCKs may be isolated from peers—particularly those raised in remote areas. This may not be a significant problem during early childhood, when parental support is more crucial than peer approval, but it can be serious during the teenage years.

Second, the dynamics in some families simply aren't suited to this type of schooling. Perhaps the parents have neither the natural nor professional skills to properly teach academic subjects. Or one or both parents may be so disorganized that instruction is haphazard or never takes place at all. Some kids habitually refuse to do anything their parents suggest, causing constant friction and confusion in the home.

In those situations, the benefits of home schooling may not be worth the frustrations. That doesn't mean the parents or children have failed. It only means that home schooling wasn't the best option for this particular family.

Satellite Schools

Pros	Cons
Living at home with parents	Labor-intensive for sponsoring agency
More chance for interaction with peers than home schooling	Still may have limited social opportunities
Trained teacher	Inadequate equipment for certain subjects
Externally organized curriculum	High teacher attrition
Parents still closely involved	

In recent years, satellite schools have been introduced as another option for TCKs. These are usually small groups of students who have clustered together into a slightly more formalized setting than the individual home. Sometimes the sponsoring agency sends out a qualified teacher to conduct the classes, which resemble the old-fashioned one-room schoolhouse. Other satellite schools depend primarily on videotapes or interactive computer programs. While an adult supervises the proceedings, the teaching itself takes place through these electronic tutors. In certain situations, these schools may also use correspondence courses.

Satellite schools usually have a good teacher/student ratio, with each child receiving individual attention. They provide a bit more socialization than a strictly home-school setting, but the TCK is still able to live at home with parents.

Local National Schools

Pros	Cons
Child lives with parents Cross-cultural relationships Language acquisition Good education in many places Relatively low cost Strong exposure to host culture	Religious/philosophical differences from parents Total cultural identification with host culture—loss of own cultural identity Tension or rejection due to nationality Competes with host nationals for available space in school

National schools may be one of the best educational options in some countries, enabling children to become immersed in the culture, learn the language quickly, make friends in the locality, and become truly bicultural. Often national schools cost far less than the international schools. In fact, in the United States, they're free. TCKs can remain home while having strong peer relationships.

However, there are special issues to consider as well. If school is taught in a language different from a child's mother language, the TCK must know enough of the local language *before* entering the school to function comfortably. We know of several sad cases where kids were put in classrooms before learning the local language. Two weeks of absolutely no communication (not even the ability to ask for directions to the toilet) is an eternity to an eight-year-old. Parents must make certain their children have at least elementary language skills before the first day of school.

Parents should also understand the basic philosophical and methodological underpinnings of this local system, as stated earlier in this chapter. Another thing to consider is the degree of animosity to the child's nationality in the host culture. If negative perceptions exist, a TCK might be designated an "outsider" and find the school situation intolerable.

Finally, there's the issue of assimilation. While one benefit of attending local schools is that it helps TCKs become part of the surrounding community faster, will this method of schooling facilitate their entering the culture more quickly and completely than the parents wish? How will acculturation affect their ultimate sense of cultural identity?

> Dave Pollock was confronted with the assimilation issue at a seminar on TCKs at the United Nations, where none of the attendees was from the U.S. To start out he asked them why they had come. After a period of silence one father said, "Most of us are here to find out how to keep our children from becoming too American." The other participants laughed and nodded in agreement.
>
> Dave replied, "Well, I have some bad news and some good news for you. Whether you knew it or not, when you decided to become a globally nomadic family and move to the United States (or any other country), you decided that your children would become third culture kids. That means they will be influenced by the culture they live in and become in some degree bi- or multicultural; it's inevitable. Now the good news: it doesn't have to ruin their lives. In fact, it will add a lot to them. It's okay to be a TCK."

While it isn't necessarily bad for TCKs to identify closely with the local culture, sometimes the cultural immersion is so complete that the TCK chooses to never repatriate. This can be a painful choice for a TCK's parents, because they may feel their child is rejecting them along with their culture. It's unfair, however, for parents to encourage in-depth cross-cultural relationships throughout their child's schooling and then object when that same child wants to marry and settle down permanently in the host country. The possible long-term implications of school and culture need to be thought through at the beginning of the TCK experience, not the end.

Local International Schools

Pros	Cons
Academically high standards	Expensive
Excellent facility and equipment	Potential lack of preparation for school in home country
Enrichment and specialized programs	Economic imbalance among students
Potential continuity with schooling during leave in home country	
Usually home with parents	
Good preparation for reentry if curriculum is based on home country's system	

International schools are another popular option for TCKs. A significant problem arises, however, in trying to identify what the term *international school* actually means. In her master's thesis, "Some of the Outcomes of International Schooling," Helen Fail raises these issues:

> Are there certain characteristics which define an international school, and if so what are they? Is it because children from several nationalities attend? If so, then many schools in Britain could be described as international. Is it determined by the curriculum? If so, then only the schools offering the International Baccalaureate would qualify. There are many schools overseas offering a U.S. or U.K. curriculum or another mixture which would presumably [result in their being] rated as national schools overseas. It may well be that many schools overseas consider themselves and indeed call themselves international yet never consider that while teaching an international curriculum to a group of students from many different nationalities, the teaching faculty is 95 percent British or American and inevitably they perpetuate certain national and cultural values.[2]

As international educators continue working on this matter, undoubtedly the term *international school* will be more precisely defined in the future. For our discussion here, we will include a broad spectrum of schools under the term *international school* and loosely define it as meaning any school that has students from various countries and whose primary curriculum is different from the one used by the national schools of the host country.

So what are particular elements to consider when thinking of sending a child to an international school? First, curriculum. Many international schools are beginning to incorporate broader choices in their subject material, including the International Baccalaureate degree and the International General Certificate of Secondary Education. Languages such as Japanese, Chinese, or Russian may now be included, when before only the more standard French, Latin, Spanish, and English were available. Many schools offer different choices in history courses, including the history of the host country.

Second, cultural framework. While offering more diversity of subject matter, most international schools still primarily operate from one cultural system of grading, style of teaching, basic curriculum, and philosophy of education. Jill and Roger Dyer write about the disadvantage Australian TCKs face when they take placement tests at many supposedly international schools which are, in reality, based on American standards in testing and curriculum content.

> Why are such [placement] tests invalid? Firstly, such aptitude testing is rarely carried out in Australian schools.... There has long been a belief among Australian educators that no scores are conclusive because of the enormous range of variables involved.... Secondly, there is no doubt that the U.S. tests are biased in content. Small children may be asked to complete a sheet by filling in the initial letter of a word represented on the page by a picture. One example of this is of a window with flowing material covering much of the glassed area. The Australian child would automatically write *C* for curtains and be

marked incorrect, as the required answer is a *D* for
drapes. Further evidence of testing which requires
cultural understanding is a general knowledge test for
primary-school children asking what is eaten with
turkey at Thanksgiving...the answer required is
cranberry sauce.[3]

Parents must look at the whole picture of any so-called international
school to make sure their child's needs will be met within the variety of subjects offered and the philosophy or cultural base of education practiced there. Probably no two international schools are alike,
given the diversity of the cultural and educational backgrounds
among those who administer them.

The above issues aside, there are several significant benefits of
international schooling. High on the list is that children usually remain at home, allowing the parents to have a more active role in
school activities and in monitoring their children's progress. In fact,
the very availability of group activities similar to those in schools
back in the home country is another advantage. One of the greatest
blessings is the diversity of backgrounds among students. When
ATCKs look back on their international school experiences, many
say they value most what they learned from their relationships with
peers from many different nationalities. These global friendships
opened the door to knowledge and understanding for a much larger
worldview.[4]

Another important benefit offered by international schools is
their general understanding of the internationally mobile experience.
Many international schools have a 30 percent turnover each year as
families are transferred in and out. Students understand what it is
like to be "the new kid in school" and typically extend themselves
toward the newcomer. Administrators, teachers, and counselors also
understand the transition experience; while some may become blasé
about what such a normative experience is, the best recognize the
mandate they hold as international educators to support students and
families in transition. Indeed, when parents have two or more inter-

national schools to choose between (not an uncommon situation in European and Asian capitals), they can factor into their decision which school provides ongoing, institutionalized transition programming. The school that offers transition activities to facilitate the adjustment of arrivals and departures and that integrates intercultural skill building and cultural identity explorations into the academic curriculum is probably the school to choose.[5]

The major drawback of international schools is their great expense. If parents are working for an agency that doesn't pay educational costs, the tuition may be prohibitive.

Overseas Boarding Schools

Pros	Cons
Academically good	Isolated from "real life"
Low or moderate expense	Early separation from parents
Usually closer than a school in the home country	Living away from parents
Peer group relationships	Separation from host culture
Good preparation for reentry if based on home-country curriculum	Individualized care difficult
	Different religious/philosophical values from parents

Many overseas boarding schools (meaning boarding schools outside the TCK's home country, though not always in the host country) originally developed in the days when strong formal educational programs of any kind were severely limited in many of the countries where third culture families worked. When missionary parents worked in remote jungles or when government officials moved to faraway lands to administer colonial regimes, few educational options were available for their children. Generally, the two choices these families had were to either home school their children or leave them behind.

In the early years of the twentieth century, however, various mission and colonial agencies founded boarding schools as an attempt to help TCKs remain closer to their parents. The schools catered to students primarily from Britain or the United States, and the curriculum was generally either British- or American-based. Children from other countries had to adjust as best they could.

Much of this has changed and is still changing. Now many of these same boarding schools not only have students from a broad spectrum of the international population, they have students and teachers from the host country as well. Some obvious benefits of these boarding schools are the opportunities students have to make close friends with their peers, to have healthy competition in sports or other areas, and to have trained teachers and a committed staff caring for them. In addition, children are usually closer to parents than they would be if left behind in the home country.

The negatives mainly have to do with the separation from parents and home. In the past, many children left home for boarding school at five or six years of age and were separated from their parents for long periods of time. This had been a common practice in Britain for years, and these schools were held up as proof that children fared well in such settings. Unfortunately, we've met many people who, as adults, have to deal with deep feelings of abandonment stemming from these early patterns of separation.

Another major problem with boarding schools is that it's almost impossible for parents to monitor what is happening on a day-to-day basis. There are many times when parents don't know until long afterwards if their child is having academic or personal problems or difficulties with a staff member. Some TCKs feel they were raised by older students, or even peers in the boarding school, rather than by adults. In the extreme, there is the risk of child abuse. While certainly not the norm, mistreatment occurs often enough to be of legitimate concern to parents.

Our suggestions for parents considering the boarding school option are to take into account the child's age and temperament, the character and reputation of the school, how often they will be able to see the child, and whether their child's communication with them is unhindered (some schools in the past have monitored their students' contact with parents).

As new findings continue to stress the importance of strong bonding with parents during a child's early years, and after listening to so many adults struggle to come to terms with early separations, we believe it's not wise, with so many other options available, to send young children—particularly those as young as five or six—to boarding school unless there are absolutely no other alternatives. It is simply impossible to measure how that kind of separation affects the children, or which ones will struggle with the effects of separation later on and which won't.

While it's good to include children in all discussions regarding their schooling, the decision about boarding school is one area in which this type of inclusion is vital. The feeling of *abandonment* expressed by ATCKs seems most often to come from those who say they were "sent off." When parents include children in the decision-making process, acknowledge the pros and cons of each schooling option, and listen carefully to the children's concerns and preferences, it makes a long-term difference. Children whose opinions are taken into account see that their thoughts and feelings matter; they do, indeed, feel valued.

Preuniversity Schooling in Home Country

Pros	Cons
Education compatible with higher education Reentry adjustment minimized Educational/enrichment opportunities	Extended separation from parents Lack of personalized care Cultural influence without parental guidance Loss of cross-cultural advantage and language acquisition

As we mentioned, leaving children with relatives or at a boarding school in the homeland used to be a common practice for third culture families. In fact, the normal practice for internationally mobile families until the late 1950s and early 1960s involved leaving TCKs in the homeland for secondary school, which often meant four or more years of separation from parents—all without benefit of e-mail, fax, or phone.[6]

Although sending preuniversity TCKs to school in the home country while parents remain overseas is no longer a common practice, it remains an option. Some families feel that nothing else suits their needs. Perhaps the TCK prefers living with relatives at home rather than going to a boarding school overseas, which was why Courtney left Saudi Arabia and returned to the States to live with her grandparents. She felt that if the only other option was to go to a boarding school where her American expatriate peers made up most of the student body, she would rather be with her grandparents. There can be any number of legitimate reasons for this choice.

The major benefit, of course, is that an early start in the school system of the home country makes it easier for TCKs to continue successfully in that system through university. But such a benefit must be weighed against the trauma of leaving their lifelong friends overseas (unless those friends are also moving) before the normally accepted time of secondary school graduation. Also, this question remains: how does changing cultures and facing all the issues of reentry during the height of identity formation in the early teen years affect TCKs compared with those who make the same switch a few years later?

For some TCKs, of course, it may be essential to return home before university. Those who face competitive exams in their midteens may find this the only real option if they wish to pursue certain careers. We've noticed a major difference in schooling patterns among Australian and New Zealand TCKs as compared with Americans. Most Americans can easily return to the States at age seventeen or eighteen and go directly to university, but TCKs from down under generally return to their home countries by the age of fifteen so they can prepare for the exams that determine which courses they will take during university.

The major drawback of schooling in the home country is the great distance from parents. In these days of e-mail and faxes, certainly communication is far easier than it was earlier in this century; nevertheless, an ocean apart is still pretty far to be away.

****

It's obvious that there are many good choices for educating TCKs, and statistics show that, as a group, they do well academically. A survey of 608 adult missionary kids carried out by the MK CART/ CORE (a research organization composed of ten mission agencies) committee came out with these statistics:

- 30 percent of the respondents graduated from high school with honors

- 27 percent were elected to National Honor Society

- 94 percent went on to university-level studies

- 73 percent graduated from university

- 25 percent graduated from university with honors

- 3 percent were Phi Beta Kappas

- 11 percent were listed in *Who's Who in American Colleges and Universities*[7]

Another survey on ATCKs confirms that a strikingly high percentage of TCKs go on to postsecondary school education. In 1993 a study of 680 ATCKs done by John and Ruth Hill Useem and their colleagues showed that while only 21 percent of the American population as a whole has graduated from a four-year college or university, 81 percent of the ATCKs they surveyed had earned at least a bachelor's degree. Half of them went on to earn master's or doctorate degrees.[8] Undoubtedly, with thoughtful planning and wise choices, the educational process for TCKs has every chance of being a rich one indeed.

Endnotes

1   Brian Hill, "The Educational Needs of the Children of Expatriates," in *International Conference on Missionary Kids: New Directions in Missions: Implications for MKs*, edited by Beth A. Tetzel and Patricia Mortenson (Compendium of the International Conference on Missionary Kids, Manila, November 1984), 340.

2   Helen Fail, "Some of the Outcomes of International Schooling" (master's thesis, Oxford Brookes University, June 1995), 8.

3   Jill Dyer and Roger Dyer, *What Makes Aussie Kids Tick?* (Kingswood, SA, Australia: MK Merimna, 1989), 139–40.

4   Fail, "Some of the Outcomes."

5   Personal correspondence to David C. Pollock by Barbara F. Schaetti, Transition Dynamics, October 1998.

6   From Ruth E. Van Reken (unpublished original research on ATCKs, 1986).

7   Leslie Andrews, "The Measurement of Adult MKs' Well-Being," *Evangelical Missions Quarterly* 31, no. 4 (October 1995): 418–26.

8   John Useem, Ruth Hill Useem, Ann Baker Cottrell, and Kathleen Jordan, "TCKs Four Times More Likely to Earn Bachelor's Degrees," *Newlinks* 12, no. 5 (May 1993): 1.

15

Enjoying the Journey

One of the best aspects of a TCK lifestyle is the fun it can be. In his book *Living Overseas,* Dr. Ted Ward emphasizes the importance of enjoying the adventure—of *living*![1] Parents of third culture kids don't need to wake up at 3:30 in the morning feeling terribly guilty because they have imposed a horrible experience on their children.

Ironically, the richness of their lives can become so routine that TCKs and their families forget to notice it. People who live at the foothills of the Alps soon take them for granted. Those living in tropical climates beside an ocean beach become so accustomed to waving palms and the roar of the sea that they rarely pause to wonder at the beauty. What's exotic and exciting to others has become ordinary for them.

How *do* third culture families make the most of their experiences in other cultures and places? Here are some practical tips.

Set Aside Special Times for Family and Make Family Traditions

At least once a week parents should close out the rest of the world and plan some family time. This might be a weekly outing, table games together one evening a week, or some other activity the family enjoys. In cultures where visitors stop by with no forewarning, families often have to leave home and find a park, beach, or restaurant to have this kind of uninterrupted time together.

Traditions bind people and groups together because they are visible markers affirming a shared history and celebrating a current unity of thought, purpose, or relationship. Every nation has them, every ethnic group has them, and, one hopes, every family has them. Traditions help families everywhere build their unique sense of identity and give each family member a sense of belonging as well.

Often a family's traditions evolve without special planning. Uncle Fred pulls out his mandolin at every reunion and family members old and young sing along. No one has consciously decided this will be a tradition, but the family gathering wouldn't be the same if Uncle Fred and his mandolin weren't there.

Third culture families have at least as much need for traditions as other families do—maybe more. But because they won't always be around to go to the family reunions and "hear Uncle Fred," they may have to do a little more conscious planning to develop traditions that are transportable and can be replicated in different places. These traditions can be as simple as giving each family member the chance to pick the menu for his or her birthday dinner every year or as complicated as making a piñata stuffed with candy for a particular holiday once a year.

Developing traditions in cross-cultural settings isn't only important, it's fun. New ideas from different places can be incorporated to help each tradition become a marker of family history. In Liberia a hot-dog roast on the beach defined Christmas Eve for some expatriates—not a traditional custom in most snow-covered lands but a nice one to carry back home (even if the hot dogs have to be roasted in a fireplace!) as a distinctive reminder of the family's history.

Build Strong Ties with the Community

TCKs usually grow up far from blood relatives, but there can be substitute "aunts," "uncles," and "grandparents" wherever TCKs live. Sometimes these people will be host country citizens; sometimes they will be from the third culture community itself. Parents can foster such relationships by inviting these special people to join in celebrating the TCK's birthday, allowing their child to go shopping with them—whatever is appropriate for the situation. This "created" extended family gives TCKs the experience of growing up in a close community, even without blood relatives. As ATCKs remember their childhood, some of these relationships rank among their fondest memories.

Build Strong Ties with Relatives

Relatives back home are another important part of a TCK's life, and relationships with them need to be fostered also. A great way to do this is to bring a grandma, grandpa, aunt, uncle, or cousin out to visit. This not only helps TCKs get to know their relatives better, it lets relatives see TCKs in their own environment—the place where they do, in fact, shine. On top of that, TCKs love to return "home" and be able to talk to family members who know what they're talking about. But even if relatives cannot make such a trip, it's important for TCKs to maintain contact with them as much as possible through letters, e-mail, faxes, telephone, and pictures.

Developing closeness with relatives at home is especially important if and when the time comes for TCKs to repatriate while parents continue living overseas.

> During the four years that Lois attended university in the States, she never once received a care package or an invitation to visit during the holidays from any of her numerous aunts and uncles. Lois was a good kid, and her relatives were warm, caring people, but it apparently never crossed their minds that she might need

them. Lois was too shy to ask, and her parents never
thought to alert their brothers and sisters that Lois
would need care from the extended family.

Fortunately Lois knew one family—friends from her
early childhood—who opened their hearts to her.
Now, many years later, Lois's own home is continually
open to other TCKs whose parents are overseas.

Build Strong Ties with Friends

To begin with, TCKs should work at making new friends everywhere they go so that they won't try to escape the challenges of
entering a new culture or dealing with reentry into their home culture by isolating themselves. Friends from the past are also important, because they validate the TCK experience and prove that the
third culture world and experience aren't a dream. It's also important, when possible, for TCKs to attend school reunions and return
to visit the home or homes of their childhood.

Return to the Same "Home" during Each Leave

Whenever practical, third culture families should return to the same
place each time they go on home leave. Children who change countries every two or three years as well as those who stay in one host
country their whole lives all need the sense that there is at least one
physical place to identify as home in their passport country. When
staying in the same physical house isn't possible, families should
try to locate nearby so TCKs can have the same school, church, and
friends. It's also helpful when taking trips to visit friends or relatives in other places to stay long enough to establish at least some
basis for a relationship that can be built upon during the next leave.

While it's good to foster all these relationships in the home country, families shouldn't spend the entire leave visiting people. When
every evening is spent with the adults chatting happily in one room
and the TCKs and children from the host family eyeing each other

warily in another, and when every night is spent in a different bed, this overload of travel can be stressful. Third culture families should also plan for nights in motels, camping trips, or other private times during their travel to reinforce their sense of being a family in this land as well as in the host country.

Tour When Traveling between Countries

As families go back and forth between host and home countries, they need to get off the plane, find a place to stay, and tour the countries in between. Making stops along the way not only expands the TCKs' world; it also creates memories that last a lifetime. Courtney had this to say about her experiences of travel:

> My memory is much bigger than most of my friends' because of all the exciting places my parents took me on our trips between Saudi and America. When we went to England or Germany, for example, knowing I loved art, my mom would take me to the museums while my sister and dad went off on other excursions. I learned so much by absorbing the cultures we encountered—we would take tours and soak up the information the guides told us.
>
> My parents may not realize that the most profound thing they did for me was to take me to Dachau. I must have been about eleven or twelve. We walked the grounds; we looked at everything; I cried. My parents did not protect me; they exposed me to everything—including the crematoriums, gas chambers, photos. When you read about World War II and the concentration camps, I can't imagine how you can truly understand it without seeing one of the camps. I just stood there, overwhelmed, and thought, how is this possible? It was so big.
>
> I am filled up when I think of all that I've seen and touched, and how much I want to return and touch it all again.

Explore and Become Involved in the Surroundings

Don't neglect actively learning about the history, geography, and culture of the host country. Families should pretend they are tourists once or twice a year and plan trips just to see the sights. Courtney's parents also helped her to explore their host country—Saudi Arabia. "My parents often took us out into the desert to look at various natural treasures such as sharks' teeth, sand roses, and arrowheads. It was exciting to imagine this place under water millions of years ago." These may seem like simple memories, but they've left Courtney with a deep sense of connection to her past.

As a corollary, a common regret we hear from ATCKs is they never really got involved with the surrounding culture when they were children. Whether it happened because they lived on a military base, went off to boarding school, or played only with expatriate friends, many consider this a loss. As adults they realize they could have learned so much more and wish they had studied the language or taken time to learn how to cook the wonderful local dishes they enjoyed when they went out to dinner.

Acquire "Sacred Objects"

As we have mentioned before, artifacts from countries where they have lived or visited eventually become the TCKs' portable history to cart around the world in future years. It helps connect all the places and experiences of their lives. During her childhood, ATCK Sandra acquired a set of carved ebony elephant bookends, a lamp (whose base included more elephants), feather paintings, and other ebony carvings to hang on the wall. At university and in the sixteen locations where she has lived since her wedding, when the bookends are in place, the paintings and carvings hung on the wall, and the lamp turned on, she's home.

****

In the end, one German TCK, Dirk, summed up best what we are trying to say. When we asked him what he thought of his experience as a TCK, he said, "The thing I like best about my life is living it!"

That's what it's all about—living and enjoying the TCKs' world.

Endnote

1   Ted Ward, *Living Overseas: A Book of Preparations* (New York: Free Press, 1984).

16

Coming "Home": Reentry

And now we have come full circle. After all these years of careful planning to make the most of their years in a host culture, the time has finally come for the family, or at least the TCKs themselves, to go "home." As we said at the beginning of this book, one of the factors that distinguishes the TCK experience from a true immigrant is the full expectation that after living for a significant period of their developmental years outside their passport culture, there will come the day when TCKs make a permanent return to that country and culture. Oddly enough, for many TCKs this is one of the most difficult transitions they go through no matter how many other moves they have already made. Commonly called *reentry,* for a great number this process more closely resembles an entry. How TCKs do or don't cope with the reentry experience can shape their lives for years to come.

Why is reentry so hard for so many?

Reentry Stresses

Many reasons for reentry stress are simply extensions of the factors we have already talked about, particularly the normal challenges of any cross-cultural transition: the grief of losing a world they have come to love, the discomfort of being out of cultural balance once more, and the struggle to find a sense of belonging in a new place with new people. There are also some very particular and additional stresses TCKs face during this transition to their home culture, however, and they are worth examining carefully.

False Expectations

One of the most basic, but unrecognized, reason for reentry stress has to do with unconscious expectations of both the TCKs and those in their home culture. As you remember, we talked earlier about the TCKs' various relational patterns with their surrounding community and used the following model to identify each one.

Foreigner	Hidden Immigrant
Look different	Look alike
Think different	Think different
Adopted	**Mirror**
Look different	Look alike
Think alike	Think alike

As we mentioned in chapter 3, traditionally most TCKs have been recognized as foreigners while they were living in their host culture. Some have lived there as hidden immigrants, and a few fit into either the adopted or mirror category. When TCKs return to their passport culture, however, almost all are hidden immigrants. Now everything Dr. Kohls talks about in his model of the iceberg and how that relates to cultural expectations and stress starts to make even more sense. People at home take one look at these returning TCKs and expect them to be in the "mirror" box—persons who think and look like themselves. Why wouldn't they? After all, these TCKs are from the same racial, ethnic, and national background as those "at home" are.

TCKs look around them and they, too, often expect to be in the mirror box. For years they've known they were "different" but excused it because they knew they were Asians living in England, Africans living in Germany, or Canadians living in Bolivia. That justification for being different is now gone, and they presume they will finally be the same as others; after all, these are their own people. Wrong. Take another look at Krista and Nicola, our look-alike TCKs who let their host culture peers in England and Scotland know how eager they were to return to their home countries where they knew they would finally fit in and belong.

> When Krista first returned to the States, she felt euphoric at finally being "home." It didn't take long, however, before Krista realized, to her horror, that she couldn't relate to her American classmates either. Somehow she was as different from them as from her English peers.
>
> The same thing happened to Nicola when she returned to England. After literally kissing the tarmac when she disembarked from the plane in London, a strange thing soon happened. Nicola found herself increasingly irritated with her English student peers. Their world seemed so small. Internally, she began resisting becoming like them, and within a year, virtually all of her friends were international students and other TCKs. She wondered why she could never completely fit into the world around her, whether it was Scottish or English. Both Krista and Nicola's disappointment was greater because they had always presumed if they could only make it "home," they would no longer feel so different from others.

Many TCKs have similar experiences to those of Krista and Nicola, where all seems well at the beginning of reentry. Relatives and old friends welcome the TCKs warmly, while the school bends over backward in its efforts to assess how transcripts from some exotic foreign school relate to the local curriculum. Soon, however, unexpected differences begin to pop up. Classmates use slang or idioms that mean nothing to the returning TCKs. Everyone else is driving a car; they only know how to ride a bike. Friends, relatives, and classmates are shocked at the TCKs' ignorance of the most common practices necessary for everyday living. If they were true immigrants, no one would expect them to know all these things, but because they are presumed to be in the mirror box, those in the home country begin to peg them as "strange" or, at least, slightly stupid.

Conversely, TCKs aren't doing much better in their opinions of newfound peers. When they saw themselves as true foreigners in Romania, they never expected their local friends to know where Utah was on the U.S. map. Now they can't believe how dumb their friends in Utah are because they have no idea where Romania is.

Reentry might not be quite so difficult if the unexpected differences were merely in some of these more obvious ways. But deeper levels of cultural dissonance lurk beneath the apparently similar surface. Every time someone takes them to McDonald's for a hamburger, the TCKs mention how many people could eat for a whole week back in their host country for the money this one meal costs. Even worse, they watch how much food people throw out and express their shock and horror. The person who bought their hamburger sees the TCKs as ungrateful at best, condemning at worst. The fact is that while TCKs and their peers at home may indeed look exactly alike, they don't share a common worldview because their life experiences have been totally different.

And so the problems continue to mount. TCKs who have grown up in a culture where the commitment to honesty and respect is accompanied by orderliness and quiet find entry into a confrontational, loud, self-centered home culture quite offensive. Those who have grown up in a boisterous, activity-centered, individualistic culture may find people from their own country docile and self-effacing. Often TCKs begin to realize they don't even like what is considered their home culture. And those in the home culture may soon realize they're not so sure they like the TCKs either. But no one stops to think through how these reactions are related to the cultural expectations they had for one another in the first place. They still presume their insides match as well as their outsides and that something is "wrong" with the other person.

Of course, there are other reasons besides erroneous expectations that make reentry a tough transition. Here are two false fears that also contribute.

False Fears

Sometimes TCKs fear that allowing themselves to repatriate totally will mean being disloyal to their host country. "If I allow myself to like it here, it may mean I really didn't like it there," or "If I adjust and fit in, I may lose my memory of and commitment to return to the place where I grew up." Such fears can make them lose the delight in their present, which is as much a part of their life experience as their past has been. They need to know it's okay to enjoy a chapati, a Big Mac, and a taco quite interchangeably—that to embrace a particular part of any of their worlds doesn't deny the reality and/or goodness of another part.

Other TCKs fear losing their identity. "If I let go of the place and the people where I have always identified most and fit in best to align myself with my home country and culture, will I lose some important part of me?" This makes for "reentry shock," a close relative to the culture shock experienced by those going to live abroad for the first time. Any threat to our identity calls up deep and complex emotions, which lead to the kinds of symptoms that signal culture shock: sleeplessness, anxiety, irritability, homesickness, depression, and others.

Common Reactions to Reentry Stress

Despite many of their contradictory feelings, however, most TCKs' basic desire is to be "home," to be "the same." How do they react when they find they are not? TCKs choose all sorts of ways to cope. Some, like Paul (our American in Australia), try to be perfect external chameleons. To fit in, they refuse to tell anyone of their past life. Where they have lived or grown up becomes a well-guarded secret. A teacher explains the whys and wherefores of the tribal practices of a group in the TCKs' host country, and they never say a word— although they're boiling inside at the misconceptions being taught. Basically these TCKs deny one entire side of their life to try and blend in with their new peers.

Others cope by getting angry. They will do almost anything to prove they aren't like their fellow citizens. One American girl refused to give up her British accent when she returned to Washington, DC, and displayed it when telling people how dumb she thought American foreign policy was.

Why is anger such a common reaction? There are several likely reasons. A cross-cultural lifestyle is so normal for TCKs that they themselves don't always understand how much it has shaped their view of the world. They easily forget that others haven't had the same exposure to different cultures and lifestyles as they have had. Also, the easiest way for anyone to deal with the stress of feeling uncomfortable in a new situation is to put others down. This impatience can be a defense against the feelings of insecurity or inferiority TCKs may have in their home culture. This impatience or judgmentalism sometimes also serves as a means of identifying with other TCKs. It becomes one of the markers of "us" versus "them." Unfortunately, a get-together of TCKs can quickly degenerate into bashing the perceived stupidity of non-TCKs.

At times it seems TCKs can be culturally tolerant anywhere but in their own culture. When people move to a new host culture, they usually keep quiet if they have strongly negative opinions about that culture. At most, they only express them to fellow expatriates. These rules seem to change, however, on reentry. Some TCKs appear to feel quite free to express every negative opinion they can possibly think of about their home culture, no matter who is around. While chronic put-downs may be an unconscious defense for the TCKs' own feelings of insecurity or rejection, such remarks further alienate them from everyone around them. But, like it or not, they are a member of this group by birth and citizenship. In affirming one part of their experience and themselves, they reject another.

Other TCKs, of course, simply withdraw. Some do it in obvious forms. They have a hard time getting out of bed, or they sit in their rooms and watch TV all day rather than joining any activities at school or church. These, too, are culture shock reactions. Withdrawal can have less obvious forms, however. Some students retreat into their studies and earn straight As—but who can fault them for that? Others spend hours practicing their favorite instrument and winning every musical contest they enter. While everyone congratulates them for their achievement, no one realizes this is another form of escape.

For a few TCKs, however, this period of looking for a way to relate to their home cultures can be a dangerous time. After trying various ways of coping, they realize that for all their external adaptation, something inside still doesn't fit, and they believe this something will never change. Psychiatrist Esther Schubert, an ATCK herself who has done research among TCKs, reports that suicide rates go up among TCKs after their first year home.[1] For them, it's the ongoing struggle to fit in that leads to despair rather than simply the initial reentry.

Helping in the Reentry Process

While there are no foolproof ways to ensure a perfect reentry, the basic key to helping TCKs find their way is to first understand what they are going through. Then there are some practical steps to help TCKs get through this process in a healthy rather than a harmful way.

When parents decide to move to another culture, they and others must accept that their children may wind up with a completely different sense of home and rootedness than their own. As we've said before, in spite of feeling so different in their home culture, many TCKs do have a sense of home, or at least cultural balance—either in one particular host culture or in the internationally mobile community and its characteristic lifestyle. Dirk, the German business TCK who grew up in Taiwan, said,

> I've always thought I felt more connected to Asia than to any other place. In fact, I glamorize Asian culture. I pick it up like my favorite pie. It's always been such a wonderful thing for me. My long-term goal is to go right back there.
>
> But I've begun to realize that it isn't only Asia that I feel so connected to. I also feel very connected to people who have lived in the international community, no matter which part of the world they have lived in. I've been doing everything I can since I've gotten here to get back to Asia, but if I can't go there, I'll have to go somewhere in the international community to feel truly at home.

Understanding that this type of reaction is normal for those with a third culture upbringing is one of the most positive ways to work through reentry. It gives TCKs the needed permission to work through reentry in much the same way they would approach coming into any new culture. Some good ways to approach the reentry process include talking with others who have already been through it, attending seminars, and reading the growing number of books available for third culture families, including *Strangers at Home,*[2] a book of essays on the reentry experience, and *The Art of Coming Home.*[3]

Instead of presuming it's everyone else's task to understand them, TCKs need to make an effort to understand the life experiences of their home peers. Asking thoughtful questions and listening more actively are great ways to learn more about the variety of backgrounds and experiences of peers in their own country. It also helps them realize that their own story is simply one of many and to understand why others may not see the world exactly as they do.

> One ATCK, Eleanor, worked in a nursing home, where most of the nurse's aides had never lived out of the state or spent one day at university. The things they talked about—boyfriends and babies—seemed

unbearably dull to her. When she tried to liven the
conversations up with stories of her past exciting life in
Chile, they listened politely but never asked a follow-
up question. At first she felt affronted and judged them
as shallow souls. But one day it occurred to Eleanor
that she knew no more about their lifestyle and
interests than they did about hers. She realized she
needed to start getting to know them better instead of
waiting for them to get to know her.

Since reentry is actually the entering stage of the larger transition experience they are going through at this point, don't forget that this is when TCKs most need a good mentor. Reentry is the key period when they are most vulnerable to being swept up in a group of friends they would never have chosen under normal circumstances, and they can get into drugs, alcohol, and other behavior they previously spurned. One thing that can make it difficult to find a good mentor, however, is that when TCKs return to their home country and are seen by others as "different" or "weird," often the peers who could be positive role models and friends don't reach out to the TCKs because they appear so odd. This means that parents often need to help identify a suitable mentor such as a relative, caring friend, youth leader, or sympathetic school staff member and enlist that person's help in positively introducing their child to this culture and community.

The chosen mentor also needs to understand that part of the mentoring process is helping the TCK learn the basic survival skills for this culture. These should include new technologies (like how to use a cell phone or the Internet) and significant changes in youth culture. Are bell-bottoms in again? What movies, rock groups, or particular shoe styles are popular? Sometimes these things are so common that the mentor may forget to specifically go over them with the TCK. Attending a transition or reentry seminar is often extremely helpful for many high school- and college-age TCKs during reentry. These seminars with other TCKs take up many of the issues

254 The Third Culture Kid Experience

discussed in this book and help TCKs realize they are not alone and aren't weird. (See the list of reentry seminars in Resources and Bibliography, pages 319–33.)

Ultimately, one of the ways to help TCKs resettle in their home country on a long-term basis is to provide an opportunity for them to revisit the host country where they feel most deeply rooted. It's easy for that past experience to become so idealized or romanticized in the transition to their home culture that it grows to larger-than-life proportions. Going back can help put it into perspective. Going back does something else as well. It connects the past and present worlds of TCKs and reminds them that their past is not a myth or totally inaccessible. In addition, such a journey reminds them that things never stay the same, and ultimately the past is now a foundation for the future.

With the increasing number of children from many cultures joining the ranks of TCKs, there are new concerns to consider. For citizens of some countries that have strong cultural traditions to which all children carefully adhere and in which the TCK is a new phenomenon, TCKs can be seen as a threat to the stability of the home culture. In one country, some government officials suggested reprogramming for TCKs because their new independent ways of thinking were unacceptable and disturbing for that culture.

We conclude with perhaps the most important matter we can mention regarding a TCK's transition home. It is this simple fact: whether parents return home with their TCK or send him or her on ahead, they must realize that ultimately it is their responsibility to help their child through the reentry phase. It's such a basic fact, it seems almost silly to say, but believe it or not, we've seen TCKs arrive at universities with no clear idea of where they will go during school breaks, for long weekends, or during summer vacations. It seems as if parents have shipped them back home in the rather vague, blissful assumption that everything will work out by itself—perhaps relying on other relatives to take care of their children, even when those relationships have never been nurtured.

It's not enough to presume that relatives at home will automatically pitch in to take care of a "homeless" TCK. We can't state this point strongly enough. Any time parents send their children back home while they themselves remain overseas, parents are still responsible for making sure their children are protected and cared for. It's their absolute responsibility to make sure their children have a designated "home-away-from-home." A strong extended family helps that process greatly, one where both the relatives and the TCKs already feel comfortable and at home with one another. If it's possible for TCKs to attend university near their relatives, this can also help ease them through reentry.

If no extended family is available, close friends can help. But if there is no safe harbor available for their TCK, parents should think seriously about staying home themselves until their child is secure in his or her new life. This may cost the parents of such TCKs a few years of their careers, but failure to do so may cause their children lifelong harm because of mistakes these TCKs make or the abandonment they feel as they try to adjust to a world they have never known.

In the end, while many TCKs look back on their reentry period as one of the more stressful parts of their TCK experience, they still wouldn't have wanted to miss much of what they learned from the process. Often they emerge from reentry with an awareness of how their own culture operates in ways that those who have never left may never see. This awareness can help them decide, perhaps more proactively than they might have otherwise, which values of their own culture they want to keep or let go of. Most also come to appreciate the special gifts they have received from each culture that has been part of their lives, including this one finally known as "home."

Endnotes

[1] Esther Schubert, "Keeping Third-Culture Kids Emotionally Healthy: Depression and Suicide among Missionary Kids," in *International Conference on Missionary Kids: New Directions for Missions: Implications for MKs,* edited by Beth A. Tetzel and Patricia Mortenson (Compendium of the International Conference on Missionary Kids, Manila, November 1984).

[2] Carolyn D. Smith, ed., *Strangers at Home* (Putnam Valley, NY: Aletheia Publications, 1996).

[3] Craig Storti, *The Art of Coming Home* (Yarmouth, ME: Intercultural Press, 1997).

17

How Sponsoring
Organizations Can Help

In addition to personal and parental choices that can help TCKs thrive in their experience, the policies and the programs (or lack thereof) of sponsoring organizations weigh heavily in the equation. Even if parents and TCKs do everything we've suggested to maximize the TCK experience, administrative decisions or policies within the sponsoring agency can still create problems. For example, a company orders its employee to move in the middle of a school year, or an organization only pays for one type of schooling. Administrators of international organizations need to realize that their personnel policies have a profound effect on the employee's family. At home, employers rarely have any influence on the schooling and living choices of their employees, but in cross-cultural situations the ramifications of corporate and organizational decisions filter down through the family of every employee affected by them.

Administrative decisions based solely on the interests of the international organization are shortsighted. Agencies should consider family needs as well as corporate needs when planning to send an employee overseas, for at least two reasons. First, it's for the long-term benefit of the company. Cross-cultural consultant Germaine

W. Shames states that "approximately 30 percent of managers from the United States return home early from an overseas assignment. The reason? Personal and family stress."[1] When agencies help employees meet their family's needs—whether for schooling, travel, or home leave—parents who work for the agencies are far more likely to stay with the company longer and be more productive. Since the cost of sending an employee overseas usually runs two to five times that employee's annual salary,[2] agencies benefit financially if they can keep their seasoned, internationally experienced employees from departing prematurely.

Keeping employees with strong cross-cultural skills also helps an agency's performance in relationship to the host culture. New people trying to learn those skills are bound to make more professional and social gaffes that hinder their effectiveness in a strange culture than someone who has already gone through the process of cross-cultural adaptation. After all, there are lessons about crossing cultures that only time can teach.

Second, sound corporate decisions and policies are for the long-term good of the family. When corporate or organizational decisions are made with families in mind, the family feels protected and cared for, a relationship that any organization should wish to cultivate as part of the organizational or corporate culture. With each family member having space to grow and develop, parents can make decisions only they are qualified to make—decisions that will help their children effectively use their cross-cultural heritage.

How Agencies Can Help Prior to the Overseas Assignment

One of the most important steps an organization can take for its overseas employees is to compile a list of schooling options well before the date of departure and make their policies and practices regarding educational costs and choices clear. Families need to know their educational options prior to accepting an assignment abroad.

A second valuable step is to plan a preassignment orientation. Some international agencies are doing an excellent job of this, offering workshops for both the employee and the employee's spouse and children. Other agencies, however, still think only of the employee and make no preparation for the intercultural adjustments that the family will inevitably face. Such agencies should seek outside help from cross-cultural training consultants and organizations.

Finally, and perhaps even preceding the two strategies above, organizational managers need to gather information on how often and why personnel are transferred to new locations. Since many challenges of the TCK experience are so closely tied to high mobility, administrators must look for ways to minimize the frequency and severity of the transition cycles. For example, why do military and embassy personnel change posts at least every two years? Is it always because of staffing needs, per se, or is it simply tradition? Some say if military or diplomatic personnel stay in one place too long and get attached to people in the host country, they will no longer be able to represent their own government effectively. Has this theory been tested? Similarly, when a business decides to send a person overseas, is it essential that the employee go in the middle of the school year?

Unnecessary, abrupt decisions by administrators can create tremendous stress for an employee's family. Simple matters like examining the options for moving a family during a school vacation or after a child graduates can make all the difference as to whether a family thrives or barely survives in a cross-cultural lifestyle.

How Agencies Can Help During the Third Culture Experience

An agency's responsibility to the family's well-being doesn't end after the final plans for departure are made or good-byes said. To increase a family's chances of success while they are abroad, the agency should have in place a plan that includes the following components.

1. *Have an entry team or a designated employee to welcome new employees on site.* Each agency should have a formal plan for introducing new people to both the host and expatriate communities as quickly as possible. It's important for newcomers to know the people they need to contact locally for business connections as well as for the practical issues of life that long-time residents take for granted. We know of one young couple who went overseas to an area where, after their initial welcome at the airport, they were left on their own to figure out how to get their driver's licenses, find someone to install a phone, and even locate a doctor to call when a family member became sick. It was three months before they met anyone who explained to them where they could buy meat they could actually chew. The problem there was that the home office presumed that families in the overseas branch would take care of properly orienting new arrivals but had no formal plan in place to make sure it was done.

   Sometimes people are assigned to a post where they are the only employees from their particular home country. Those from the local culture may work hard to make the newcomers feel welcome and to introduce them to local customs and stores, but it is also helpful during this time if they can find others from their home culture as well. These people are the ones who know the types of products the newcomers can substitute for things they have been accustomed to using at home. They are also the only ones who might think to explain, for example, that a siren going off in bad weather means a tornado may be approaching. Local residents are so accustomed to this warning system that they don't even think to explain it or realize these new friends have never been around tornadoes before.

2. *Help employees evaluate schooling options using the compiled list put together before departure.* Agencies should never insist on one particular method of schooling for their families. As

we've said, parents must have freedom to consider each child's personality and special needs when making this critical choice.

Agencies must also take into account the additional costs of education for expatriate children. Part of the employee's salary and benefits should include helping with those costs. In the home country, educational expenses for children are rarely discussed when negotiating a job contract, but schooling is often a complex and costly issue for expatriates, especially in certain countries.

3. *Establish a flexible leave policy.* Policies for leave vary from agency to agency. Some insist their employees remain on site for four years, followed by a one-year home leave. Others have a cycle of sending people overseas for eleven months, then home for a month. Between those two ends of the spectrum lie other alternatives. There are pros and cons to each—both for the sponsoring organizations and for the families. Wise administrators are willing to negotiate mutually beneficial leave packages if the standard policy for that organization doesn't work for a particular person or family.

4. *Make provision for children who are attending school in the home country to visit parents during vacations.* Traditionally, many sponsoring organizations have paid for TCKs to return home for vacations if they were away for schooling through secondary school, but once those children returned to their home culture for university, those benefits ended. It's during those postsecondary years, however, that many major life decisions are made, years when parental support and guidance are crucial. Many organizations lose valuable employees whose children are at this critical life juncture; many would rather resign than be separated for several years—particularly if they are in a situation where they can't afford to pay personally for such trips.

We believe there is a fairly simple answer. Paying for children attending postsecondary institutions in the home country to visit their parents for vacations should be a normal benefit for those working for international organizations. That policy change alone would likely prolong the careers of many of their employees, and it would also go a long way toward reducing many of the most challenging aspects of this globally mobile lifestyle.

5. *Support international community efforts to provide ongoing expatriate family services.* Research surveys that assess the factors contributing to the relative success or failure of an overseas assignment now include the degree to which a sponsoring organization provides ongoing assistance abroad.[3] Barbara F. Schaetti, a consultant to the international expatriate community, suggests that the challenge for a company lies in how to provide such assistance in every one of its international locations. She notes that, historically, most have relied upon their network of expatriate spouses. Support has been limited to paying membership dues to international women's clubs and contributing funds to international school parent/teacher association programs. Increasingly, however, companies are taking a more proactive approach. Many are now contracting with International Employee Assistance Programs (IEAPs) to provide expatriates with access to confidential mental-health services on demand. Others are underwriting spouse-managed information centers and providing access to the Internet so that spouses in diverse locations may link together. Still others sponsor such regional events as the European-based Women on the Move conferences.[4]

One of the most exciting developments in the way companies are providing ongoing expatriate family services is their support of community-based transition programs. Schaetti describes this corporate/community partnership as one in which local operating companies provide the funding, while the community, often with the leadership of the international school, provides a "transition resource team." This team is typically composed of ten to fifteen parents, educators, and students and represents the diversity of the community in terms of nationality and international experience. Its purpose is to design and implement ongoing, institutionalized, year-round transition programming customized to the needs of its own community. Although the specific goals will thus vary by community, the common commitment of community-based transition programs is to help expatriates take the lead regarding their own experience.[5]

6. *Help families prepare for repatriation and organizational re-entry.* Not only do companies lose valuable employees during the posting abroad, but disappointing statistics indicate that 20 to 25 percent of expatriate families leave the company within one year of repatriation.[6] Repatriating, or returning home, is frequently more difficult than moving abroad in the first place. Many, especially corporate employees, have been out of the loop while they were overseas. Their old job has been filled by someone else, their career is off track, and the company doesn't know what to do with them or how to use the international and cross-cultural skills they have acquired. Also, overseas these employees may have had a good bit of autonomy as decision makers or leaders, but at home their position is subordinate. Plus, they no longer fit into old patterns—not only at work but also at home in their former community.

Unfortunately, agencies and employees who prepared well for the original cross-cultural transition often forget to prepare equally carefully for the transition home. Ideally, before the family leaves the host country, a formal or informal briefing should be provided by people who have experienced this type of transition before. Families should be reminded that it is as important to build the RAFT we discussed earlier during this transition home as it is prior to a transition anywhere else. If the family has been overseas for a long time, agencies should provide a mentor to help the family navigate the various changes that have occurred at home in their absence.

7. *Offer reentry seminars for both parents and TCKs soon after repatriation.* Several organizations sponsor week-long seminars every summer for TCKs who are returning to their home country, and some agencies hold debriefing seminars for the adults. Recently, some groups have begun offering programs for the entire family (see Resources and Bibliography, pages 319–33, for a list of reentry seminars).

How Agencies Can Help Their TCKs in the Long Term

Because so many TCKs grow up with a strong sense that friends from the sponsoring agency or their international school are a part of their extended family, belonging to this group becomes part of their very identity. It may be the one place outside their family where they have a deep sense of belonging. They want and need to stay connected with this support system in some way.

Helping TCKs and ATCKs stay connected with one another and their past is beneficial for those directly involved as well as for the organization. Think of the benefit it would be for a company if these children return with their cross-cultural skills when they are ready for their own careers. Here are some ways administrators can play a vital role in helping TCKs who have grown up in their communities continue to thrive, ways that can also help in the healing process for those ATCKs who still need help dealing with some of these matters of adjustment.

1. *Support an alumni newsletter.* A growing number of agencies and international schools already help their TCKs and ATCKs maintain a sense of connectedness by helping them put out a newsletter. This forum not only distributes information, it also

gives them the opportunity to discuss relevant issues from their past, to offer suggestions for the present, and to stay part of the "family."

2. *Use the experience of TCKs and ATCKs.* It's ironic to see an organization bring in "experts" about a particular subject or country while ignoring the wealth of knowledge and experience of their own ATCKs.

> One ATCK sat through a meeting where a medical facility to be established in Brazil—modeled after one in the States—was being described and discussed. She knew from the beginning that the project would fail, because the philosophical concepts on which it was based were very different from those which shaped Brazilian thinking. When she attempted to raise a few questions, she was disdainfully put down. Three years later, after vast sums of money had been spent on the project, it folded, a complete failure.

Perhaps all prophets are without honor in their own country, but agencies shouldn't overlook the great resources they have in their ATCKs.

3. *Apologize for past organizational mistakes.* Unfortunately, as a direct result of poor administrative decisions from the company or sponsoring agency, some TCKs suffer the consequences. Some policies on relocating families, for example, have caused needless separations. An unfortunate choice of caregiver in a boarding school may have done harm to some children. The errors may not have been willful but they happened nonetheless. Even though those who made the decision may have since left the organization, it helps the employees—and the TCKs who were hurt by those policies—to know that the system itself is taking responsibility and that someone representing that system or organization is willing to apologize for past mistakes and, where needed, offer restitution.

4. *Pay for a TCK's "journey of clarification."* Some agencies already offer a trip back to the host culture during or immediately after university for all of their TCKs who grew up overseas, even if the parents are no longer abroad. As mentioned before, going back to their roots and validating past experiences helps TCKs move on more smoothly to the next stages of life, but when the agency itself is willing to pay for such a trip, the journey becomes even more healing. TCKs receive the important message that they do indeed belong to a community that cares for them—not one that discards them at a certain age with no concern for the impact growing up as a member of that overseas community had on them. It's another way of validating the value of their heritage and inviting them to build on that heritage rather than disowning it.

****

In conclusion, international organizations must face the fact that they bear responsibility not only to their individual employees but also to their families once they begin to transplant their workers cross-culturally and ask them to be global nomads. Too often administrators have blamed failures totally on the person who failed rather than looking at the part their agency or corporate policies and decisions may have played in the matter. We're grateful for the growing awareness among companies and sponsoring organizations of their role in helping cross-cultural families be successful.

Endnotes

[1]   Germaine W. Shames, "Transnational Burnout," *Hemispheres,* (February 1995), 39.

[2]   Mel Mandell and Lindsey Biel, "Global Repatriation," *Solutions,* (February 1994), 23–26.

[3]   Berlitz International and HFS Mobility Services, 1996–1997 International Assignee Research Project, Princeton, NJ.

[4]   Personal correspondence to David C. Pollock from Barbara F. Schaetti, Transition Dynamics, October 1998.

[5]   Ibid.

[6]   Cornelius Grove and Willa Hallowell, "On Trade and Cultures," *Trade and Culture* (September–October 1994), 4–6.

18

It's Never Too Late

In spite of the growing efforts to help current TCKs better understand and use their cross-cultural experiences, most TCKs from previous generations grew up with little assistance in sorting out the full effect of their third culture upbringing. No one understood that help might be needed, let alone what to do if it were.

Even so, many ATCKs have successfully found their way through the morass of conflicting cultures and lifestyles, come to terms with the inherent losses, and developed a positive sense of identity. They have learned to use their heritage in personally and/or professionally productive ways. But what about ATCKs who are still struggling to put it all together?

Unfortunately, we have met many who continue to be so confused or wounded by the challenges of their childhood that they have never been free as adults to celebrate the benefits. Depression, isolation, loneliness, anger, rebellion, and despair have ruled their lives instead of joy. Some ATCKs may outwardly continue to be successful chameleons, but inwardly the questions "Who am I?" "Where am I from?" "Why can't I seem to move on in life?" still rage. They can't figure out why they have always felt different from their peers.

Other ATCKs believe they are just fine, but spouses, children, friends, and coworkers know better. There is a shell around them that no one can penetrate—even in the closest of relationships. Some of them grew up in organizational systems where extended periods of separation from their family seemed so normal at the time that they never considered how these separations might have affected their lives. Others went through periods of war or conflict in their host country with or without their parents being present. TCKs have experienced emotional, mental, physical, and spiritual abuse, or at least trauma, as they have traversed their worlds, but because these worlds vanished with a plane ride, they have never stopped to sort things out. The experiences and their contexts simply disappeared. Often ATCKs are stuck in one of the stages of unresolved grief without realizing it. All they know is that they are trapped in some place or behavior from which they can't break free.

So what can they do now? Is it too late for wounded ATCKs to put the pieces together? When they have been stuck for a long time in a self-destructive lifestyle, is it possible for them to learn to use their past constructively rather than be bound by it? The answer is, simply, yes. It's never too late to deal with unresolved grief, identity issues, or other challenges related to the TCK lifestyle.

But how does healing occur? Obviously, ATCKs and their parents can't go back and relive their transitional experiences, nor can they undo the separations. The years of family life lost are irretrievable. In fact, most ATCKs can't recover any of their hidden losses. They can't reclaim the sights, sounds, or smells that made home "home" as a child. They can't stop the war that displaced them or the abuser who stole their innocence. What they can do is learn to put words to their past, name their experiences, validate the benefits as well as the losses, and ask for help from their families and others.

What ATCKS Can Do

Name Themselves and Their Experience

For many ATCKs, putting a name to their past—"I grew up as a third culture kid"—opens a new perspective on life. Discovering there are legitimate reasons for their life experiences and the resulting feelings not only helps them understand themselves better, it also normalizes the experience. Some, who have spent a lifetime thinking they're alone in their differentness, discover they have lived a normal life after all—at least normal for a TCK.

Somehow the concept of normality is very liberating. It doesn't solve every problem, but it gives permission for a lot of self-discovery and frees ATCKs to make some changes they may not have thought possible. For example, rather than remaining eternal chameleons and continuing to try fitting in everywhere, they can focus on examining who they are, where they do fit, and where they can best use their gifts. If ATCKs can understand, for example, why they chronically withdraw before saying good-bye to others, they can purposefully choose to stay engaged in relationships until the end.

> Since one ATCK discovered withdrawal was her consistent pattern before moving, she now tells her friends a month before the departure date, "I want to let you know what a great friend you've been, because I might not be able to tell you at the end. I also need to tell you that I've hurt a lot of people by acting like I don't care when it comes time to say good-bye. I'm going to try not to do that, but if I start to withdraw, you let me know." And her friends do.

This simple acknowledgment both helps others understand this ATCK's potential behavior and helps her remain emotionally present in relationships both before and after she leaves.

For other ATCKs, discovering they have a name—that they are adult third culture kids—and are members of a group whose membership extends around the world finally gives them a feeling of belonging. Instead of feeling their history is a piece of life's puzzle that will never fit, they now see it as the key piece around which so many others fall into place.

Name Their Behavioral Patterns

Once ATCKs realize their past has undoubtedly influenced their present life and their choices, it's time for them to make an honest assessment. Are there certain lifelong, repetitive behaviors (such as constantly moving or failure to allow intimacy in one relationship after another) that they have always excused as "That's just the way I am"? Is their anger, depression, or other behavior often out of proportion to its context?

After looking at such repetitive cycles of behavior, ATCKs need to ask themselves some questions: Is this behavior related to a confusion of identities? Is it related to one of the expressions of unresolved grief? Is it totally unrelated to anything except a personal or family matter? If it seems to be a personal matter, how might the influences of cross-culturalism and high mobility have added to that stress?

Name Their Fears

Often a major barrier to healing is fear—fear of facing the pain, fear of taking a risk again, fear of rejection. This fear is hidden behind such statements as "I don't see any reason to look back. Life is to be lived in a forward direction." Or "That TCK stuff is bunk. I'm just me, and my life experiences have nothing to do with the way I am. I'd have been the same no matter where or when I grew up."

It is scary to go back, but it can be helpful for ATCKs to realize that no matter how badly a certain situation hurt, they have already survived it and that situation is now past. Facing the pain will hurt for a bit, but it can be grieved and dealt with in the end. Not facing it may well continue to drive the ATCK into far more pain-producing behaviors than they can currently imagine.

Name Their Losses

After deciding that healing is worth the risk of pain, it's important for ATCKs to look back and try to identify some of the losses they haven't been fully aware of before. Journaling is one effective way to do this, answering such questions as these:

> Did you properly say good-bye to a country you loved dearly?
>
> What ever happened to your pets?
>
> Where is your amah now?
>
> Have your relationships with your siblings ever been restored?
>
> What do you need to do to heal parental relationships?
>
> Have you rediscovered your role in a group?

Having named the losses, it's not too late to go back and do the work of grieving that should have been processed as the losses occurred. We have been astounded at the severity of losses some ATCKs have experienced in their childhood: death in the family while the TCKs were away at boarding school, sexual abuse they never told anyone about, war that uprooted them in the middle of the night. So many of these have been covered over with no proper period of mourning or comfort to deal with the losses. Many ATCKs have simply disassociated themselves from the pain, but the grief merely surfaces in all the other forms mentioned earlier.

If ATCKs dare to face the losses in their lives, to acknowledge and grieve for them, they will discover that proper mourning takes away the power of those losses to drive their behavior in ever more destructive ways. When the pain has been severe, good friends who listen well are essential. Therapists with understanding of the TCK experience can be helpful in identifying and dealing with the ATCK's losses from the past if he or she finds it difficult to do alone or with friends.

One word of warning: we have noticed that when ATCKs first acknowledge some of their hidden losses, part of the grief process is a newly found or at least newly expressed anger at various people whom they feel are responsible for those losses. Lots of ATCKs (to say nothing of the people they're angry at) are so upset by this phase that they back off from going further. Don't give up on the process if this begins to happen! The anger phase *can* be a very difficult period of the healing process for everyone involved, but remember it is a normal stage of grief, which can be worked through to a stage of resolution as the ATCKs (and those around them) persist and give the healing process time.

Name Their Wounds

Even retrospectively, it's important for ATCKs to name not only their losses but also the ways in which they have been hurt and how they have hurt others. Why is this important? Everyone has been hurt by other people, and each of us has hurt others. Some of the wounds, whether intentional or not, have been significant, and they must be acknowledged to be dealt with properly.

Once we have identified a wound, we then have to make a critical decision. Will we hold on to our anger forever or will we forgive the ones who have hurt us? Some ATCKs we have met are living lives bound by bitterness. They have turned their pain into a weapon with which they beat not only the offender but themselves and everyone else as well. It seems that the hurt becomes part of their identity. To let it go would be to leave them hollow, empty. The problem is that the anger and bitterness destroy as much as, or more than, the original wound. Many are unwilling to forgive because they feel the offender will "go free." They believe that saying "I forgive you" means "It doesn't really matter what happened."

Forgiveness is not something lightly given, bestowed without looking at what the situation cost the person who was wounded. Without forgiveness, however, the offended person's life continues to be ruled by the offender. It's important to acknowledge the offense, but forgiveness is making a decision to let go of the need and desire for vengeance—even if the offender never has to pay. Forgiveness is the only thing that ultimately frees the wounded one to move on to true healing.

None of us is perfect. Healing also involves looking at how we ourselves have knowingly or unknowingly hurt others and asking their forgiveness. It's amazing to listen to stories of rage against parents, siblings, relatives, friends, and administrators in the sponsoring organizations from ATCKs who seem to have no perception that they are doing similar damage to their own children. Some who complain of emotional abuse or separation from parents one moment are yelling at their own children the next. Some who complain of abandonment in their childhood are workaholics who may not send their children away to boarding school but still never seem to have time for them.

Until and unless we are willing to acknowledge our own sins and failures against others, true healing is stymied, for we will have to continue living in our self-protective modes, shutting out those who would dare approach us and mention our offenses against them. We need to identify specific occurrences where we have wounded others, and when we recognize the offense, we need to be the first ones to go and ask for forgiveness, not waiting for them to approach us. Doing this both heals important relationships in our lives and also frees us from having to defend and protect ourselves. Instead, we can begin to live more openly and with greater joy.

Name Their Choices

Dealing with the past in a healthy way frees us to make choices about the future. We are no longer victims. Each of us must ultimately accept responsibility for our own behavior, regardless of the past. That doesn't mean that we are responsible for all that happened to us. A sexually abused child isn't responsible for the abuse, a child who felt abandoned is not responsible for the parents' choices. But as adults, we *are* responsible for how we deal with our past, how we relate to those around us in the present, and what we choose for the future. ATCKs must ask themselves several questions as they sort through their past in order to get on with their future: Will I forgive? Will I retaliate? Will I succumb to the message that I am worthless? Will I look at what it means to be a person and realize that it's okay to think, to create, to have emotion? Will I dare to find ways to express these parts of myself?

The choices ATCKs make in response to these questions can make all the difference for those who feel bound by the past but are longing to move on to freedom in the future.

We have started this final chapter focusing on what ATCKs can do for themselves because, in the end, how they deal with their history and how they can best use it is ultimately their responsibility. They can heal and find fulfillment in life even if others never understand their background. However, those close to the ATCKs can be immensely helpful if they try to understand the struggle and freely give their support during the time of healing.

How Can Parents Help Their ATCKs?

We have been saying throughout this book that family relationships are key to a TCK's well-being while he or she is growing up. This is also true for ATCKs who are still struggling with the challenges from their TCK experience. Parents can often be partners with their ATCKs during this healing process. If parents can be supportive and understanding rather than defensive or threatened when ATCKs are sorting through the past, they can help open the way to much faster healing for their adult children. Support throughout an ATCK's healing process is the greatest gift a parent can give. Here are some specific ways that parents can help.

Listen and Try to Understand

This may seem simple, but it's not. ATCKs sometimes turn against their parents when they begin verbalizing their feelings about the past. When the accusations rage, parents often try to defend themselves with the facts: "We *didn't* send you away for six months. It was only three." "We never *made* you wear those hand-me-down clothes. You *wanted* to."

The facts aren't the main issue here. The issue is how ATCKs *perceived* the event. For them, the separation *felt* like six months. In other words, they really missed their parents. When they were laughed at for their attire, they felt they had had no choice in what to wear. Like everyone else in the world, the ATCKs' perceptions of reality have been shaped by the emotional impact of their experiences. That emotional reaction is real, and it's far more important at this point for parents to deal with those perceptions of certain events and the feelings behind them than to argue about the facts. Arguing the facts only proves to the ATCK that the parents never understood any-way—and still don't.

Sometimes parents not only argue with the facts ATCKs bring up during this time but also with the feelings ATCKs express. For example, the ATCK tries to express how lonely he or she felt when leaving for boarding school, and the parent replies, "You never minded going off to school. Why, you smiled and waved and always said you had a great time there." Or the ATCK talks of how hard it was to leave the host country and the parent interjects, "How can you say you were heartbroken to leave Port-au-Prince? You always told us it was too hot and you couldn't wait to get back to France." Perhaps nothing will shut down communication faster between parents and their ATCK than such a response, because no one can tell what another person did or did not feel. Outer behavior often masks inner feelings. That's why it is critical that when ATCKs try to tell their parents, even years later, what they were feeling as they grew up, parents need to listen and accept those feelings. This kind of acceptance opens doors for far more fruitful discussion between parents and ATCKs than trying to prove this isn't what the ATCKs felt.

Parents may be stunned when suddenly confronted with feel-ings their ATCKs have never expressed before—especially when the ATCKs are in their thirties and forties. This won't be easy, but it's important for parents to realize that life has stages and that, often, people can't fully deal with or understand what is happening at a certain time in their lives. They wait until later, when it is safer to examine the full impact of a situation. This applies not only to ATCKs. It happens to adults from all sorts of backgrounds. Children basically have to deal with life's traumas in a survival mode—whether it be someone calling them a bad name, their own physical handicap, parental divorce, a major separation from either or both parents, abuse, or death. Some kids escape into fantasy. Others block out the feelings of pain with denial or rationalization. Compulsions may be another child's attempt to control the pain. It's not the *how* that's significant; it's the fact that children have to survive, and they must use everything at their disposal to do so.

As life proceeds, however, the pain remains until, finally, the day comes when adults decide to face their inner wounds.

> Many people have asked Ruth how she remembered so many details of her childhood to include in *Letters Never Sent*. She always explains, "I didn't remember; I reexperienced those moments. But as an adult, I had words to describe the feelings I felt but couldn't explain as a child." After one such discussion, Faye, another ATCK who had been through a similar process of retracing her own childhood, challenged Ruth: "I don't think we reexperience those feelings. I think we allow them to be felt for the first time."
>
> On further reflection, Ruth agreed. She realized that when she was six and the lights went off at bedtime her first night in boarding school, she felt an immense sense of isolation, aloneness, and homesickness that threatened to squeeze her to death. To give in to that much pain would surely have meant annihilation. So, like most kids, she tried everything she knew to dull the pain, to control it somehow. Ruth's solution involved "trying harder." She prayed with great attention to style—carefully kneeling, giving thanks in alphabetical order for everyone and everything she

could think of. This so God would stay happy with her and grant the requests that she would sneak onto the end of the prayer to see her family again. She tried to meticulously obey all the rules at school so she wouldn't get in trouble. Keeping track of the details of life took a lot of focus and attention away from the pain.

When she picked up her pen at age thirty-nine and wrote, "I want my mommy and daddy" as part of the letter her six-year-old self would have written if she'd had the words, Ruth felt that same horrible squeezing in her chest that she had known as that six-year-old child. This time, however, she didn't need to put it away or work against it. She had already survived it and could allow herself to feel the anguish all the way to the bottom of her soul in a way she couldn't have when the separation actually happened.

This pattern of midlife clarification of the past seems to be common for many ATCKs, but it's a process that brings great consternation to some parents. It's helpful for parents to accept that their ATCKs may need to deal with their emotions many years after the events themselves. They also need to see that their ATCKs' attempts to share feelings with them—though initially expressed in anger—are because the ATCKs still want and need their parents to understand what they felt during their moments of separation or other experiences of childhood. Consciously or unconsciously, the ATCKs want to be in a closer relationship with their parents or they wouldn't bother trying to communicate these feelings. After all, these are the only parents the ATCK will ever have.

Dialogue and healing can begin if parents will listen and try to understand their adult child's accounting of the past without defending themselves, their sponsoring organization, the facts, or anything else. They also need to remember that just because their ATCK never told them these things before doesn't mean the ATCK didn't feel them.

Comfort and Be Gentle

Offering comfort is a key factor in any grieving process—even when that process is delayed by decades. Remember, comfort is not encouragement. It is being there with understanding and love, not trying to change or fix things.

> One ATCK took courage and finally wrote his parents some of the things he had felt through some of the early separations from them as a child. His mother wrote back, "Thank you for telling us how you felt. As I read your letter, of course I cried. I wish I could give you a big hug right now. I'm sorry we didn't know then what you expressed now or we might have made some different decisions—but we didn't. I love you and trust your story will help others."

Obviously, the first piece of comfort came with the acknowledgment that his mom understood the feelings he had expressed. The second came with the words, "I wish I could give you a big hug." Then his mom expressed her own sorrow with a simple acknowledgment that as parents they had not realized what he was feeling. His mother never denied his feelings, nor did she wallow in self-blame or defensiveness. Instead, she blessed her son. Parental listening, understanding, comfort, and blessing are huge, wonderful steps in the healing process that parents can provide for their children—even when those children are now adults.

Don't Preach

Almost all parents find it difficult not to preach, but this may be especially so for parents of adult missionary kids. These parents have spent their lives dedicated to a religious cause. There is probably no greater anguish parents can feel than when their ATCKs reject the system for which the parents have stood—particularly when it is the faith they have gone halfway around the world to share. Often, the sense of urgency to convince their children to believe in what they themselves believe grows as parents watch their ATCKs fall into increasingly self-destructive behavior: "If they'd just get their lives right with God, they'd be fine."

To that we would respond with a "yes, but" answer. Yes, what the parents desire for their children is valuable, but ATCKs who suffered within a religious system must first sort out their pain in terms of who God actually is compared with the rules and culture of the religious system that seeks to represent God. Until then, preaching, or worse, words of spiritual reprimand, will only fuel the anger.

Is there never a time for third culture parents to talk forthrightly with their ATCKs in response to both the accusations that are being made as well as the destructive behavior parents see? Of course there is. When parents have listened and understood what their adult child is feeling, there *is* an appropriate time to express their own feelings and beliefs. But it must come as a sharing of who they are and their perspectives rather than as a denial of what the ATCK has shared or is feeling.

Forgive

Sometimes parents need to ask their ATCKs for forgiveness. They have made mistakes too and shouldn't run from acknowledging them. If their ATCK has been extremely hurtful and rebellious toward them, parents will also have much to forgive. This can be very difficult, particularly if their child is not yet acknowledging how badly he or she has hurt them. But if parents are able to forgive and ask for forgiveness, it can be a major factor in their adult child's healing process.

Assume You Are Needed

Parents should assume their adult children still need and want them as part of their lives. They may tell parents not to bother coming for a birth, graduation, or wedding, saying "It isn't that big a deal," and these ATCKs probably believe that's how they really feel. But it makes a big difference—even to those who don't think they need their parents any longer—when parents make the effort to remain involved in a caring way in their children's lives as adults. Sometimes those years together as adults finally make up for the separations of the past.

What Friends and Other Relatives Can Do

Sometimes friends and other relatives can help ATCKs take the first major step in the healing process because they stand outside the emotionally reactive space occupied by the ATCKs and their parents. What can they do for the ATCKs they love to help in the healing process?

Listen to the Story and Ask Good Questions

Many ATCKs feel their childhood story is so far removed from their present lives that they have nearly forgotten it themselves. Few people cared to know more than the cursory details when they first returned from their third culture experience, and they quit talking about it long ago. To have someone invite them for lunch, ask to hear about their experiences, and then actually listen may be such a shock to some that they seem to at least temporarily forget everything that has happened to them. But persist. When friends or relatives initiate the conversation and clearly express their interest, the ATCK knows it's bona fide. It may even give them the first chance they've ever had to put words to their experiences.

Questions such as these can also help the process: "How did you feel when you said good-bye to your grandma?" "What was the hardest thing about returning to your home country?" "What did you like best about growing up that way?"

These kinds of questions prove the friend is listening closely enough to hear the behind-the-scenes story and may even challenge ATCKs to consider issues they never stopped to think about before.

Don't Compare Stories

Friends and relatives shouldn't point out how many other people have had it worse. Generally, ATCKs already know they have had a wonderful life compared with many others. That has often been part of their problem in trying to understand their struggles.

Most ATCKs will first relate the positive parts of their story. They won't tell the difficult aspects until they feel safe and comfortable with the listener. Once they do begin to share the darker times, don't try to cheer them up by reminding them of the positives. Both sides of the story are valid.

Comfort If Possible

Sometimes friends are the first ever to comfort an ATCK, and it can be hard initially for the ATCK to accept it. Many feel as if admitting to any pain is the same as disowning their parents, their faith, or the organizational system in which they grew up. Sometimes ATCKs become angry when others try to comfort them, because they refuse to admit they might need it. So, offer comfort—but don't push if your friend isn't ready to receive it.

How Therapists Can Help

We don't presume to tell therapists how to counsel ATCKs, since professional therapy is outside our domain. We hope, however, that we can help therapists understand the problems specific to the TCK experience, such as where TCK grief often comes from, where the early attachments between parents and children might have been broken, and how TCKs' concepts of identity and worldview have been affected by cultural and mobility issues. Our goal is to help therapists understand the basic life patterns of the third culture experience so they will be better prepared to assist their TCK clients. An interesting occurrence when we have given seminars for therapists is that after our presentations, our audience begins to redefine the topic by explaining it back to us—and to each other—from therapeutic models such as attachment theory or post-traumatic stress syndrome with which they are already familiar.

> After attending a conference on TCK issues, one
> therapist said, "We used to think that if a child was

adopted at birth, that child would have no different issues to deal with than a child born to the adoptive couple. Now we know anytime a client comes in who was adopted, there are certain questions to ask.

It seems to me the TCK issue falls in that category. Being aware of this experience can help us ask better questions when we realize our clients are TCKs or ATCKs.

Recognize Hidden Losses

Therapists who understand the nature of the third culture experience may be the first to help ATCKs identify the hidden losses that are part of the TCK experience but that the TCKs themselves are often not aware of. A "Cycles of Mobility" chart (see Chart 1) can be a useful tool in this process. Many ATCKs do not recognize the degree to which separation has been an integral part of their lives and how it has contributed to feelings of loss and grief.

Chart 1 Cycles of Mobility

Instructions: Make a time chart of the separation patterns for the first eighteen years of the ATCK's life, using different colors to fill in the spaces for when and where he or she lived, for example:

Blue = time living with parents in home country

Green = time living with parents in host country #1

Purple = time living with parents in host country #2

Yellow = time living with parents in host country #3

Brown = time spent away from parents in boarding school in host country

Pink = time spent away from parents in boarding school in home country

Orange = time living with anyone other than parents or in boarding school

Chart 1
Cycles of Mobility

	1	2	3	4	5	6	7	8	9	10	11	12	13	14	15	16	17	18
January																		
February																		
March																		
April																		
May																		
June																		
July																		
August																		
September																		
October																		
November																		
December																		

Age in years

This chart can be modified to fit the specific situation of each ATCK. What's important is for the therapist—and the ATCK—to see the overall patterns of mobility—where the transitions between various cultures occurred, at what ages, and so forth. As the times of transition, separation, and loss become obvious, therapists may discover the roots of some of the issues they see in their ATCK clients. This insight can help them aid their ATCK clients in recognizing the areas that need healing.

Therapists should also help their ATCK clients carefully think through the issues regarding the impact of culture on a TCK's developmental process. Some of the feelings ATCKs struggle with may, in fact, be largely a result of cultural imbalance.

Recognize the Impact of the System

One major factor that many therapists of ATCKs overlook or fail to understand is the powerful influence of the military, mission, business, or other organizational system under which these ATCKs grew up. Often the ATCKs' anger or hurt stems directly from policies that either controlled their lives on a daily basis or took away choice when it came to schooling, moving, and so on. On the flip side, ATCKs who were used to being protected or nurtured in that system (for example, the perks like free medical care or inexpensive housing) may not know how to cope comfortably in a larger, less structured world, where they are expected to depend more on themselves. Therapy is sometimes stymied if issues are dealt with only in the context of family relationships rather than understanding the operative system that often superseded family decisions.

Recognize the Paradox

Often ATCKs are defensive in therapy when asked about the painful parts of their past. They don't want to negate the way of life that is the only one they have known and is a core element of their identity. Missionary kids may have particular trouble acknowledging the pain because they feel that to do so will negate their faith. It is hard for many to know how much of that system they can examine, and potentially give up, without giving up God in the process.

Acknowledging the paradoxical nature of his or her experience may be particularly important in relationship to a client who attended a boarding school. These ATCKs may have so many great memories of the camaraderie experienced there and friendships made and maintained down through the years that they can't imagine there could be any negatives. In addition, for some TCKs who were boarding students for as long as twelve years, their identity is deeply tied to the boarding school experience. To acknowledge anything but the good could threaten their entire sense of self. But young boarding students often feel unprotected; a six-year-old child going to boarding school may actually experience something akin to becoming an orphan. How can ATCKs acknowledge the loneliness they felt without seeing it as a denial of the good they have also known at school? For these, or any ATCKs who grew up in strong systems and feel closely identified to that system, questions about system policies can be such a threat to their core identity that they may refuse to go on with the therapy they need.

That is why those working with ATCKs must never forget to recognize—and help the ATCK recognize—that when we look at the TCK experience from the perspective of the adult TCK, we will see many paradoxes. Therapists must affirm the positive elements as well as identify the stress points to give their ATCK clients the permission they need to look at all sides of their past experiences. It's also helpful to remind them once more that if there hadn't been so much good to lose, there often wouldn't have been so much grief at its passing.

Final Thoughts

We have now reached both an ending and a beginning—the end of sharing what we have already learned from and about TCKs and ATCKs and the beginning of watching the rest of this story unfold. We haven't begun to look fully at the many possible variations in the TCKs' world. Instead of the traditional pattern of having parents among the elite of the community, some TCKs grow up in the homes of migrant workers or domestic servants. Does that shade the picture differently? If so, how? What about TCKs who, for reasons of war or some other unforeseen event, never have the choice of returning to their home country? There is so much more to study and learn not only about TCKs themselves but also about how their experience compares with others who are raised outside their home culture because they have been adopted cross-culturally or their parents are immigrants or refugees.

We're also encouraged to see the end of apathy and the beginning of real awareness that there are some valid issues to deal with in this lifestyle. Sponsoring agencies are developing new strategies for taking better care of their families. Schools throughout the world are making changes in curriculum and approaches to teaching that will make it easier for students of any country to fit back into the school system of their home country. Parents are making careful, thoughtful decisions that take into account their own TCKs' needs. Everywhere, we see ATCKs taking ownership of their past so that they may use it well.

On the other hand, as the world tries to move toward increased globalization, we also see that many of the same challenges TCKs have faced in their multicultural upbringings will be encountered in the larger world arena as well. We hope this book will help all of us begin to consider some of the ramifications of globalization so that we can avoid at least some of the major pitfalls of intercultural living.

But after all is said and done, we say this: it's exciting to be a TCK or an ATCK. It's also exciting to know, love, and work with them. We wish each of you, our readers, much joy in your own journeys as well.

Appendix A
Adult Third Culture Kid Survey Results

An Historical Overview of Mobility Patterns for TCKs and Their Long-Term Impact on ATCKs

People often ask, "Is it fair to look at adult TCKs and project their experience onto current TCKs when conditions for third culture living are so different [and presumably better] than they were during the first half of the twentieth century?"

That's a valid question, and in our early days of working with TCKs, we wanted to find an answer. Were the long-term effects of both benefits and challenges of the third culture experience valid for current and future TCKs or simply fading products of an earlier day and way of life?

In 1986, the few surveys that had already been done among TCKs mostly reflected the benefits of the experience but seemed to miss any major discussion of the challenges. We soon realized that because boarding schools and universities were the easiest place to access this population, every survey that had been conducted among TCKs picked up mostly missionary kids, and all were teenagers or in their early twenties. That raised the next question. Did the "positive only" nature reflect that the younger TCKs didn't face the issues of former generations or did it reflect another possibility—that young people often don't have a full perspective on their life experiences and perhaps haven't yet started to deal with some of the long-term ramifications of their experience? Certainly we had found a pattern among the many ATCKs we had talked to. Most had not begun to deal consciously with issues relating to their TCK experience until their mid to late twenties—or even into their thirties. Armed with this information, we decided to do a simple survey ourselves.

In 1986 we gathered 800 names of ATCKs from a variety of sources—personal contacts, referrals by friends, and alumni lists of various TCK boarding schools. Most of these prospects were adult missionary kids, so our sample pool in parental occupational orientation closely reflected that of the initial surveys we had seen. All were postuniversity ATCKs, and the 282 who responded ranged in age from twenty-two to seventy-five years of age.

The questionnaire focused on two major issues:

1. What were the patterns of separation from family, home, and host countries—both in kind and amount—during the first eighteen years of the ATCK's life?

2. How did the respondent think these separations had affected him or her?

The results were revealing. We not only learned the ways many ATCKs felt their lives had been affected by these patterns of separation, but a vivid picture of the changes occurring in the third culture community emerged as well. The findings painted a clear historical picture of the TCK world as well as showing changing trends.

When we began noticing some significant differences in certain statistics among ATCKs of the pre- and post-World War II eras, we decided we could best compare the past and present world of TCKs by dividing our respondents into two major categories. Those born before 1947 we called the "older ATCKs"; those born in 1947 and later we called the "younger ATCKs." To study the data more precisely, we broke these two larger groups down into subgroups representing all the respondents born within five-year spans. Each of the following graphs and discussions is based on this framework.

Graph 1
Place of Birth—Home or Host Country

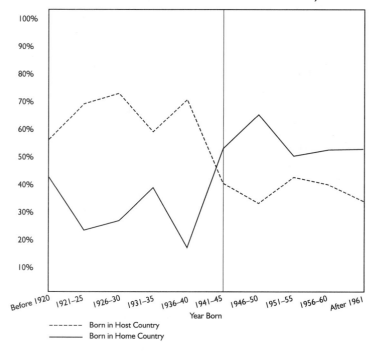

Our first clue about the changing patterns in the third culture world came when we graphed out place of birth. In every five-year group of the older ATCKs—those born during or before World War II—the majority were born in the host country. It was exactly the opposite for every five-year age group of TCKs born after the war. The majority of these younger ATCKs were born in their home countries.

There are undoubtedly several reasons for this marked difference. In the prewar years, most missionaries (the major group from which our sample came) went overseas for at least four years at a time—some much longer. It could easily take six weeks to three months on an ocean freighter before they arrived at their destination.

In those early days, many mission boards didn't accept people over thirty years of age, feeling that by the time anyone older than that learned the language in a new country, they would be too old for useful, long-term service. Agencies also believed only younger people could better stand up to the health risks involved in overseas living. This meant people went overseas in their early twenties, often before the birth of their children. When babies came later, they were born wherever their parents were—usually in the host country.

In the post-World War II era, children were and are still being born wherever parents are, but patterns for how and when people engage in international careers are vastly different from before. Long, uninterrupted stints in faraway lands are less common now than they used to be. Because people can travel by jet rather than ship, it means they come and go between countries far more easily. Leaves or furloughs are scheduled more frequently. Women who choose to do so can fly home for the delivery of their babies rather than stay in a host culture that may have less adequate facilities. Short-term assignments are also possible because the business or mission started by the lifelong pioneers of earlier days is now well established. It's easy to identify a place where people can plug in to meet a specific need of the moment. For these reasons, and doubtless others, more TCKs are being born in their home country now than formerly.

Graph 2
Those Separated from Parents for a
Significant Period before Age Six

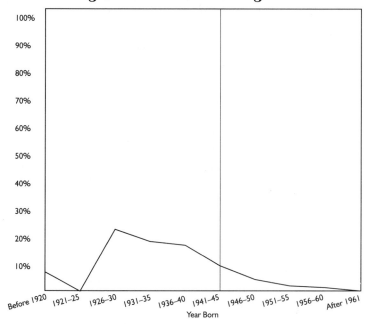

Year Born

The next difference between the older and younger ATCK groups became clear when we looked at how many had been separated from their parents for a significant period of time before the age of six. Many ATCKs born just before and during World War II were in this category. There were two common reasons children were left in the home country at an extremely early age while parents went overseas.

1. Children weren't allowed to travel overseas during the war because of the risks involved. In 1944 this ban on children traveling across the ocean meant Ruth Van Reken's parents faced a major dilemma when they discovered Ruth's mom, Betty, was pregnant while they were preparing to go to Africa for the first

time. They could either go while Betty was pregnant, not go at all, or wait in the States for the baby to be born and then go on to Africa, leaving the baby with caregivers until the war was over. Ruth's folks chose to cross the ocean while her mom was still pregnant. (Sadly, the ship that carried them to Europe was torpedoed and sunk by enemy fire on its return trip to the States; there were obviously good reasons for the ban on travel for children.)

2. Even before the war, many parents chose to leave their young children at home for educational purposes. Others left their children behind because they feared the disease and other perils they might face in an overseas post such as West Africa, which in the colonial era was called "the white man's grave."

Graph 3
Those Who Lost a Family Member to Death before Respondent Was Eighteen

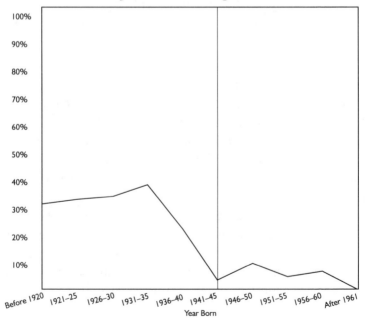

During their first eighteen years of life, the older ATCKs surveyed had suffered a much higher mortality rate in their immediate family than had the younger ATCKs. Before antibiotics and antimalarial drugs became available, death rates were high for expatriates in many tropical countries. When an article came out in the early 1990s in *Christianity Today* discussing the children's graves at a mission station in Nigeria, Ruth realized she'd known every one of those children personally except for two. They'd either been her friends, or she had baby-sat them, or they were the children of her parents' close friends. Death was a sad, but common, occurrence among the expatriate community in those earlier days.

Graph 4
Total Years of Separation from Parents
before Age Eighteen and Longest Single Stretch of Time
without Seeing Parents Even Once in First Eighteen Years

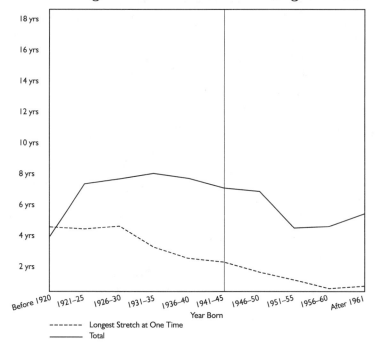

Aside from the TCKs mentioned in Graph 2, who were left at home for fear of war or disease, most separations for TCKs occurred because of schooling. The figures in this graph reflect some interesting possibilities regarding educational patterns. The higher number of total years away for the oldest ATCKs likely reflects not only time away in boarding school overseas but long stretches in their home country as well.

The graph stays relatively steady until we see those born after the war, in the fifties and sixties. Suddenly, the total number of years away drops. The trend toward home schooling and the more varied options offered by satellite schools and by local national and international schools are likely reflected in these statistics.

The greatest difference between the older and younger ATCKs, however, is in the average *longest* period of time TCKs went without seeing their parents at all during those same first eighteen years of life. These figures tell a remarkable story.

In the older group, the average length of time for not seeing parents even once was 3.6 years. The normal pattern for most missionaries in those days was four years overseas and one year back in the home country for furlough. With few American or British secondary schools available overseas, many TCKs stayed in the States, Canada, or England and went to boarding schools or lived with relatives in the home country during their teenage years. Meanwhile, parents returned overseas for the next four-year stint. With slower transportation and the high costs involved for travel, TCKs rarely visited their parents overseas during those four-or-more-year stretches.

The average length of time the younger TCKs went without seeing parents once was only eleven months. Quite a change.

Graph 5
Percent of Those Separated from Parents for Longer
Than One Year at a Time before Age Eighteen

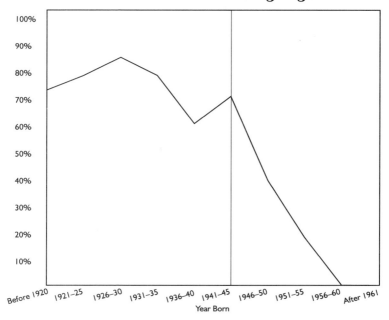

A quick look at this graph shows how common these long separations were for older ATCKs. They were accepted as a normal and inevitable part of an international, or at least a missionary, career. The dramatic lowering in this pattern of extended separations for the younger ATCKs (among those born in 1956 and later, not one ATCK during the first eighteen years had gone a full year without seeing parents at least once) clearly reflects several points. Like Graph 4, this decline no doubt reflects the trend toward home schooling and the more varied options offered by satellite schools and by local national and international schools. These figures also reflect the trend for sending children who are in their home country back to see their parents in the host country during the school vacation periods.

Graph 6
Age at Permanent Return to Home Country

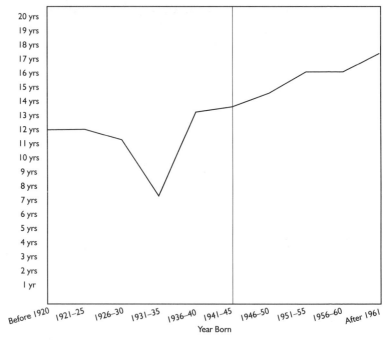

The rising average age when TCKs permanently reentered the home country clearly reflects the increased availability of international schooling options around the world. Instead of returning at age twelve or thirteen for secondary school in the home country as the older ATCKs did, the great majority of younger TCKs stayed in the host country until an average age of almost seventeen. They only returned to the home country for university.

Graph 7
Impact of Multiple Separations on Relationships

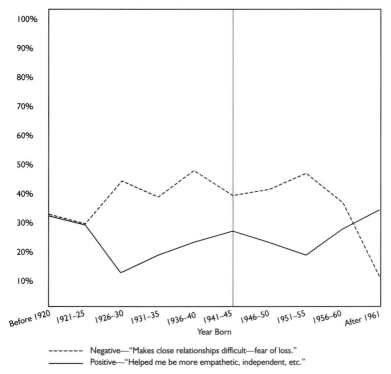

------ Negative—"Makes close relationships difficult—fear of loss."
——— Positive—"Helped me be more empathetic, independent, etc."

After looking at the notable differences in type, amount, and patterns of separation experienced by the older and younger ATCK groups, we expected to find that the issues TCKs from previous generations faced weren't relevant for today's culturally mobile kids. We presumed there would be a significant difference in how the older and younger groups responded to our question of how the separations had affected them—with the older generation saying they had been hard and the younger group barely noticing them.

The specific question we asked was "How do you feel the cycle of separations affected you?" Here are some of the replies.

"Don't know."

"Hard to communicate and make friends."

> "I am sympathetic with those who have to be separated from loved ones."
> "Have never made intimate friends."
> "Because of internment by Japanese, I was spared separation. [Apparently this ATCK was in internment camp with the parents.] My brother, who was separated, was affected."
> "Am very interested in people and their needs."

There were three basic types of response: positive, negative, and both. Positive responses were judged as those that included such statements as "It made me more independent," although we have no way to assess if that is a healthy independence or the isolation we talked about in chapter 6. We judged as negative those remarks which included *only* challenges with no benefits listed. Here's one example. "I have become very protective emotionally. I do not easily let others get close emotionally. I find it very hard to communicate in an intimate relationship for fear of rejection. It has crippled my marriage." A major recurring theme in many of the remarks reflected the ATCKs' fear of intimacy because of the fear of loss.

The responses we marked as "both" included replies such as this respondent's: "I struggled with depression for years but now find my own struggle gives me greater empathy for others." None of these were listed in the negative responses.

To our surprise, in spite of all the differences in separation patterns between older and younger ATCKs, 47 (40.1%) of the 117 respondents in the older group said the chronic cycles of separation had a negative impact on them and 62 (39.2%) of the 158 in the younger group said the same thing. A mere 1 percent difference!

How could this be? With further reflection, and many intervening years to test our hypothesis, our conclusion was, and remains, that it is the *cycles* of separation and the loss itself that affect TCKs and ATCKs—not merely the longevity or amount. Though TCKs may now return from boarding school every three months instead of being separated from parents for four years, these children still know, and internally stay prepared for, the fact that they will soon be leaving again. If TCKs see grandparents and relatives back home more often than before, they know it's not a permanent settling down. In fact, some ATCKs who experienced the long periods of separation from parents adjusted to it much as they would to death. Perhaps they experienced less of the *cycle* of separation by staying with the same relatives in one place rather than saying "hello" and "goodbye" to parents every three months—although other types of losses are certainly inherent in such prolonged separations between parents and children. It was this graph which made us begin to look more carefully at the hidden—rather than the obvious—losses we discuss in this book.

Surely there is much more research to do in this whole area. While other surveys have been done in the intervening years on ATCKs as well as TCKs, many questions remained unanswered. Perhaps because this is such a highly paradoxical experience, it is hard to measure the "both/andedness" in any quantitative survey. For those interested, we would suggest that any survey designed for TCKs and ATCKs take into account the inherent paradoxes and leave room for open-ended responses as well as those designed to gather statistical data.

Appendix B
Writings by Adult
Third Culture Kids

Let Us Possess One World

Sophia Morton

Sophia is an Australian TCK who grew up in Papua
New Guinea and now lives in Sydney. This fictional
piece reflects the struggle for intimacy many TCKs
know well.

You stare out the window in hurt defeat. I suppress a sigh and continue to stir my coffee aimlessly, casting my mind back into the depths of high school geography, trying to remember whether flotsam or jetsam is the appropriate name for the froth on top of the coffee. The levels of my mind continually amaze me. While I'm pondering the flotsam-jetsam dilemma, I'm simultaneously recognising the pondering as an attempt to distract myself from the question at hand, which threatens to overwhelm me. It's an old coping strategy. At another level I'm observing you and wondering what you'd think of my ponderings. I am indeed a curious mix.

We have circumnavigated the proverbial bush often and ferociously in the afternoon. It's not that I don't want to push through, but I don't know how. I can't make you understand. Instead of communicating myself to you, I get stuck defining and redefining the terms of reference. I thought we spoke the same language. But it seems that even though our words are the same, their meanings must be different.

Sometimes I think the cement of my being was taken from one cultural mould before it cured and was forced into other moulds, one after the other, retaining bits of the form of each but producing a finished sculpture that fitted into none. At other times I think of myself as the fish we caught snorkeling off Wewak. My basic shape camouflages itself in the colours of whatever surroundings I find myself in. I am adept at playing the appropriate roles. But do I have a colour of my own apart from those I appropriate? If I cease to play any role, would I be transparent? To mix metaphors, if I peeled away the layers of the roles I adopt, would I find nothing at the centre? Am I, after all, an onion—nothing but the sum of my layers?

The slipping sun casts its rays across the table, creating a wall of light and dancing dust particles between us. An intangible but definite barrier. I am halfway through thinking cynically that if communication can't be achieved between individuals, then it must be truly impossible across cultures, before I remember I am communicating across cultures—that is the problem.

You came to me with questions. We had promised each other honesty and openness, but you felt mine could be queried. I gave but I didn't share. There was a depth of intimacy we weren't achieving. You said I was shutting doors in your face. Staring out across the light barrier, I realise I have no answers for you, only a plea for understanding, which you think is an excuse, a justification for my lack of commitment (read: a commitment less than yours).

I tried to explain I was as committed to you as you are to me but that I find it nearly impossible to demonstrate that fact. You said I was splitting hairs. How can I make you understand I'm afraid? You got mad. You wanted to know why I didn't trust you. I said I do trust you. I'm not afraid of you necessarily; I'm just afraid. You said that people are always afraid of something. I agreed there's always a reason for fear but it's not necessarily a fear of something. So you wanted to know what the reason was. Words failed me. I tried. I tried to explain.

How can I make you understand that? Once my world stopped spinning, people, places, things, behaviours, and even a language were ripped from my life and I was thrust naked, except for the skimpy garment of family and the rags of memory, into a cold, new, and unfamiliar world. The more I invest in the world you and I are creating, the more there will be to grieve for when our world stops spinning.

If, I think quickly, *if*.

I am training myself slowly to the belief that worlds don't have to end. It is a measure of my intimacy with and trust in you that I can change the "when" to "if," even as an afterthought.

It is a mark of how much I trust you that I don't play the roles completely with you. I forget to. I lapse into pidgin, point with my chin, pick things up with my toes in your presence. You are amused. I've tried to explain to you that this is who I am. But I'm beginning to realise you have no way of understanding. It is totally outside your experience.

There was the day we went to the cricket match and I borrowed your binoculars. You asked me what was going on in the centre. I had to say I didn't know. I'd been watching a West Indian outfielder chewing gum. You laughed, yet a trifle impatiently. But I scarcely noticed. The sight of brown faces, with the occasional contrastive glimpse of shell-white teeth and dusky pink tongue, chewing casually but continuously, had brought the pungent smell of betel nut vividly to mind. I fully expected their saliva to be saffron when they spit. I was lost in my childhood. It is now that I remember.

Or the day we were shopping at the Queen Victoria Building and I dragged you into the Papua New Guinea shop. I was madly examining bilems and carvings, staring at story boards, transfixed by the chilling evil that fear fetishes always cast over me, and inhaling deeply the odour of the market and the village. I sensed your restless movements beside me and looked up into a bored but inquiring glance. We left. You exhaled suddenly and commented on the smell. For me it was a familiar and pleasant odour.

I was reexamining the world I lost, giving the globe in my mind a flick. In the part of me that belongs to that world, I was pretending the few revolutions caused by the flick were the continuous spinning of a living world, however unsatisfactory, artificial, and transient the indulgence. That globe haunts my present world. The truth is the old world informs the present. I am a composite, a citizen of the two. You couldn't participate in my other world. How can I expect you to accept the fear its loss creates and accommodate it? You have often questioned the veracity of my effort in maintaining contact with friends down south. Simply, I refuse to let another world stop. Spin more slowly, yes; halt, no.

If I could make you understand, I know what you'd say. As you grasped at the fragments of the conversation that made sense to you, I could see you heading down that track. *Willpower*, you'd say. *You simply have to push your fears to one side, take a risk, and open up to me. I won't fail you.*

And if I told you I can't, you'd interpret my insufficient willpower as a lack of real desire to do so. That's not it. I yearn for oneness with you with every fibre of my being. I don't like the still sparse landscape I inhabit. The people I've let into my heart have been like the tropical downpour that ends the dry season and fills up the tank again. I know it would be worthwhile. But fear creates an inertia that I, for all my oft-discussed strength of character, willpower, even stubbornness, cannot simply set aside. It's not you I fear, it's losing you. I'm trying to minimise the loss.

The last Christmas someone gave us two giant teddy bears—three months before we left. I remember sorting through my possessions, trying to decide what to take and what to leave. It was the teddy bears I cried for. I remember Mum trying to comfort me, pointing out all the things I could take and saying that I really hadn't had the teddies for long, they weren't my favourite toys. But that was precisely why I was so upset. I didn't have a chance for them to become well-loved favourites. I was crying not for the past I was leaving, nor even the present, but for the future, the might-have-beens. I think I sensed I could take my history with me but not my future. My world was slowly grinding to a halt. It was going to be arrested at a fixed point. While I would always have it, while I could examine it, while I could mount it on a stand and have it as a globe in my memory to give an occasional spin, I could never give it life, never keep it spinning, never develop it beyond the point at which it stopped.

Your hands come down onto the table. *Long, lean, attractive hands*, I muse absentmindedly.

The coping strategy again. You look searchingly into my face. I hope the desperate need, the pleading are clear in my eyes, but I fear the mask of independence I have long since learnt to wear has been permanently grafted onto my face. I want you to know without me having to tell you. I want you to cross the barriers within, without me having to open them. I want intimacy without vulnerability, I realise in a blinding flash of insight. The ludicrousness of it is nearly overwhelming.

"I have to go," you say wearily. Your knuckles whiten as you push yourself to a standing position. There is a luminosity to this moment. I have been here before.

"Call me?" I hear myself asking.

It is an effort to display even that much need, to make myself that vulnerable. Your smile is whimsical, and a shadow chills your calm blue eyes. Inside me the little girl is weeping for her teddy bears again. *Don't do it*, I think. *If you bring this world to a close, how will I ever find the courage to begin another?*

You stop to kiss me good-bye and your lips are cool against my mouth. For the first time I begin to doubt my logic. Suddenly my fear of investing too heavily in an uncertain future is swamped by the knowledge of losing a present that is just starting to pay dividends on my past investments. The realisation slams into my consciousness. Now is a future that *has* arrived. Tears fill my eyes and overflow down my cheeks. You feel the wetness and pull back in surprise.

"I need you." The words come out in a sob, surprising me more than I think they surprise you. I weep, my eyes drowning in the warm, equatorial waters of grief, guilt, and relief. I am vaguely aware of the group at the next table staring, but adrift in a liberating moment of nakedness I couldn't care less. In my mind I see children playing naked and carefree on the banks of the Sepik and I recognise their wisdom—*naked and unashamed.*

The child in me is weeping too—for the market, for favourite toys, for the lagoon, for school friends and courtesy relatives, for the everyday sights, sounds, and smell. She is weeping for her present.

I am aware also of your indecision. If our world has stopped spinning, I will have myself to blame as much as my history. I hate my own culpable blindness. Amazingly, I feel your hands under my elbows drawing me up into your arms. A line flows up from my memory—*Let us possess one world, each hath one and is one.* And I recognise its truth. Now is reality.

The Long Good-bye: Honoring Unresolved Grief

Paul Asbury Seaman

Paul is the son of United Methodist missionaries and grew up in Pakistan. He is also a former president of Global Nomads, Washington area, and author of *Paper Airplanes in the Himalayas: The Unfinished Path Home* and *Far above the Plain*.

Dealing with the accumulated grief of too many leavings is an essential part of the global nomad legacy. Why then are we so reluctant to talk about it? Hushing up heartache only means that it will take longer to let go and move on.

I moved recently, bringing to an end the longest period of geographic stability in my life. It was a big event. After three and a half years in the same apartment, I packed up and moved...a block down the street. I didn't have to say good-bye to any friends, learn a new currency, or adjust to a new job. The new apartment was comparatively spacious, filled with light, and, most importantly, contained the woman I loved. Like "an outward sign of an inward grace," this transition reflected some very positive developments in my life.

So why, a month later, was I so depressed? Stress counselors emphasize that even good changes are stressful. But I suspect there was another factor: the grief of leaving familiar places is a distinctive part of my identity as a global nomad. Many of us have experienced such transitions multiple times, and because they occurred during our formative years, their impact is deeply embedded. We might deny or may not recognize the effects of accumulated losses, but they will make their influence felt through other voices. Depression, anger, withdrawal, arrogance, exhaustion, and righteousness are some of the voices grief has borrowed in my life.

Grief is a current that goes unarticulated in many people's lives, and even within the very organizations that seek to understand and serve global nomads, grief seems almost like a taboo subject. There is a curious reticence about publicly exploring this key aspect of our experience. Informal discussions of grief as a global nomad issue are often characterized by hyperbole and judgmental generalizations: "Everyone who says that they had a great experience growing up and that they are content now is in denial." Or "Everyone who is grieving is using their global nomad background as a crutch, as a catchall excuse, for all their current problems"; they are "wallowing in a victim mentality" and need to "get a life."

I readily grant that some global nomads had perfectly happy childhoods; others have experienced horrendous disorientation, abandonment, or abuse, the impact of which they will struggle with for the rest of their lives. And, yes, some individuals are obsessed and crippled by grief, allowing themselves to be defined by it. I suspect, however, that the majority of us simply live with ambivalent memories, and whether the dominant feeling is nostalgia, regret, or bitterness, the sense of loss is essentially the same.

Sometimes we cushion our grief under blankets of explanations and pillows of dimming memories. To hear someone articulate a vaguely familiar pain can be quite threatening to these careful arrangements. Even if there is nothing unresolved within ourselves to be disturbed, most of us aren't very good with public expression of vulnerability. It is too intimate and may often be viewed as a sign of weakness or social maladjustment. Dealing with an emotional individual is awkward enough, but a whole group of people displaying their raw feelings can really make us uncomfortable.

Some time after the Second International Conference for Global Nomads in September 1992, one person remarked to me that the event seemed to be "overrun with grieving MKs [missionary kids]." This was not my experience, but supposing grief was an insistent if unofficial theme at the conference, it is worth asking why this was the case—and why among missionary kids more than other global nomads. An emotional atmosphere can seem manipulated, ungenuine, or self-absorbed, but genuine opportunities to face grief directly and honestly will be missed—or can be comfortably avoided—as long as the topic itself remains so highly charged.

A curious phenomenon happens when global nomads are called upon to talk about their past, especially in more formal situations such as a panel discussion or interviews. Invariably, they end their already very positive accounts with "...but it was great. I wouldn't trade it for anything." There is a subtle defensiveness in this kind of summary that begs the question: What is it that they feel needs this reassurance? Or are they reassuring themselves?

The parents of many global nomads were involved in high-profile or morally weighty service professions. They were on a mission, representing the home country, a particular ideology, or even God. Sacrifice—of family or emotional stability, of reliable friends or circumstances—was just part of pursuing the noble cause. We were trained from an early age to believe in the cause; to show our pain, to acknowledge the cost, was disloyal.

But acknowledging grief or anger does not invalidate the positive aspects of an otherwise cherished experience. When I unexpectedly shed a few tears at the loss of my old apartment, it did not mean I regretted the decision to move. Rather, it was honoring all that place had given me, the things that I had learned and experienced during the time I lived there, and acknowledging that a particular period of my life, not just my location, had come to an end.

Give Grief a Chance: Acknowledgment and Closure

Why is grief such a persistent, unresolved issue for many of us? There are at least four reasons:

1. incomplete good-byes or a lack of closure at the time a loss occurs;

2. not recognizing the symptoms, such as anger and depression;

3. guilt or embarrassment about having "negative" feelings, which can lead to denial or repression; or

4. the lack of adequate forums for expressing grief.

David Pollock's presentations of the TCK Profile and transition workshops by Norma McCaig always emphasize the importance of having closure rituals. These can take many forms, from simply having the opportunity to say farewell to your friends to something more elaborate, perhaps with spiritual overtones. This may include saying good-bye privately to familiar buildings, to a favorite spot, or to the landscape itself. The day I left my old apartment I stood in the empty rooms and suddenly felt the pangs of parting. I took a few minutes to cherish the many memories contained in that place. Going back to the places where we were raised to complete our good-byes can be a powerful release and brings an added dimension to what might otherwise be merely a nostalgic trip.

Our backgrounds were often wondrously unusual, sometimes exotic, even glamorous. We do feel privileged. Often there was excitement in the transitions themselves: the anticipation of going "home" or to an interesting new place. In the eager hustle and earnest efforts to embrace a new setting, we often didn't understand how much we were leaving behind. When grief showed up as depression or other forms of stress, we attributed it to culture shock. Years later we are confused by an uncharacteristic sentimentality, triggered by certain movies, even television advertisements, that evoke a sense of community or home. What we think is nostalgia may really be some part of ourselves that is being given permission to grieve. The tears may be as much from relief, from finally letting go, as they are about the grief itself. I remember seeing *Out of Africa* several years ago when it was first released. After the movie ended, I sat in the theater and wept for twenty minutes.

We need to give dignity to our grief and create social structures—personal ones, if not institutional—where we can name the pain of lost friendships, lost places, lost identities. To finally bring closure and healing to lingering grief some people may need to practice "constructive indulgence" for a time.

Western society is famously bad about dealing with grief. Death is the only severe loss for which we have public grieving rituals (and *they* are usually pretty restrained). We have no tradition that offers socially sanctioned support for the many other causes of grief. Severe illnesses or natural disasters may be exceptions, but even in these cases, when the symptoms are gone, the affected individual or family is expected to return to "normal."

From my own struggles with grief and depression I have learned that the process of healing always takes longer than other people think it should and, further, that those who have not experienced a similar loss or identity struggle will never really understand.

How then, once we face our grief, can we know if the way we are dealing with it and the length of time it takes are appropriate? Some questions to ask might be:

- Can we see progress—is the grief evolving, going deeper, beginning to dissipate?

- Is the grief clearly not the primary attribute that defines our identity?

- Does it lead to a sense of solidarity and kinship with others that is healing, empowering, change-inducing?

- Are we moving away from a sense of victimization, or powerlessness, toward a greater sense of control of our life that is still connected with but not overly dependent on others?

Trauma experts emphasize that talking is a critical step in healing. If survivors of an airplane crash or victims of a hurricane simply describe *what happened* in detail, while difficult, it significantly hastens the recovery from shock and helplessness. Like Vietnam veterans, global nomads have been deprived of social validation of their experience. We didn't get a hero's welcome. For the most part society—friends, relatives, school officials, parents' sponsoring agencies—couldn't appreciate the "big deal" about what had happened to us. They did not recognize the trauma of uprooting and cultural dislocation, because many aspects of this were beyond their own experience and, thus, their ability to comprehend.

For friends and family the importance of listening cannot be overstated. For some global nomads, the chance to reminisce with an empathetic group, to laugh together about the hard memories, is enough. Others need to express their grief more directly. Grieving people sometimes talk a lot because they've never really felt heard. This is, of course, a vicious cycle, as impatience sometimes causes others to tune out. But when a grieving person finally feels accepted and understood, the compelling need to talk about his or her woundedness usually dissipates. A pain that has been named and honored by the empathy of others can be let go of. This is one reason that the company of other global nomads can be so exhilarating and healing.

While we cannot recover what we've lost, we can celebrate those aspects of ourselves that we may associate with another time and place. For instance, we cannot become children again, but we can seek to recover a childlike sense of wonder, spontaneity, and vulnerability—or perhaps just a sense of contentment about our place in the world. Ultimately, coming to terms with grief means learning to feel at home within ourselves.

Resources and Bibliography

Resources for TCKs and ATCKs

Australia/New Zealand

Australasian MK Association
23 Bundoran Parade
Box Hill North
Victoria 3129
Australia
Group of primarily adult missionary kids helping one another and new returnees in adjusting to home country.

MK Merimna
PO Box 205
Kingswood, South Australia 5062
Australia
61 08 272-5419
"Committed to caring for cross-cultural kids." Directors Roger and Jill Dyer have been involved in issues relating to helping international schools with curriculum development so non-North American TCKs can fit better into their own culture.

Denmark

DUO-Denmark, Borgmestervej 12,
DK-6070 Christiansfeld, Denmark
Postal Giro 1199-081 88 36
Organization working with returned TCKs through conferences and seminars.

United States

Around the World in a Lifetime (AWAL)
c/o FSYF
PO Box 39185
Washington, DC 20016
Organization for Foreign Service teens. Circulates newsletter and sponsors local meetings for TCKs.

Cultural Connexions
PO Box 90402
Indianapolis, IN 46290-0402
Phone: 317-465-8760
Fax: 317-251-4933
e-mail: RDvanreken@aol.com
Organization of conferences and seminars for internationally mobile families. Special focus on issues related to non-North American families living and raising their TCKs in the United States.

Global Nomads International
PO Box 9584
Washington, DC 20016-9584
Phone: 202-466-2244
e-mail: info@gni.org
Website: globalnomadsassociation.com
Organization founded for those with internationally mobile childhoods of all backgrounds. Sponsors conferences and publishes newsletter with articles pertaining to such a lifestyle.

Global Nomad Resources
Norma M. McCaig, President
PO Box 8066
Reston, VA 20191
Phone/Fax: 703-758-7766
e-mail: gmu.edu
Workshops, presentations, consultations, and publications related to global nomads and their families.

Interaction, Inc.
PO Box 158
Houghton, NY 14744-0158
716-567-8774
Directed by David C. Pollock. Conducts reentry seminars and TCK profile seminars throughout the year for international organizations and individuals throughout the world.

Intercultural Press, Inc.
PO Box 700
374 US Route One
Yarmouth, ME 04096
Phone: 207-846-5168
Fax: 207-846-5181
e-mail: books@interculturalpress.com
Website: www.interculturalpress.com
The premier publisher and distributor of books, videos, simulations, and other materials on intercultural topics.

Mu Kappa International
PO Box 1388
De Soto, TX 75115
One of the first support groups started by and for TCKs. Primarily for missionary kids.

Overseas Brats
PO Box 29805
San Antonio, TX 78229
Group designed to help adults raised as dependents of parents in U.S. military, government, or civilian organizations to connect with one another.

Third Culture Family Services
Elsie Purnell, Director
2685 Meguiar Drive
Pasadena, CA 91107
Phone: 626-794-9406
Strong emphasis on organizing and facilitating support groups for ACTKs. Presentations for international organizations on how to maximize third culture experience for families involved.

Transition Dynamics
Barbara F. (Bobbie) Schaetti, Principal
2448 NW 63rd St.
Seattle, WA 98107
Phone: 206-789-3290
Fax: 206-781-2439
e-mail: bfschaetti@transition-dynamics.com
Website: www.transition-dynamics.com
A consultancy committed to serving the children, women, and men for whom international mobility and cultural transitions are a part of daily life.

Practical Books on TCK Issues

Austin, Clyde N., ed. *Cross-cultural Reentry: A Book of Readings.*
1986. Abilene, TX: Abilene Christian University.
> A collection of articles on how to identify and deal
> with problems which occur when reentering the home
> country after a period overseas.

———. *Cross-cultural Reentry: An Annotated Bibliography.* 1983.
Abilene, TX: Abilene Christian University.
> A review of literature on cross-cultural reentry
> issues.

Bell, Linda. *Hidden Immigrants: Legacies of Growing Up Abroad.*
1997. Cross Cultural Publications, PO Box 506, Notre Dame,
IN 46556.
> Linda explores the TCK experience by interviewing
> six men and seven women who were raised as TCKs.
> They share their reactions to things such as culture
> shock and matters of identity, marriage, career, and
> grief along with what helped or hindered them in
> dealing with these matters.

Blohm, Judith M. *Where in the World Are You Going?* 1996. Intercultural Press, PO Box 700, Yarmouth, ME 04096. 800-370-
2665; fax: 207-846-5181.
e-mail: books@interculturalpress.com
Website: www.interculturalpress.com
> An entertaining activity book for children ages five
> to ten to help them prepare for an overseas move
> with their families.

Bowers, Joyce, ed. *Raising Resilient MKs: Resources for Caregivers,
Parents, and Teachers.* 1998. ACSI, PO Box 35097, Colo-
rado Springs, CO 80935.
> A collection of materials from a variety of authors
> all designed to be helpful for caregivers, teachers, and
> parents of TCKs. Many of the articles were originally

presented as seminars at the first three International Conferences on Missionary Kids. Other chapters are from various magazine articles published later on this topic.

Dyer, Jill. *Harold and Stanley Say Goodbye*. 1998. MK Merimna, PO Box 205, Kingswood, SA, Australia 5062.

This delightful story featuring a bear family about to make a cross-cultural transition is designed to help young TCKs understand and talk about their own feelings as they face a similar uprooting. A great tool for parents to use with their children.

Dyer, Jill, and Roger Dyer, eds. *"...and Bees Make Honey."* 1995. MK Merimna, PO Box 205, Kingswood, SA, Australia 5062.

Second anthology of TCK writings—including many from non-North American TCKs. Interesting—and short—readings.

———, eds. *Scamps, Scholars, and Saints*. 1991. MK Merimna, PO Box 205, Kingswood, SA, Australia 5062.

First volume of collected anecdotes, reflections, poems, and drawings by TCKs. Many good insights expressed even by young TCKs.

———. *What Makes Aussie TCKs Tick?* 1989. MK Merimna, PO Box 205, Kingswood, SA, Australia 5062.

A practical resource book primarily written for Australian families living overseas, but also helpful to any non-North American family in dealing with the strong North American influences in schooling and culture present in many expatriate communities.

Eakin, K. B. *The Foreign Service Teenager—At Home in the U.S.: A Few Thoughts for Parents Returning with Teenagers*. 1988. Washington, DC: Overseas Briefing Center/Foreign Service Institute, Department of State.

Written by a veteran diplomat spouse, educator, and officer in the Family Liaison Office of the State

Department, this book deals with specific issues of teenage children whose parents are in the diplomatic corps.

Echerd, Pam, and Alice Arathoon, eds. *Understanding and Nurturing the Missionary Family.* 1989. (Compendium of the International Conference on Missionary Kids, Quito, Ecuador, January 4-8, 1987, vol. 1). William Carey Library, PO Box 41029, Pasadena, CA 91114.

————. *Planning for MK Nurture.* 1987. (Compendium of the International Conference on Missionary Kids, Quito, Ecuador, January, 1989, vol. 2.) William Carey Library, PO Box 41029, Pasadena, CA 91114.

The above two books contain transcripts of the various plenary sessions and seminars from the conference held in January 1987.

Foyle, Marjory. *Missionary Stress.* 1987. EMIS, PO Box 794, Wheaton, IL 60189. (Originally published in Britain as *Honourably Wounded.*)

British psychiatrist Marjory Foyle, herself an experienced missionary, writes of particular stresses faced by the missionary community in its cross-cultural endeavors.

Gordon, Alma. *Don't Pig Out on Junk Food: The MKs Guide to Survival in the U.S.* 1993. EMIS, PO Box 794, Wheaton, IL 60189. 708-653-2158.

A humorous yet practical guide by ATCK Alma Gordon, based on her years of experience as the daughter of an ATCK, as a TCK herself, and in raising her own TCKs in South America.

Hess, J. Daniel. *The Whole World Guide to Culture Learning.* 1994. Intercultural Press, PO Box 700, Yarmouth, ME 04096. 800-370-2665; fax: 207-846-5181.
e-mail: books@interculturalpress.com
Website: www.interculturalpress.com

A substantive introduction to culture learning, designed especially for students going abroad. Contains a series of guides to help students get the most out of their overseas experience.

Hughes, Katherine L. *The Accidental Diplomat: Dilemmas of the Trailing Spouse.* 1998. Aletheia Publications, 46 Bell Hollow Road, Putnam Valley, NY 10579. 914-526-2873; fax: 914-526-2905.

e-mail: AlethPub@aol.com

Website: http://members.AOL.com/AlethPub

A close-up look at the world of women whose identities are shaped by the professional commitments of their husbands to the Foreign Service. In the context of frequently shifting locales, they are often forced to reinvent their lives every two or three years.

Janssen, Gretchen. *Women on the Move: A Christian Perspective on Cross-Cultural Adaptation.* 1989. Intercultural Press, PO Box 700, Yarmouth, ME 04096. 800-370-2665; fax: 207-846-5181. Out of print.

e-mail: books@interculturalpress.com

Website: www.interculturalpress.com

Kalb, Rosalind, and Penelope Welch. *Moving Your Family Overseas.* 1992. Intercultural Press, PO Box 700, Yarmouth, ME 04096. 800-370-2665; fax: 207-846-5181.

e-mail: books@interculturalpress.com

Website: www.interculturalpress.com

Designed for use by the entire family, this book provides practical information on the steps involved in preparing for and successfully managing an overseas move.

Kohls, L. Robert. *Survival Kit for Overseas Living.* 3d ed. 1996. Intercultural Press, PO Box 700, Yarmouth, ME, 04096. 800-370-2665; fax: 207-846-5181.

e-mail: books@interculturalpress.com

Website: www.interculturalpress.com

Practical information and insights into the process of cross-cultural adaptation along with suggestions on how best to go about it.

Marshall, Terry. *The Whole World Guide to Language Learning.* 1990. Intercultural Press, PO Box 700, Yarmouth, ME 04096. 800-370-2665; fax: 207-846-5181.
e-mail: books@interculturalpress.com
Website: www.interculturalpress.com
Practical guide to successful, self-directed language learning while abroad. The learning program includes maximum use of and involvement with the local community.

McCluskey, Karen Curnow, ed. *Notes from a Traveling Childhood: Readings for Internationally Mobile Parents and Children.* 1994. Foreign Service Youth Foundation, PO Box 39185, Washington, DC 20016.
A helpful, easily readable handbook filled with short essays and writings by ATCKs and others on not only the issues involved for internationally mobile families, but practical charts on what to do.

Pascoe, Robin. *Culture Shock: Successful Living Abroad.* 1953, 1993. Graphic Arts, Portland OR. 800-452-3032.
Website: www.gacpc.
Robin takes a critical look at the issues of settlement for the entire family in the light of the role and relationships of the trailing spouse in maintaining sanity in the home.

―――. *Surviving Overseas: A Wife's Guide to Successful Living Abroad.* 1953, 1992. Times Books International, Times Centre, 1 New Industrial Road, Singapore.
Robin's sensitivity to the issues she so clearly spells out regarding the "trailing spouse"—and how to best deal with them—stems from her own firsthand experience as a Canadian diplomat's wife who served in China and Korea.

Piet-Pelon, Nancy J., and Barbara Hornby. *Women's Guide to Overseas Living.* 2d ed. 1992. Intercultural Press, PO Box 700, Yarmouth, ME 04096. 800-370-2665; fax: 207-846-5181.
e-mail: books@interculturalpress.com
Website: www.interculturalpress.com
A perceptive examination of issues critical to women (and their families) who relocate abroad.

Romano, Dugan. *Intercultural Marriage: Promises and Pitfalls.* 2d ed. 1997. Intercultural Press, PO Box 700, Yarmouth, ME 04096. 800-370-2665; fax: 207-846-5181.
e-mail: books@interculturalpress.com
Website: www.interculturalpress.com
A wise look at the various factors and stresses of intercultural marriage from one who has been there.

Schmeil, Gene, and Kathryn Schmeil. *Welcome Home: Who are You? Tales of a Foreign Service Family.* 1998. Aletheia Publications, 46 Bell Hollow Road, Putnam Valley, NY 10579. 914-526-2873; fax: 914-526-2905
e-mail: AlethPub@aol.com
Website: http://members.AOL.com/ AlethPub
From the bizarre and unpredictable to the peaceful and reassuring, the vignettes offer vivid portrayals of the life of a Foreign Service family living and working on three continents.

Shames, Germaine W. *Transcultural Odysseys: The Evolving Global Consciousness.* 1997. Intercultural Press, PO Box 700, Yarmouth, ME 04096. 800-370-2665; fax: 207-846-5181.
e-mail: books@interculturalpress.com
Website: www.interculturalpress.com
Through stories of those who have gone overseas, the author explores how an individual can become a "global" person.

Smith, Carolyn D. *The Absentee American.* 1991; reprint, 1994. Aletheia Publications, 46 Bell Hollow Road, Putnam Valley, NY 10579. 914-526-2873.
e-mail: AlethPub@aol.com
Website: www.members.AOL.com/ AlethPub
> A Foreign Service ATCK writes specifically about how American ATCKs view their home country and its place in the contemporary world. Includes helpful statistical data about the American expatriate community as well as stories gathered from over three hundred questionnaires to which ATCKs responded.

———, ed. *Strangers at Home.* 1996. Aletheia Publications, 46 Bell Hollow Road, Putnam Valley, NY 10579. 914-526-2873
e-mail: AlethPub@aol.com
Website: www.members.AOL.com/ AlethPub
> Essays on the reentry experience of TCKs. Includes the findings of the ATCK survey done by sociologists Ruth Hill Useem and Ann Baker Cottrell along with reflections by ATCKs themselves. David Pollock, Norma McCaig, and Ruth Van Reken are among the authors.

Storti, Craig. *The Art of Coming Home.* 1997. Intercultural Press, PO Box 700, Yarmouth, ME 04096. 800-370-2665; fax: 207-846-5181.
e-mail: books@interculturalpress.com
Website: www.interculturalpress.com
> This book addresses in detail the reentry process after a cross-cultural sojourn.

———. *The Art of Crossing Cultures.* 1990. Intercultural Press, PO Box 700, Yarmouth, ME 04096. 800-370-2665; fax: 207-846-5181.
e-mail: books@interculturalpress.com
Website: www.interculturalpress.com

An essential book for anyone returning to his or her country after a time abroad. Storti also discusses the substantial emotional and financial costs of unsuccessful reentry for the sending organizations as well.

Taber, Sara Mansfield. *Of Many Lands: Journal of a Traveling Childhood.* 1997. Foreign Service Youth Foundation (Publications), PO Box 39185, Washington, DC 20016. Fax 703-875-7979.
Evocative "snapshots" of the author's life as a TCK invite response from fellow TCKs or ATCKs as they reflect on their own experience. Written in journal form, this workbook can be used both personally and also as a tool for family members or groups of TCKs or ATCKs to share their stories.

Tetzel, Beth A., and Patricia Mortenson, eds. *International Conference on Missionary Kids: New Directions in Missions: Implications for MKs.* (Compendium of the International Conference on Missionary Kids, Manila, November 1984.) Missionary Internship, Box 457, Farmington, MI 48024. 313-474-9110.
Based on the plenary sessions and workshops of the first international conference on TCKs in Manila, specifically missionary TCKs.

Walters, Doris L. *An Assessment of Reentry Issues for Missionary Children.* New York: Vantage Press, 1991.
Psychologist Walters reports on what she considers the primary reentry issues facing missionary children based on her work with them through the Southern Baptist mission.

Ward, Ted. *Living Overseas: A Book of Preparations.* New York: Free Press, 1984.
This book specifically deals with preparing to make the move overseas; what to look for, how to deal with conflicts, and much more useful advice.

Wertsch, Mary Edwards. *Military Brats*. 1991. Reprint, 1996. Aletheia Publications, 46 Bell Hollow Road, Putnam Valley, NY 10579. 914-526-2873.
e-mail: AlethPub@aol.com
Website: www.members.AOL.com/AlethPub
> A groundbreaking book on life in the military. Filled with stories, facts, and philosophizing about this subset of the TCK world. Insightful and helpful.

Williams, K. L. *When Africa Was Home*. New York: Orchard Books, 1991.
> Many beautiful pictures accompany the text of this story about a TCK childhood. It is written for children of all ages.

Biographies, Autobiographies, and Fictionalized Personal Accounts of TCK Experience

Addleton, Jonathan. *Some Far and Distant Place*. Athens and London: University of Georgia Press, 1996.
> A memoir of a TCK childhood spent in Pakistan. Addleton was born in the mountains of northern Pakistan in 1957, the son of missionary parents who had themselves grown up in rural Georgia. The book includes many reflections on the challenges that come with continuously confronting and, on occasion, crossing boundaries of race, class, religion, and ethnicity. It offers an interesting perspective on the various subcultures arising within missionary communities and within overseas boarding schools established by and large to educate the children of expatriates.

Fritz, Jean. *Homesick: My Own Story*. Santa Barbara, CA: Cornerstone Books, 1987.
> A charming, slightly fictionalized story of a childhood spent in China in the prerevolutionary days. It covers not only time in China but also reentry to a

country Fritz had always considered home without having once been there. TCKs everywhere will recognize much in this story as their own.

Gilkey, Langdon. *Shantung Compound.* San Francisco: Harper-Collins, 1975.

This is a story based on Langdon Gilkey's two and a half years spent in Japanese internment camps with two thousand other expatriates, including many TCKs. It is a reflection on people's reaction under stress as well as an accounting of prison life.

Michell, David J. *A Boy's War.* Republic of Singapore: Overseas Missionary Fellowship, 1988.

One man's account of his internment in a Japanese concentration camp along with his fellow students from the Chefoo School in China. Includes interesting insights of fellow detainee, Eric Liddell, the runner featured in *Chariots of Fire.*

Seaman, Paul, ed. *Far above the Plain.* Pasadena, CA: William Carey Library, 1996.

An anthology of stories written by alumni of Murree Christian School, a missionary kid boarding school in Pakistan.

———. *Paper Airplanes in the Himalayas: The Unfinished Path Home.* Notre Dame, IN: Cross Cultural Publications, 1997.

A well-written account of Seaman's life as a TCK growing up in Pakistan. Includes a powerful history of the era and country as well as accounts of his school days. The description of "the train ride"—that long trek back and forth from boarding school—will move any who have made similar journeys.

Van Reken, Ruth E. *Letters Never Sent* (formerly *Letters I Never Wrote*). 1986. "Letters," PO Box 90084, Indianapolis, IN 46290-0084. 317-251-4933.

This is a thoughtful look at the hitherto unexamined

impact of the many cycles of separation and loss from Ruth Van Reken's missionary kid childhood. Using the format of letters to her parents, Ruth explains—at the age of thirty-nine—the feelings she could never articulate to them when she was a child.